WAREHOUSE MANAGEMENT AND INVENTORY CONTROL

2nd edition

P.M. Price, Ph.D.

N.J. Harrison, M.Ed.

Access
EDUCATION

ISBN 978-1-934231-04-3

Table of Contents

Chapter 4: Internal Processes: Materials Handling 75

Chapter 5: Internal Processes: The Unit Load 97

Chapter 1

The Role of Warehousing in Logistics and Supply Chain Management

Believe it or not, you already know how to manage a warehouse. You go to this warehouse at least once every day. Its exterior may be white or black or even of the stainless steel variety. You store goods in a temperature-controlled setting in this warehouse and later distribute them to their end consumers.

Have you guessed what this warehouse is that you so skillfully manage every day? I'll give you a final clue: It's actually located in your home and, unless you're a Hollywood celebrity, Rachel Ray, or President of the United States, it typically takes up no larger than a 3' X 3' X 6' space in your kitchen. Guessed it yet? Your refrigerator!

In your refrigerator, you may have a gallon of milk, a six-pack of yoghurt, a couple of bags of frozen vegetables, and many other perishable goods in quantities that it would take more than a day or even a week to consume. Without a refrigerator, you would have to purchase many perishable foods on a daily basis, unless you wanted to keep your home cooled to 32° to 50°F, which even those of us in Alaska might find a bit uncomfortable. Having your temperature-controlled refrigerator allows you to buy milk, cheese, meat, and vegetables in large quantities and store them for future use. Also, because your refrigerator allows you to buy these items in bulk, you get better shopping discounts, have plenty of extra food on hand in case unexpected guests arrive, and do not have to spend time going to the grocery store every day. Just imagine settling down to watch the Super Bowl and having to go to the local grocery store each time you want a cold can of your favorite beverage!

Our personal, temperature-controlled, kitchen warehouses, otherwise known as *refrigerators*, operate on the same principles as large, commercial warehouses. We purchase goods in greater quantities than we immediately need; we inspect them; we store them; we issue them when we are going to use them; and, every so often, we have a look to see if we need to replace our old or used inventory. Just like a refrigerator, a warehouse plays a major supporting role in receiving, storing, and issuing inventory.

In this chapter, we introduce the concept of a warehouse: what warehouses are and why we need them; the functions of a warehouse; the role a warehouse can play in the internal logistics and external supply chain management of a company; and what logistics and supply chain management are and how they are related to warehouse management. Throughout this chapter and later chapters, we will also explore the world of warehousing and inventory in a variety of settings, including the manufacturing retail, and service settings. Whether it's a warehouse , distribution center, or retail store, the principles of warehouse management and inventory control are the same!

So... What Is Warehouse?

We already mentioned that a warehouse is a place to receive, store, and issue inventory, which is a more academically-friendly way of saying a place to take in, hold, and give out stuff. (More on all this later!) The great thing about warehouses, too, is that anyone can have one. When we take a look at the stuff around us, chances are, it passed through multiple warehouses on its way to us!

Most goods have either producers or manufacturers. **Producers** are those companies who gather and supply natural products at their most basic form, such as fruits and vegetables or metal and timber. Similar to producers are **manufacturers**, who build, mix, or assemble products, such cars, computers, and loaves of bread. Both producers and manufacturers need to store and issue the products they produce and manufacture, which means they need warehouses!

Many goods also pass through the hands of suppliers and retailers. **Suppliers** (also known as **vendors**) are companies that provide things that other companies need. For example, a computer manufacturer might make the most highly complex and intricately detailed computers, but it's not likely to also manufacture the cardboard and styrofoam packaging our computers come in. Therefore, out computer manufacturer needs a packaging supplier. Similarly, our computer manufacturer might be so busy building millions of computers that it doesn't have the time or expertise to sell them. Instead, it uses **retailers**, businesses that sell goods to consumers - often end users like you and me! Retailers that sell the computers we've been talking so much about could include electronics stores, big box discount stores, and online-only sellers. Both suppliers and retailers need to be able to receive, store, and issue out goods, which means they need warehouses, too!

To get down to a more formal definition, a **warehouse** is a facility or an area within a facility in which an organization may receive, inspect, store, pick, pack,and ship any of a variety of materials needed for manufacturing, distribution, maintenance, and packaging within the organization. Warehouses may range greatly in size and structure, from the back storeroom of your favorite local restaurant to the mammoth complex of warehouses of the top online sellers

POP QUIZ!

Which of the following locations pictured are warehouses according to our definition above?

Retailer's Regional Distribution Center

Fish Processor's Storeroom and Distribution Area

Local Restaurant's Cold Storage

You got it! They're all warehouses!
Because they are all warehouses, the lessons to be learned from this book can apply to all of these settings!

like Amazon.com. While a *warehouse* may be an enormous building or just a back corner of a neighborhood shop, there are couple of examples of special kinds of warehouses that are worth mentioning: distribution centers and cross-docking facilities.

A *distribution center (or DC)* is a type of large warehouse that receives large quantities of goods from manufacturers to be stored for short periods of time and sent on to multiple retail locations. When we think of a warehouse, we often think of a place to store goods for one business or manufacturer at one location. Distribution centers are a bit different and are built to store goods and prepare them for shipments to multiple locations across a specific region. They are typically located according to access to transportation (such as interstate highway systems, railroads, and airports) and lower labor and utilities costs. Because of their geographic nature of being established to meet the needs of particular regions, they are also called *regional distribution centers (or RDCs)*.

A *cross-docking facility* is a specialized distribution center that doesn't store goods because it moves them so quickly from a wide range of suppliers' incoming trucks to multiple outbound trucks headed for different locations. Goods from a variety of suppliers or locations are received at one end of the facility, immediately sorted, and then immediately placed into trucks or containers at the other end of the facility for shipping. This entire process usually takes less than 24 hours and can sometimes take less than a single hour! Essentially, cross- docking eliminates the need for storage because items from incoming shipments are transferred directly onto outgoing shipments. In a traditional warehouse, goods are held until a purchase order is received from a customer. At a cross-docking warehouse or distribution center, it is already known who the customers will be for each item in the incoming shipment long before they reach the cross-docking facility. For example, the home improvement retailer, Home Depot, operates an enormous cross-docking facility in Philadelphia that services more than 100 of its stores across the northeastern United States. When large truckloads of finished goods come into the cross-docking facility, employees immediately transfer items to different trucks heading for any of the retail chain's 100 plus stores in the region. Typically, cross-docking occurs throughout the day as different suppliers arrive with their different items.

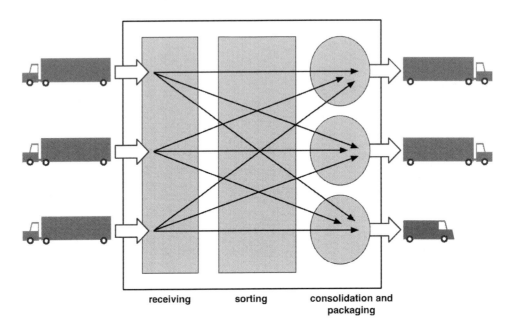

receiving   sorting   consolidation and
                                    packaging

Figure 1.1 - Cross-Docking Illustrated

A few more important types of warehouses are related to the ownership structure of the warehouse. Warehouses can be owned by the company supplying the goods, the company buying the goods, or an entirely different company. A *private warehouse* is a facility that is owned and managed by a company for the goods it manufactures, supplies, or receives. For example, a shoe manufacturer will have its own warehouse to store both newly manufactured shoes and the leather, thread, rubber, and other raw materials it uses to make their shoes. A *public warehouse* is a facility that is owned by a third party (one not supplying or purchasing goods) and is paid on a month-to-month basis to store goods. A public warehouse stores goods for multiple organizations and often charges by the pallet.

Similar to a public warehouse is a *contract warehouse*, which is also owned by a third party and stores goods for multiple organizations, but it involves a longer term contract, such as one to three years. Unlike public warehouses, which operate more along a "pallet in - pallet out" basis, contract warehouses often offer more warehouse services, such as order picking and packing. Finally, a *third party logistics provider (3PL)* can be used as a warehouse for a company's goods, but the 3PL provides services beyond simple storing of goods, such as collection, picking, packing, inventory management, and information documentation. A 3PL is typically the costliest option, but it takes all of the warehouse-related work away from a company and allows them to focus on their core business.

WHAT'S IN A WAREHOUSE?

So what is in a warehouse? Just about anything and everything! Getting a little bit more technical, however, when we talk about the contents of a warehouse, we typically mean its ***inventory***, the raw, in-process, finished materials, and other inputs needed for the creation of a company's goods and/or services. Basically, all the stuff in a warehouse except for the equipment used to to store or move goods is its inventory! For example, the following list includes typical inventory items found in the warehouse of a medium-sized manufacturing operation: *raw materials*; *component parts*; *packaging*; *spare parts*; *tools and equipment*; *work in progress*; *finished inventory*; and *maintenance materials*.

The range, value, and complexity of items held by any particular warehouse will depend upon the size and complexity of the operations involved. For example, picture the difference between the inventory of a lumberyard and the inventory of a luxury automobile manufacturer's warehouse. Because warehouses and their corresponding operations and inventory can vary greatly, warehouse managers and staff need to have an extensive knowledge of a large number of material types and operations. Throughout later chapters in this book, we will examine examples of different types of inventory in the warehouses of manufacturing, retail, and service operations. No matter what type of inventory or warehouse is involved, one common term that you must know in the world of warehousing is ***SKU, or stock keeping unit***, which refers to a distinct type of item held in inventory. For example, in a coffee retailer's warehouse, each size and type of container of coffee will have a unique SKU, which means that the SKU for the 1 pound bag of the decaf Sumatra-blend coffee is different from the SKU for the 2 pound bag of the decaf Sumatra-blend coffee.

WAREHOUSES AND WAREHOUSING

We mentioned earlier that most goods we encounter likely passed through multiple warehouses on their way to us. But why do companies go to all the time and expense of building and using warehouses? To keep us - the consumers - happy! As customers, when we want something, we want it immediately in the exact color, size, and quantity we desire. When we can't find what we need from one store or supplier, we immediately move on to other stores and suppliers. Companies need us to survive and don't want to lose our business, so they want to make sure they have enough goods on hand to meet our desires, or enough supply to meet our demand. To ensure that supply can meed demand, companies have to be able to store and quickly access the goods that customers want.

Warehouses fill the need of keeping enough goods nearby so that they can be accessed easily when customers need them. In fact, warehouses are so important to organizations that *warehousing* has become a core business function for most organizations. ***Warehousing*** is a business function of an organization that is concerned with the following six activities:

1. receiving goods from suppliers and putting them away

2. picking goods from storage when needed

3. consolidating and packing goods to prepare them for shipment

4. shipping goods

5. controlling inventory

6. keeping records and documenting the flow and inventory of goods within the organization

Depending upon the size and structure of a company, its warehousing function may be housed in one department, such as the Warehousing Department, or it may be spread across many departments with names like the Goods Inward or Goods Receipt Department, the Packaging Department, and the Inventory Control Department. In addition, although the physical receipt, storage, and issuing of goods have historically been linked with the term *warehousing*, they are now increasingly becoming linked under the broader heading of *logistics*. (More on that later in this chapter.)

Warehouses and warehouse management have become increasing important as customer demand has increased in complexity. As consumers, we are becoming increasingly accustomed to instant gratification. This expectation makes customer demand a complex problem to tackle because demand does not always remain static, with the same customers wanting the same quantity of goods at the same locations all the time. Instead, customer demand is often an uncertain and **dynamic demand**, constantly changing based on any number of reasons from weather patterns to customer whims and fashion trends. Warehouse management must ensure that goods are held in places that can be readily accessed to fill this dynamic demand while balancing this with the cost implications of storing too many goods.

A FEW OF THE FUNCTIONS OF A WAREHOUSE

Now that we have a basic understanding of what's inside a warehouse, let's take a brief look at the role of a warehouse and what a warehouse does for an organization. In later chapters of this text, we will explore these functions in greater depth and examine how they relate to different kinds of warehouses and companies.

Function#1: Customer Service. First and foremost, the primary reason to have a warehouse is all about customer service and making sure that an organization has the goods a customer wants when and where the customer needs them.

Function #2: Economy. A warehouse manager must ensure that all operations within the warehouse are performed as effectively and economically as possible. Warehouses can be quite expensive to operate, so the concept of economic levels of inventory is of vital importance because it ensures that minimum costs of operations are clear to every member of the warehouse team. (Don't worry. We'll tell you more about how to do this in later chapters.)

Function #3: Inventory Receipt. Warehouse managers and staff must receive and handle all of the items delivered to the warehouse. In doing so, they must also check all incoming inventory documentation (such as delivery notes and packing notes) and inform those in the Purchasing Department about all goods received.

Function #4: Inspection. Warehouse managers must work with the Quality Control Department to inspect and check all deliveries made to the warehouse. The factors checked include correct quantity, requested quality, and possible damage. In many cases, suppliers will not accept responsibility for damaged or missing quantities of goods unless they are reported within a specified number of days of delivery. Therefore, it is critical that warehouse managers conduct these inspections and report their results to the Purchasing Department in a timely manner.

Function #5: Inventory Storage. Another one of the core duties of warehouse managers and their staff is to unload, unpack, and store all of the goods delivered to the warehouse. This storage process also entails establishing the correct storage conditions of goods in connection with suppliers' instructions. This requires specialist skills and knowledge, especially when unique storage conditions are required, such as when goods must be kept refrigerated, dry, warm, etc.. It is the warehouse manager's responsibility to ensure that goods do not suffer damage or deterioration as a result of improper storage conditions.

Function #6: Inventory Identification and Location. Warehouse managers must also formulate and update a system of warehouse coding so that goods and services stored within a warehouse may be put away and located quickly and efficiently. Furthermore, a good warehouse manager has the added responsibility of ensuring that, when an item is not available, a suitable and authorized alternative that is in inventory is recommended.

Function #7: Safety and Security. Another important duty of warehouse management and staff is to ensure that security is maintained at all times within all warehouse buildings and external inventory yards, which involves protection from theft, damage, fire, and spillage. It also includes ensuring that all doors, windows, and external fences are secure.

Function #8: Physical Inventory Control and Checking. A warehouse manager is responsible for organizing, supervising, and collating all physical inventory checks carried out by an organization. These checks may be made on a continuous schedule or at set periods of time, such as the end of the fiscal year.

Function #9: Inventory Records. In many organizations, it is the responsibility of warehouse management to ensure that adequate and up-to-date inventory records are maintained for every item held in inventory, whether on-site or in an external contract warehouse. These records, whether paper or IT-based, provide information required to control and maintain the inventory levels the organizations has established, such as recording inventory levels, order levels, code numbers, and suppliers' reference information.

Function #10: Picking, Packing, Issue, and Dispatch. It is also the duty of warehouse management and staff to ensure that the goods and services required for an organization's operation are picked (selected from the storage area) and issued (given to the requestor) as and when required, while maintaining proper authorization procedures and strict clerical control of all inventory issues. Before issued, most items will need to be packaged for subsequent dispatch and transportation. Inferior packaging could lead to costly physical materials and customer loyalty losses.

Function #11: Product Flow. The issuance and dispatch of goods must have a smooth flow and be as efficient as possible because it is often the efficiency and effectiveness of inventory issuance that determines the image and status of the warehouse function throughout the entire organization. Goods must get to the factory exactly when needed so that manufacturing processes can continue without having to stop and wait for inventory!

Function #12: Materials Handling. Finally, perhaps the most fundamental duty of warehouse management and staff is the quick and safe handling of all materials. This core task of moving goods to, from, and between factories and warehouses can be achieved manually, mechanically, or with automated equipment. In later chapters, we will look at some of these techniques and the fascinating mechanical and automated tools at the disposal of today's modern warehouse manager.

WAREHOUSING AND OTHER DEPARTMENTS

Although we have focused on the importance of external customers (those outside of the company or organization) and how warehousing benefits them (having the right quantity of goods where and when they want them), the warehousing function also provides vital services to an organization's internal customers (those inside the company or organization receiving goods or services). For example, how efficiently and effectively a warehouse is run affects the overall efficiency and effectiveness of the whole company. Therefore, the relationships between a warehouse and the other major functions (or departments) of an organization very important. In addition, no warehouse is an island; it needs participation and information from an organization;s other major functions to ensure that a company's warehousing practices are efficient, effective, and meet corporate needs and goals.

Below are brief descriptions of the relationship between the warehousing and an organization's other departments and functions.

Warehousing and Manufacturing. In a manufacturing organization, the manufacturing function is one of the most important users of a warehouse. Warehouse managers must ensure that all materials needed for continued manufacturing operations are available in the right quantity, with the right quality, at the right time, and at the right place. If any of these rights become a wrong, the manufacturing function may have to cease production, which may result in extra cost, angry customers, an irate manufacturing department and company president, and a very embarrassed and berated warehouse manager. Therefore, it is critical that warehouse and manufacturing managers work together to keep open lines of communication about each function's needs and timeframes.

Warehousing and Physical Distribution. Physical distribution is concerned with the movement of finished goods from manufacturing plants to warehouses and then on to external customers. The physical distribution function must get finished goods to depots, regional distribution centers, and other warehouses throughout the organization's national and international distribution network. The warehousing function must ensure that adequate inventory is available in the correct quantities picked and is packaged and ready for loading on to the mode of transport chosen by the physical distribution function. Open and continuous communication is also important in this relationship. For example. physical distribution managers must supply warehouse managers with up-to-date information about the needs and wants of the distribution system, making every effort to give adequate notice of loading quantities, destinations, types, and marshaling points, to ensure efficient service from the warehouse system.

Warehousing and Maintenance. An organization's maintenance function is responsible for ensuring that the manufacturing plant, its machinery, and other machinery used by the organization are kept in working order and performing to designed efficiency standards. The warehousing function plays a critical supporting, ensuring that all required maintenance spare parts, tools, and equipment are held in inventory or are easily available from a supplier's inventory. For example, a warehouse must hold emergency spare parts in case of unscheduled machine breakdowns. Again, open communication is critical because the maintenance department will often work to a set schedule of engineering maintenance activities covering two or three months. The warehouse manager then plans according to this maintenance schedule, making sure that specialized maintenance materials are available in advance to avoid the dreaded scenario of disassembled machines sitting out of commission for weeks while awaiting spare parts.

Warehousing and Quality Control and Inspection. Organizations set standards for the materials it both uses and produces. The quality control function or department inspects goods and ensures that these standards are followed. Warehousing plays a role by holding all delivered goods aside until they are checked by Quality Control and making sure that the items labeled for rejection are not allowed to become part of the organization's acceptable working inventory. When rejected items are used, costly problems may arise, damaging an organization's budget and reputation.

Warehousing and Purchasing. Historically, the link between warehousing and purchasing has been very close. In many organizations, these two functions are united under the heading of *integrated materials management*. Where two separate operations do exist, a smooth relationship between them is vital. As a separate function, purchasing is responsible for buying all of the goods and services needed by the organization.

The purchasing function relies on the warehousing function for a wide variety of support activities. For example, purchasing managers depend on warehousing managers to keep them constantly informed about physical inventory levels and condition. When inventory loss, damage, or deterioration occurs, warehouse managers inform purchasing managers so that problem inventory may be replaced immediately, ensuring a balanced and economic flow of goods and services to the end users. Today, much of this is done through automated warehouse management and inventory control systems.

The purchasing function in many organizations is physically separated from the warehouse area or manufacturing floor, often located in different buildings, states, or even countries. Therefore, the purchasing function relies on warehousing to provide real time, up-to-date, accurate information about the performance of goods and services it is providing, based on manufacturing and user feedback. Such inventory performance information can be critical in ensuring maximum efficiency of the purchasing operation and its evaluation of the materials purchased.

Because they typically receive goods directly from suppliers, those in the warehousing function must resist the temptation to become directly involved with suppliers unless they are directed to do so by those in the purchasing function. Such a situation can cause problems when warehouse management makes decisions about delivery, quality, progress, and goods selection without the full background information that purchasing managers will have. Organizations that employ the integrated logistics management approach tend to suffer less from this type of problem.

Warehousing and Marketing. The marketing department relies on the warehousing department to ensure that finished inventory is available to be sold to customers as and when required, which is especially important for sales promotions and other marketing events. Warehousing is sometimes also responsible for the control of spare parts and accessories used in connection with an organization's finished products, which are supplied to users by the After-Sales Service function. Finally, warehouse managers must be aware of future sales forecasts in order to plan for possible increases or decreases of inventory and corresponding warehouse space and staff.

Warehousing and Accounting and Finance. Accounting and finance functions rely on the warehousing department for information about the value of inventory held and items damaged that need to be written off the organization's assets list. The accounting function also asks warehousing to confirm the receipt of goods as invoiced, especially in the case of doubt or query. The warehousing function also provides a continuous supply of data on inventory use in operations, which is especially useful for accounting in cost allocation to particular batches or jobs as carried out by operations. In addition, warehousing supplies information on physical stocktaking which helps accounting and finance prepare annual financial statements for an organization.

WAREHOUSING, LOGISTICS, AND SUPPLY CHAIN MANAGEMENT

As we mentioned earlier in the chapter, warehouse management resides within the realm of *logistics* at the individual company level or *supply chain management* at the cross-company strategic level. But what on earth do we mean by *logistics* and *supply chain management*?

Logistics is the name of the business discipline and the function within an organization that handles the flow of goods and information into, within, and out from that organization. Similar yet distinctly different, **supply chain management** is the business discipline and function within an organization that focuses on the flow of goods, information, and related finance across multiple organizations, often as goods move and transform from a raw materials or unfinished stage to a finished product received by an end user. Although these terms technically have different meanings, they are often used interchangeably by organizations in the real world to signify anything at all that has to do with the movement of goods. As goods - and their supporting information and documentation - flow into and depart from an organization, they follow a path known as a **supply chain**. If the perspective of the supply chain is from the internal workings of one organization, the supply chain has a *logistics focus*. If its perspective is broader and spread across multiple organizations, the supply chain has a *supply chain management focus*.

Figure 1.2 shows a *simple supply chain*, in which a supplier provides goods to a manufacturer, who in turn supplies manufactured finished goods to a retailer, who, at the end of it all, provides these finished goods to customers or end users. For example, a local apple orchard may have a glass

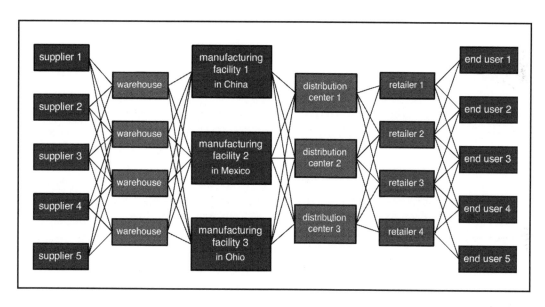

Figure 1.2 - Simple Supply Chain

container supplier for the cider and apple butter that it produces. When the orchard orders and receives the glass containers from its suppliers, it stores them in its warehouse until they are needed when cider and apple butter are produced in their manufacturing facility. Finished containers of cider and apple butter are then stored in the orchard's warehouse until they are delivered to a regional distribution center and then to local grocery stores and other retail locations across the state, where they are sold to end users like you and me.

Figure 1.3 - Complex Supply Chain

Most supply chains today are not that simple, however. Actual supply chains may look less like the simple supply chain of Figure 1.2 and more like the global supply chain in Figure 1.3, which spans many organizations in multiple locations around the world. For example, unlike the local apple orchard's simple supply chain, a popular breakfast cereal manufacturer might have many suppliers, manufacturing facilities, and retail sellers across the world, resulting in a complex *global supply chain*. For example, the cereal manufacturer may have separate suppliers for wheat, oats, vegetable oil, milk, preservatives, and cardboard packaging, with items going to the warehouses of the cereal company's different manufacturing facilities across the country and across the world. After the cereal is produced at each of the company's multiple manufacturing facilities, it is shipped to different regional distribution centers and then on to the multiple grocery stores within their region. As we will see later in this chapter, all of the locations indicated in the boxes in Figure 1.3 above may have their own warehouses associated with them, even if the box is not labelled *warehouse*. For example, "retailer 4" above might be a specific grocery store in Akron, Ohio. This grocery store is likely to have a small warehouse area in the back of the store to receive the cereal when it comes in and hold the extra boxes that don't currently fit on the grocery store shelves.

Warehouse management plays a significantly strategic role in the realm of logistics and supply chain management. In Price and Harrison's model of logistics management from *Looking at Logistics, 2nd Edition*, as shown in Figure 1.4, warehouse management plays a key role in inbound processes, internal processes, and outbound processes in logistics management. Internal warehouse management is a part of **materials management** and spans across logistics management process that are both **inbound** (into the company) and **internal** (within the company). Warehouse management is also the critical component of the **outbound** (out from the company) process of external distribution center management. No matter where you look within the world of logistics management, you are likely to find a warehouse!

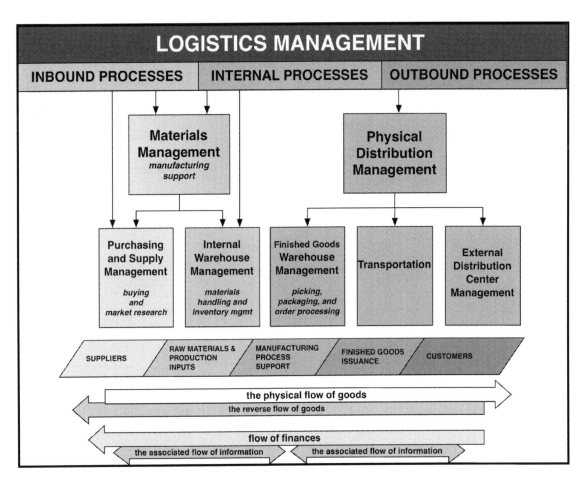

Figure 1.4 - Model for Logistics Management

Earlier in this chapter, we explored may of the functions of a warehouse. In Figure 1.5, many of these functions of a warehouse have been mapped out into a logistics management framework, showing which functions are associated with each *inbound*, *internal*, or *outbound* processes. Subsequent chapters of this text will first cover each of these inbound, internal, and outbound processes in warehouse management and will then follow with explorations of safety and security, technology and information technology, the people side of warehousing, and the future of warehouse management and inventory control.

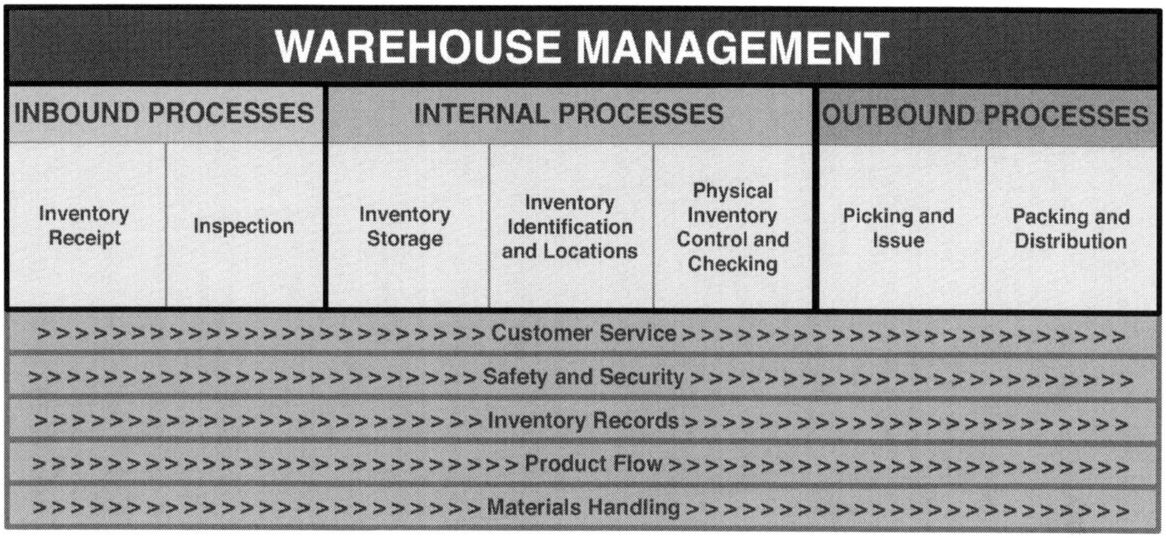

WAREHOUSE MANAGEMENT						
INBOUND PROCESSES		**INTERNAL PROCESSES**			**OUTBOUND PROCESSES**	
Inventory Receipt	Inspection	Inventory Storage	Inventory Identification and Locations	Physical Inventory Control and Checking	Picking and Issue	Packing and Distribution

> Customer Service >

> Safety and Security >

> Inventory Records >

> Product Flow >

> Materials Handling >

Figure 1.5 - The Functions of Warehouse Management

CHAPTER 1 REVIEW QUESTIONS

1. What is a warehouse? What is the size of a warehouse?

2. What are some examples of inventory held in warehouses?

3. What is the inspection function of warehousing? Why is it important?

4. What are the security and safety functions of warehousing? Why are they important?

5. What is the inventory records function of warehousing? What kind of information is kept and in what form is it recorded?

6. What is the difference between an internal customer and an external customer?

7. What is the relationship between warehousing and manufacturing?

8. What is physical distribution? What is its relationship to warehousing?

9. What is an organization's maintenance function? In the relationship between maintenance and warehousing, why is communication important?

10. What is materials management? What are its two primary functions?

CHAPTER 1 CASE STUDY

Three Examples of Real Life Warehouse Management

The chapters to follow will include examples of the inbound, internal, and outbound functions of warehouse management from three businesses: a retail chain, a manufacturer, and a service provider.

The retail chain we will examine is an Alaska gift and souvenir chain of retail stores called Once in a Blue Moose, which is a family-owned and family-run business headquartered in Anchorage, Alaska. Perhaps the best known and most highly regarded gift shop chain in Anchorage, Once in a Blue Moose regularly receives award and accolades from its customers, such as the 2015 Channel 2 Viewer's Choice Award for Best Gift Shop. Once in a Blue Moose has been a feature in downtown Anchorage since 1969 and is now run by two sisters and was run by their mother before them who founded the company. Two children of the sisters who are now running the company are currently in training to take over the company leadership. Once in a Blue Moose has seven retail locations across Anchorage and two retail locations in Seward, Alaska, which is a three-hour drive south of Anchorage. It also has an online storefront (https://store.bluemoosealaska.com) and ships goods to customers around the world. Once in a Blue Moose has a positive impact on the local economy, too, by working with local vendors and encouraging artisans to stop by to show and sell their creations. As a result, the company purchases products made both overseas and locally. Of its 732 vendors, an impressive 284 of them are located in Alaska. The company's headquarters and central warehouse are located in the same building in midtown Anchorage. As the company has grown, its owners have come up with innovative solutions for warehouse management and inventory control, especially in its creation of a tailor-made inventory management system. As a local retail chain, without the warehousing and inventory management resources available to larger chains, Once in a Blue Moose has come up with efficient, effective, and cost-effective solutions for managing and moving its inventory, such as in its use of coding and clever use of low cost materials handling solutions.

At Once in a Blue Moose, special floor tile designs serve as an immediate visual location code for different types of incoming inventory. Although difficult to tell in a black and white photo, color coding is also used in the movable storage racks for incoming inventory to indicate information about the inventory and its stage in the inventory receipt process.

The manufacturer we will examine is an internationally renowned winery called Tabalí, which is located in the Limarí Valley of Northern Chile. The winery owns three vineyards, from which all of its wines are sourced. The first plantings for the vineyards began in 1993 and the beautiful, open-air winery was built in 2004. The Tabalí winery processes 1300 tons of wine per year and many of its wines have received multiple national and international award and scores of 90+ points. Tabalí ships large quantities of its fragile bottles of wine around the world and must provide exceptional care and customer service throughout its inbound, internal, and outbound warehouse management processes to ensure that its bottles of wine get to their end consumers in perfect condition. Careful packaging and meticulous materials handling, while still maintaining a good speed of service, are the company's keys to exceptional customer service, with a perfectly balanced and consistent tasting wine hitting the customers' palates every time, wherever they may be.

In the northern desert of Chile, Tabalí, creates exceptional wines and must ensure that its customers receive the same exceptional wines. The winery does an outstanding job paying special attention to internal customer service in their outbound processes of warehouse management.

Finally, the service provider we will examine is an Alaskan telecommunications service provider called Alaska Communications. The company began as a utility and has been in operation for more than 100 years. It is now provides broadband and managed IT services for businesses and private customers. Alaska Communications employs approximately 700 people across Alaska and has a central warehouse in Anchorage. The company is an Alaskan leader in warehouse management and supply chain management with its forward thinking. Alaska Communications is one of the state's shining examples of vendor managed inventory, with vendors taking ownership for managing their items in the company's warehouse.The company also significantly streamlined its supply chain operations, including its warehouse management and inventory control, through an extensive lean initiative, completely changing its way of thinking about processes and waste.

At Alaska Communications, the company-wide lean initiative to streamline and standardize processes is reinforced visually throughout the company's warehouse.

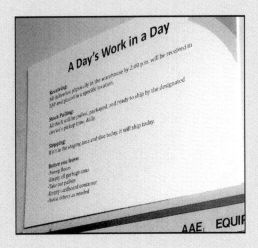

INSTRUCTIONS:

For the three companies described, which of the twelve functions of a warehouse might each of the company's warehouses engage in? Please explain your answer.

What might the supply chains for each of the three companies look like?

Do you think they will have simple or complex supply chains? Please explain your answer.

Chapter 2

Inbound Processes in Warehouse Management

In Chapter 1, we introduced the concept of *inbound* (into the company), *internal* (within the company), and *outbound* (out from the company) *processes* in logistics and warehouse management. This chapter focuses on the exciting world of the inbound processes of warehouse management! But before we begin talking about taking in and receiving inventory in inbound processes, let's examine what we mean by the word *inventory*.

INVENTORY: WHAT'S IN A WAREHOUSE?

Inventory is the collection of goods, materials, and physical resources being held by an organization, typically in warehouse facilities, distribution centers, or external inventory yards. Inventory may include, but is not limited to: components to be used in product assembly, finished products to be delivered to customers, and equipment maintenance or repair supplies.

More specifically, inventory can be classified into the following five categories:

1. *raw materials*, which are all goods used to assemble or produce the finished product (i.e., the product which will be sold and delivered to the customer). Examples of raw materials include: raw timber for a furniture manufacturer, 3/8" Philips head screws for a mechanical toy company, and flour for a bread bakery.

2. *work-in-process*, which are partially finished goods. They are no longer raw materials but are not quite yet fully assembled, produced, or manufactured. Because it is becoming economically advantageous for many industries, work-in-process goods are increasingly being transported and held by organizations. Examples of work-in-process goods include: lumber

cut, shaped, and sanded to be used in bookshelf production; crates of programmed computer chips to be placed in automobiles being assembled; and barrels of non-carbonated syrup base for soft drink bottling.

3. *finished goods*, which are the fully assembled, produced, or manufactured goods to be delivered to the customer. Examples of finished goods include: boxes of Quaker chocolate chip granola bars; Huffy bikes rolling off the assembly line; and 3/8" screws, with a toy manufacturer as the final customer. From this example, we see that one company's raw material (i.e., the toy manufacturer) is another company's finished goods (i.e., the screw manufacturer).

4. *maintenance, repair, and operating (MRO) supplies*, which are those goods not used to become part of the finished product but essential to the operation of an organization. Examples of MRO supplies include: cleaning liquids, machine parts and oils, equipment replacement hardware, paper, and light bulbs.

5. *distribution channel inventory*, which refers to any items and components currently located in the distribution system. These are likely to also fall into any of four previous categories of inventory; the important distinction is that they are not in static storage but are in movement in the distribution system.

As shown in Figure 2.1 below, inventory can be found throughout a product's entire supply chain, from the suppliers of raw materials to the finished goods being delivered to the final customer.

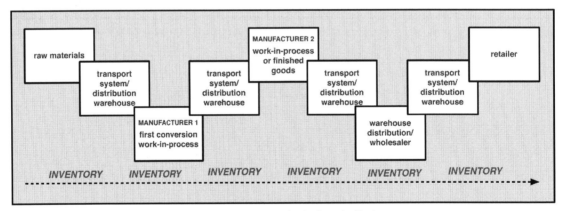

Figure 2.1 - Inventory in the Supply Chain

In the past twenty years, inventory has gotten a bad rap. The term has been saddled with negative connotations and is viewed with disdain because of the recent push to streamline supply chains and shed any and all excess inventory to cut costs. (We'll cover this in greater detail when we discuss Just-in-Time inventory management.) However, inventory and inventory holding are critical to an organization's ability to produce quality goods and deliver them to customers in a timely manner. For example, if a carbonated soft drink bottling plant did not hold an inventory of bottle caps, the drink would lose its defining fizz with bottles sitting idly, waiting for caps to be produced as they are needed. Therefore, let's charge forth and embrace the beauty that is inventory!

INVENTORY TERMINOLOGY AND MANAGEMENT

Understanding the primary types of inventory can also help us understand the importance of holding inventory. The two primary types of inventory are: *cycle stock* and *safety stock*. **Cycle stock** is the inventory that is most often "in action." Goods in cycle stock are continuously being issued and replenished and their holding times are typically brief and temporary. **Safety stock**, which is also called **buffer stock**, is inventory that is held and used as supply and demand dictate. These are basically the extra quantities of items held to protect an organization from losses that might be incurred from fluctuating supply availability and customer and market demands.

Although cycle and safety stock are categorized as different types of inventory, they are essentially the same goods held in the same location. Cycle and safety stock quantities are determined, contained, and tracked within a computer warehousing or inventory management information system. A few additional terms commonly associated with types of inventory are:

- **anticipation stock** - a form of safety stock in which raw materials, work-in-process goods, or finished goods are held in anticipation of a particular event that will occur, such as an upcoming holiday or a supplier phasing out a product line

- **hedging stock** - another form of safety stock in which raw materials, work-in-process goods, or finished goods are held in anticipation of an event that may or may not occur, such as a forecasted weather pattern, a potential increase in gasoline prices, a potential plant shutdown for a nearby supplier, or a potential transportation worker strike. For example, most large home improvement and grocery stores carry a hedging stock of snow shovels when television meteorologists forecast large winter storm fronts approaching.

- **allocated inventory** - inventory that is allocated and held for specific customers based on their orders or regular purchase patterns

- **decoupling inventory** - a form of safety stock in which an inventory of work-in-process goods is held at work stations within a manufacturing or assembling facility. These work-in-process goods are held to prevent operations from slowing down or halting entirely when delays, both expected (perhaps caused by shift changes or trainee employees) or unexpected (perhaps caused by machine failure or injury).

- **pipeline (or transportation) inventory** - a form of cycle stock which is simply that inventory (raw materials, work-in-process, or finished goods) which is in transit or "in the pipeline." Pipeline inventory is often examined in inventory efficiency studies of finished goods focusing on the amounts of time inventory spends in transit throughout different segments of its transportation pipeline.

Much of the inventory terminology above deals with having enough inventory to keep companies from having to go through the costly process of shutting down operations because they don't have enough inventory on hand. Inventory is also managed to help companies reduce their inventory holding costs. With **inventory management**, an organization examines and determines the amount of inventory (raw materials, work-in-process, finished goods, and supplies) needed to hold stock to keep the organization operating most efficiently and effectively as it faces fluctuating supply availability, customer demands, and an array of anticipated and unanticipated events.

Inventory management can provide a range of benefits, some of which act in conflict with one another. These benefits of inventory management include:

- **Increased Customer Service.** For organizations that don't practice inventory management or the many wonderful systems and models it has to offer (we'll cover these later in the book), maintaining a stock of excess inventory is a common method of ensuring that customers get their goods on time. With inventory management, however, forecasting is used to reduce inventory levels held while maintaining the same timeliness of delivery to customers. Furthermore, the cost to the customer can be reduced or additional services can be provided with the storage cost savings or reduced inventory levels.

- **Increased Efficiency.** Organizations can use inventory management to help them achieve greater efficiency in production and purchasing operations. For example, inventory management can help organizations determine the most efficient production run sizes (i.e., how many products to manufacture) based on customer demand forecasts and cost efficiencies to be achieved from longer runs of the same product. Similarly, inventory management can help organizations determine the most efficient purchasing volumes (i.e., how many supplies are ordered) based on forecasted amounts of supplies actually needed and discounts offered by suppliers for purchasing bulk volumes.

- **Reduced Cost.** As previously mentioned, organizations can use inventory management to help reduce operating costs. Holding excess inventory across its supply chain creates negative cash flow and drains a company of potential profits. Companies use effective inventory management systems every day to mitigate these potentially disastrous effects.

Inventory management plays a balancing act between the needs of those in an organization's operations and marketing departments and those in its finance department. The inventory goals of those in operations and marketing are to hold enough (or even more than enough) inventory to maintain a constant production and inventory flow to meet customers' demands and to keep sufficient safety stock levels to cover all anticipated events and unforeseen demands. Conversely, the inventory goals of those in finance is to minimize inventory levels as much as possible to

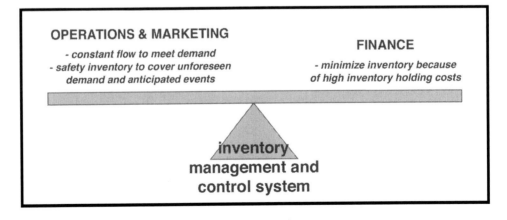

Figure 2.2 - Balancing Act Between the Needs of Operations/Marketing and Finance

minimize high holding costs. Inventory management and inventory control systems balance these conflicting needs to achieve optimum inventory efficiency levels.

When goods start rolling in through the doors of your warehouse, you need to examine how you will control this incoming inventory. Within a warehouse, the ***inventory receipt team*** is responsible for receiving all materials and items supplied to the organization, from both internal transfers (such as from another part of the organization) and external sources (such as deliveries from suppliers). Both must be strictly controlled to ensure efficient warehouse management and inventory control. This inventory control, which is the domain of our diligent inventory receipt team, is made up of the following five elements: *inventory receipt process*; *planning for and unloading inventory*; *inventory documentation*; *inspecting inventory*; and *inventory coding*.

THE INVENTORY RECEIPT PROCESS

The inventory receipt team of an organization typically follows a standard and logical sequence of events, known as the ***inventory receipt cycle*** or the ***inventory receipt cycle process***. Each stage of the inventory receipt cycle is important for efficient and cost effective inventory management and must be carefully controlled and supervised by the warehouse. The eleven uniquely important stages of this process are:

1. **Notification of Order Placement.** In this stage of the inventory receipt cycle process, the Purchasing Department notifies the warehouse that goods have been ordered and that a provisional delivery date and method of delivery have been set. Warehouse managers can then make provisional plans within the inventory receipt system, which is especially important for larger orders. (Imagine the chaos of an unexpected container load of eggs arriving at a Florida warehouse on a hot August day.)

2. **Confirmation of Delivery.** In this second stage of the inventory receipt cycle process, the warehouse confirms the upcoming delivery date, time, and contents with the distributor, who may be either internal or external to the organization. This allows the warehouse manager to make definite arrangements for the delivery within the warehouse, especially if any last minute changes have been made.

3. **Inventory Space Allocation.** After the delivery has been confirmed, the warehouse manager then ensures that sufficient space has been allocated within the warehouse for this new delivery, which may include inventory rearrangement. Space allocation is vital if double handling is to be avoided!

4. **Labor Allocation.** In almost every situation, inventory unloading requires some degree of manual or mechanical handling. In some cases, a large number of staff may be needed. The warehouse manager, therefore, make plans to ensure that the necessary amount of staff will be available at the time of delivery.

5. **Materials Handling Equipment Allocation.** The warehouse manager also needs to plan for the materials handling equipment to be used during inventory unloading and storage. Certain types of materials and packaging will require specialized materials

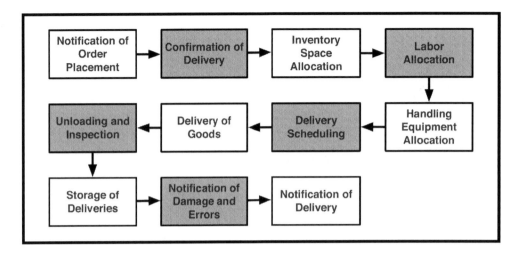

Figure 2.3 - The Inventory Receipt Process

handling equipment to unload and store them properly (e.g., palletized goods require forklift trucks). The warehouse manager must ensure that this equipment and their operators will be available.

6. **Delivery Scheduling.** Upon confirmation of delivery and simultaneously with inventory, labor, and materials handling equipment allocation, scheduling the delivery of the goods into the warehouse's operating systems calendar is the sixth step of the inventory receipt cycle process. Proper scheduling enables deliveries to be handled using the full resources of the warehouse operation. The ideal schedule provides a steady stream of deliveries throughout the warehouse working day.

7. **Delivery of Goods.** At this stage of the cycle, the goods actually arrive at the warehouse. The delivery note is checked against the inventory supplied. If the warehouse is not able to check a load (perhaps if it is undermanned or experiencing too many simultaneous deliveries), the delivery document must be signed and the word unchecked must be written so that any claim for shortage or damage will not be complicated by a delivery note signature alone, which typically indicates that the delivery was received and checked as acceptable.

8. **Unloading and Inspection.** This eighth stage of the inventory receipt cycle process is unloading and inspecting the inventory delivered. This eighth step is so important that many portions of subsequent section of this book are devoted to it.

9. **Storage of Deliveries.** After the goods have been delivered, unloaded, and inspected, they must then be stored. This is not as simple as it sounds, however. In some cases, deliveries have to be broken down into smaller units and then stored on the shelves, bins, racks, or whatever storage equipment is available and most appropriate. At this stage, it is essential that goods be placed in their correct storage location so that the entire inventory issuance and checking system is not adversely affected.

10. **Notification of Damages, Shortages, or Errors.** As goods are received and stored, warehouse personnel sometimes uncover damage, shortages, or errors. When this happens, warehouse management must send notification of the damage, shortage, or error to the Purchasing, Production Planning, Quality Control, and Inventory Control/Records departments.

11. **Notification of Delivery.** In addition to notification of damages, shortages, and errors, the warehouse must notify the Purchasing, Production Planning, Quality Control, and Inventory Control/Records departments that the goods have been delivered and accepted as inventory so that the other departments can adjust their records accordingly to note the increase in inventory.

The eleven stages of the inventory receipt cycle process outlined above are standard for most warehouse situations. Depending on the nature of the organization, its products, the goods being delivered, and the warehouse itself, there is a range of other elements, which may also influence the inventory receipt cycle process. These elements include: special deliveries, special handling, communications between the Warehouse and Purchasing departments, and internal transfers. In some instances, different arrangements may need to be made for certain types of *special deliveries* and materials. An example of such a special arrangement might be to accommodate a delivery outside of normal working hours, such as nighttime deliveries of unusually large items to avoid roadway and even warehouse traffic and congestion. In addition, some materials, such as hazardous explosives and chemicals, may require *special handling* upon receipt into the warehouse. These instances require careful planning by warehouse managers to ensure that all preparations and safety measures are taken to reduce the risk of accident or damage.

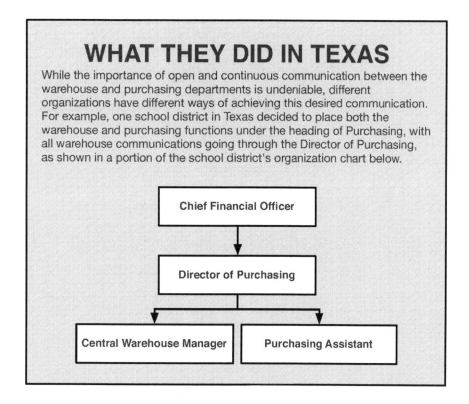

WHAT THEY DID IN TEXAS

While the importance of open and continuous communication between the warehouse and purchasing departments is undeniable, different organizations have different ways of achieving this desired communication. For example, one school district in Texas decided to place both the warehouse and purchasing functions under the heading of Purchasing, with all warehouse communications going through the Director of Purchasing, as shown in a portion of the school district's organization chart below.

Chief Financial Officer

Director of Purchasing

Central Warehouse Manager   Purchasing Assistant

During the inventory receipt cycle process, sound and meaningful communication between the warehouse and the purchasing department is vital. Purchasing must keep the warehouse fully informed of all development concerning inventory delivery. Changes in delivery schedules occur often due to factors beyond the control of the supplier or buyer. Unless the warehouse is advised of these changes, however, much preparation and work will go to waste and the warehouse will continue to work to a schedule that has no real meaning, making management of the whole operation very difficult. It is equally vital for the warehouse to inform the purchasing department of any faults, shortages, or errors made by the supplier so that Purchasing can contact the supplier immediately to arrange for a new delivery. If the warehouse does not contact them, those in the Purchasing department may incorrectly assume that all was well with the delivery and thus take no action.

An *internal transfer* is the process of moving inventory from one location to another within the organization. Each location, such as a depot or warehouse, may have its own inventory record and inventory control system, making properly documented control of inventory transfer a necessity. One important part of internal transfers is the *internal transfer note*, the standard document used to transfer inventory and check all internal deliveries. The internal transfer note is very similar to the *supplier's delivery note*, described later in this chapter.

PLANNING FOR AND UNLOADING INVENTORY

One of the key warehouse management activities is getting goods into and out from the warehouse facility. Getting goods into a warehouse is called *inventory receipt* and involves something as simple as receiving and signing for a single package from a delivery person to something as complex as unloading endless streams of trucks and railroad cars into a cross-docking distribution center for subsequent sorting and delivery while continually checking the accompanying paperwork to make sure that the tens of thousands of items being received are the ones that were actually ordered. The more goods a company receives, the more likely it is to have a *shipping and receiving department*, dedicated solely to making sure the inventory receipt cycle process is followed efficiently and effectively. This department manages the flow of goods into and out from warehouse facilities, keeps track of who owns the goods at which stage of the process (more on this later), and keeps accurate inventory control records of the goods.

The receiving and shipping department also holds a tight control over the schedule of incoming receipts. They must work with the purchasing department to make sure that the flow of goods into warehouse facilities are timed so that the warehouse docks aren't cluttered with too many trucks, with truck drivers idly sitting in line racking up unnecessary cost in labor hours for the company. On top of that, if trucks or railcars are held too long at a warehouse facility, the organization may incur *detention and demurrage charges*, extra fees charged by the shipper. Warehouses also have a limited amount of materials handling equipment to move the goods from the trucks or trains into the warehouse (or onto other trucks if it's a cross-docking facility), so deliveries must be timed to make sure that there will be enough of the needed equipment on hand to handle the type and amount of inventory being received.

Even when deliveries are timed and scheduled well, the receiving and shipping department must also plan for individual incoming delivery vehicles. Some trucks may need assistance and direction in backing in to the assigned dock. Trucks may also need **dock levelers**, which the trucks drive onto to ensure that the floor of the truck's trailer is level with the warehouse floor. (Just imagine having to drive a forklift or wheel a hand truck into a truck that is eight inches below the warehouse floor!) Warehouse receiving personnel should also check to make sure that truck drivers place **chocks** (wooden or metal barriers) against the truck's tires to prevent it from moving while it is parked in the warehouse dock. Finally, warehouse receipt personnel must do an initial inspection of goods in the truck or train car to make sure their is not major damage, deterioration, contamination, or insect infestations before unloading it into the warehouse. (Imagine a warehouse worker forgetting this step as damp and roach-infested bags of sugar are unloaded into a doughnut factory!)

When a truck or rail car has arrived, goods must be unloaded from the container or truck and placed into inventory in the warehouse facility. Depending on the needs of the company receiving the goods, either the people delivering the goods unload them or the company receiving the goods has their own crew to handle all unloading. For example, if heavy goods are received that need forklifts to get them out of the truck, the company receiving them may want their own forklift-trained drivers to handle all unloading. In especially busy facilities, such as larger distribution centers and cross-docking facilities, drivers delivering goods may drop off the trailers and detach them from their trucks so that they can be on their way to work on other deliveries and the company receiving the goods can handle the goods when they are ready.

When companies receive goods into a warehouse facility, it is often not placed directly into the far reaches of the warehouse shelves. Instead, goods are often first unloaded into a **staging area**, which is typically located close to the bays where goods are received. Items typically wait here until they are inspected and checked formally by the quality control department. (More on this later in this chapter.)

INVENTORY DOCUMENTATION

One vital element of the inventory receipt procedure is **documentation**. Organizations engaged in any aspect of warehouse management have developed a comprehensive set of documents to facilitate control of the inventory receipt process. Each of these documents has a specific and important role to play. Although documents will vary as individual organizations develop them to meet their own unique needs, the logic behind inventory receipt documentation remains constant. Examples of categories of inventory receipt documents include: *Bill of Lading, Need to Reorder Notification, Purchase Order Copies, Advice Note of Intended Delivery, Delivery Note, 3rd Party Carrier's Consignment Note, Internal Packing Note,* and *Receiver Report.* As we explore each of these document categories below, you will see that documentation may occur in a variety of forms, including both computer-based and hard copy varieties. Despite the fact that the documentation of larger companies is almost entirely digital, many small- to medium-sized companies still rely heavily on a mix of digital and paper-based documentation.

Bill of Lading. A Bill of Lading (also referred to as *BOL* or *B/L*) is a document issued by a shipper, which may or may not be the supplier itself. The document acknowledges that specific, listed goods have been received as cargo for conveyance to a specific, listed place for delivery to an identified consignee. This is perhaps one of the most important documents in the inventory receipt process because it serves as paper to digital proof of and controls the acceptance, transport, and delivery of goods. The Bill of Lading contains a wealth of information about the shipment, including: shipment date and weight, order number, city of shipment origin, whether to not the shipment charges have been prepaid, the shipper's identification information (again, thing may or may not be the supplier itself), the destination name and address, a BOL tracking number, and special handling and payment instructions.

Date: **BILL OF LADING** Page 1 of ______

SHIP FROM	
Name: Address: City/State/Zip: SID#: FOB: ☐	**Bill of Lading Number:** ____________ BAR CODE SPACE
SHIP TO	
Name: Location #: ____ Address: City/State/Zip: CID#: FOB: ☐	**CARRIER NAME:** ____________ Trailer number: Seal number(s): **SCAC:** **Pro number:**
THIRD PARTY FREIGHT CHARGES BILL TO:	
Name: Address: City/State/Zip:	BAR CODE SPACE
SPECIAL INSTRUCTIONS:	**Freight Charge Terms:** Prepaid ______ Collect ______ 3rd Party ______
	☐ (check box) Master Bill of Lading: with attached underlying Bills of Lading

CUSTOMER ORDER INFORMATION

CUSTOMER ORDER NUMBER	# PKGS	WEIGHT	PALLET/SLIP Y	or N	ADDITIONAL SHIPPER INFO
GRAND TOTAL					

CARRIER INFORMATION

HANDLING UNIT		PACKAGE				**COMMODITY DESCRIPTION**	**LTL ONLY**	
QTY	TYPE	QTY	TYPE	**WEIGHT**	H.M. (X)	Commodities requiring special or additional care or attention in handling or stowing must be so marked and packaged as to ensure safe transportation with ordinary care.	NMFC #	CLASS
						RECEIVING		
						STAMP SPACE		
						GRAND TOTAL		

Where the rate is dependent on value, shippers are required to state specifically in writing the agreed or declared value of the property as follows:

"The agreed or declared value of the property is specifically stated by the shipper to be not exceeding ______ per ______."

COD Amount: $ ____________

Fee Terms: Collect: ☐ Prepaid: ☐
Customer check acceptable: ☐

NOTE Liability Limitation for loss or damage in this shipment may be applicable. See 49 U.S.C. - 14706(c)(1)(A) and (B).

RECEIVED, subject to individually determined rates or contracts that have been agreed upon in writing between the carrier and shipper, if applicable, otherwise to the rates, classifications and rules that have been established by the carrier and are available to the shipper, on request, and to all applicable state and federal regulations.

The carrier shall not make delivery of this shipment without payment of freight and all other lawful charges.

____________ **Shipper Signature**

SHIPPER SIGNATURE / DATE	Trailer Loaded:	Freight Counted:	**CARRIER SIGNATURE / PICKUP DATE**
This is to certify that the above named materials are properly classified, packaged, marked and labeled, and are in proper condition for transportation according to the applicable regulations of the DOT.	☐ By Shipper ☐ By Driver	☐ By Shipper ☐ By Driver/pallets said to contain ☐ By Driver/Pieces	Carrier acknowledges receipt of packages and required placards. Carrier certifies emergency response information was made available and/or carrier has the DOT emergency response guidebook or equivalent documentation in the vehicle.

Figure 2.4 - Blank Bill of Lading Form

Need to Reorder Notification. A Need to Reorder Notification is typically created by an organization's Inventory Control/ Records section and is sent to the Purchasing department, who, in turn, places an order with the appropriate supplier based on the information supplied in the reorder notification. The warehouse is also typically sent a copy of this notification so that it is aware of the impending inventory delivery, even though it may be some time before the goods actually arrive at the warehouse.

Purchase Order Copies. A copy of the Purchase Order, which is typically issued by the purchasing department and sent to the supplier, is also sent to the warehouse receiving area. This purchasing order contains information including: the code number and description of goods, quantity ordered, method of delivery, required delivery date, the purchase order number, date of the order being placed, the supplier's made and address, and special instructions for inventory receipt and quality control inspections. The price of items might also be included in some copies of the purchase order but typically not on the copies received by the warehouse.

Advice Note of Intended Delivery. The supplier, who is contracted by the Purchasing department to supply the inventory ordered, issues the Advice Note of Intended Delivery. This note is issued when the goods are dispatched and is designed to provide the following data: *confirmation that the order will be delivered, a provisional delivery date and time, the method of delivery to be used by the supplier, the quantity of goods that will be supplied,* and *the code number and description of the inventory concerned.*

Delivery Note. The Delivery Note (or *Delivery Slip*) is usually supplied with the goods as they are delivered, describing what the supplier has actually delivered to the warehouse. When goods arrive at the warehouse, the Delivery Note must be carefully checked by the warehouse receiving area staff against the inventory unloaded to ensure that the figures and details on the delivery note are accurate. The Delivery Note is one of the most important inventory receipt documents, largely because of the information it contains, which includes inventory: *quantity, type, color, code, delivery date,* and *cost.*

3rd Party Carrier's Consignment Note. This Consignment Note (or *Consignment Slip*) is used when the supplier has outsourced (i.e., contracted out) the actual physical delivery of inventory to a third party carrier. The third party organization provides its own form and delivery note so that delivery control can be maintained and claims for non-delivery may be processed properly. In most cases, the goods delivered will have both a supplier's delivery note and a carrier's consignment note.

Packing Slip. The Packing Slip also provided by the supplier at the time of delivery, is used to carry out a more detailed check of the inventory delivered after the shipment has been broken down for storage. Unlike the Delivery Note, which describes the content of the entire shipment, the Packing Slip lists what is actually within each individual unit (parcel, box, drum, etc.) delivered. It typically includes specific data about quantities, types, sizes, colors, and specifications of the inventory within the unit.

Receiver Report. The Receiver Report is generated by the company receiving the goods and a new report is created for each shipment received. It typically lists the items received, the time and location they are received, and, most importantly, notes if there are discrepancies between the suppliers' and shippers' documentation and the actual goods received, such as if incorrect quantities of items were received or if there has been initial visible damage that occurred to items in shipment.

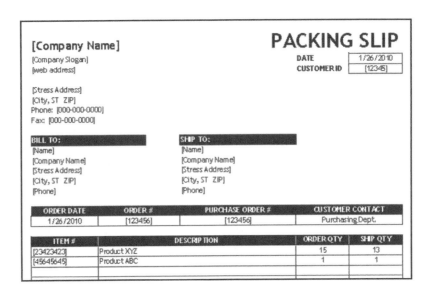

Figure 2.5 - Packing Slip Template

INSPECTING INVENTORY

As goods arrive into the warehouse, one of the primary steps taken to control the incoming inventory is inspecting the incoming materials. Inventory inspection begins with the shipping and receiving department, or whoever receives goods into the company that has ordered them. This department checks the order to make sure the goods received match the goods listed in the accompanying paperwork, such as the delivery note or internal packing note. When someone from this department signs off on the delivery, whether in a longhand signature or digital form, the ownership of the goods transfers from the sender to the receiver. Therefore, the person handling and initially inspecting the goods upon receipt must check the accuracy of the shipment and make sure the quantity and quality of the items matches the documentation. There must also be procedures in place in when there are discrepancies or if damage has occurred during the shipping process and some incoming goods must be rejected. There must also be procedures in place for how to handle special inspection and handling requirements for specific goods.

In many situations, the truck driver delivering the goods cannot leave until the goods have been check and signed for by the receiver, so the more streamlined the inventory inspection and receipt process, the more efficient and cost-effective the process is for all involved. For example, a company may plan for such contingencies by allowing partially damaged shipments to be accepted if the following rules are followed:

1. *Check all incoming goods for quantity and accuracy.*

2. *Check all incoming goods for immediate signs of visible damage.*

3. *If there are any discrepancies with #1 or #2 above, take photographs of the items involved, especially damaged items. Make sure to take the photos of the items while they are still on the shipper's truck or container.*

4. *Write down all of these discrepancies on the Bill of Lading and any additional documentation that the driver or deliverer asks you to sign. Such discrepancies could include differences in pallet counts or specific damage to goods. Initial all areas where you have written additional information and ask the driver to initial these areas, too.*

5. *Sign the required documentation and make sure to get a copy of the signed documentation from the driver. If the quality of your copy is poor, make sure to take a photograph of the original copy held by the driver.*

In addition to this initial eyeball inspection of goods as soon as they are received, there is also a more thorough inspection of goods received as they are unpacked. Depending upon the size of the company and the nature of the goods being received, warehouse staff or specially trained employees from the company's **quality control department** may perform this inspection. Sometimes both may be involved, with the warehouse is often responsible for ensuring that physical quantities are correct and the quality control department responsible for checking the quality of the incoming inventory.

When the quality of goods are checked, this inspection is typically made against predetermined levels of acceptability using one of two basic inspection methods: **the 100% method**, in which all items are tested, or **the sampling method**, in which only a sample of each batch delivered is tested. If the sampling method is used, the warehouse might supply samples of each delivery to the quality control department so that regular quality checks and tests can be made for each delivery, thus maintaining consistency in supply quality. If inspected items are rejected upon delivery, the warehouse must notify the quality control department immediately. The warehouse typically holds this rejected inventory aside in a dedicated area to ensure that these faulty materials are not used, which might subsequently cause faulty manufacturing output or customer dissatisfaction. Similarly, the warehouse must store accepted incoming goods in a manner that ensures that they will not be damaged while in storage.

The reputation and survival of an organization depend upon its ability to satisfy its customers' needs. Poor product and service quality can lead to a loss of credibility and increased cost due to scrap, rework, and late deliveries, all caused by the need to repeat tasks that were not completed correctly the first time. One measure developed to address this pivotal issue of quality is **TQC**, or **total quality control**. Total quality control was developed in Japan in the 1970s as a means of preventing waste by not producing defective products. In TQC, everything is important in the goal of achieving first-class quality. Rather than follow the traditional approach, in which goods not meeting specification are detected, in TQC, the relationship between the supplier, buyer, and ultimate customer is fully integrated to prevent poor quality.

From the Japanese idea of TQC, quality control has become a standard practice in organizations throughout the world. **Quality control** is today known as the process of setting standards of acceptability for goods purchased and produced by an organization and then accepting or rejecting goods based on these standards. In setting quality control standards, **specifications** or detailed item descriptions are outlined, which include information about its: size; dimensions; performance; characteristics, such as color, texture, and form; quality; chemical analysis; and functions. Once an item's specifications have been drawn up, all goods of this type received by the warehouse will have to meet the requirements of the specifications. If they are found to be below the standards set within the specifications, they will not be accepted into the warehouse and will instead be classified as ***rejected inventory***. Once an item has been rejected, a procedure like the one below is typically followed carefully:

- *The rejected goods are double checked to ensure that the real cause for rejection exists. A senior member of the warehouse staff is typically involved with this step.*

- *The quality control department is then notified so that it can inspect the items to confirm the rejection order.*

- *The purchasing department is then informed of the rejection so that it can contact the supplier to arrange for collection and replacement of the faulty items.*

- *The production/planning department is then informed so that it will be aware of the shortage of inventory caused by the rejection. This step is a vital one because inventory shortages can affect the organization's production output.*

In order to carry out this quality control function, many organizations have their own ***quality control department***, whose sole function is to monitor the standards and quality of the goods used and produced by the organization. In an ideal world, organizations would only buy items from suppliers whose items were all consistently of acceptable quality, thus never needing inspection. In the real world, however, even the best suppliers can make mistakes. In addition, many organizations do not have the market power needed to demand consistently perfect quality from their suppliers. This leaves the average organization with the need for a quality control department, which inspects incoming inventory to prevent faulty items from making their way into the production process or into the hands of end users.

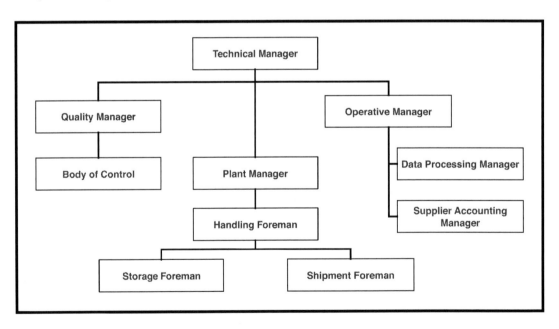

Figure 2.6 - Example of a Quality Control Department. This Italian steelworks company's organization chart outlines a separate quality control department headed by a Quality Manager.

Once it is formed, a quality control department sets its aims and objectives. Examples of the aims and objectives for a standard Quality Control department would include:

- *To set and monitor standards of quality for all items handled by the organization.*

- *To eliminate the possibility of faulty production from becoming distributed and sold to the consumer, which might damage the organization's reputation.*

- *To act as a liaison between all departments involved with setting standards to ensure that all standards set are acceptable and workable for all those concerned.*

- *To ensure that the quality and performance of all items delivered from suppliers and internal sources into the warehouse is acceptable.*

For a quality control department to function effectively, the organization must first establish a system of standards based on its own needs and objectives. These standards, which vary in stringency from organization to organization, are influenced by a range of factors, including: *company policy, complexity of the items,* and *agreement between departments.*

Most organizations set a global company policy regarding their reputation and the quality of their products. A company facing strong competition, especially when quality is a factor of this competition, will need very stringent quality control standards so that it won't fall behind its rivals. In addition, the degree and nature of quality control inspections depends largely upon the type and nature of the goods involved, i.e., how complex they are. Effective inspection of highly specialized and technically advanced materials will require highly skilled and knowledgeable quality control inspectors.

Finally, when an organization's quality control standards are being set, an effective and productive working environment is created when all of the organization's departments affected by these standards agree on and accept them. This desired acceptance of standards is best achieved when a representative of each department participates in initially setting the standards. If the approach used to set quality control standards is indeed one of joint consultation among departments, for most organizations, the departments involved are the:

- **Production Department.** Because the production department (or manufacturing department) must work with the materials purchased during the production process, it is most interested in establishing standards that guarantee a high quality of input. With higher quality input materials, productive output improves because machine output improves and delays arising from rejected materials are reduced.

- **Marketing Department.** Because the marketing department has to sell the organization's products in the marketplace, it is most interested in establishing quality control standards, which will result in high quality output in terms of finish, performance, design, and packaging.

- **Design Department**. Designers must be involved in setting quality control standards because they are responsible for meeting the quality and performance requirements set by the company and the customers.

- **Quality Control Department.** While it seems obvious that the quality control department would be involved in setting quality control standards, it is important to note quality inspectors and monitors themselves should be involved in setting the standards because it will be their responsibility to enforce them.

- **Warehouse Management.** In many cases, the warehouse is the first line of defense against faulty materials being introduced into the organization. The warehouse has traditionally been responsible for the initial inspection of all materials, both internal goods and those from external suppliers, delivered to the warehouse. Warehouse managers are now responsible for initial inspections and for liaising with the Quality Control department for quality control standards inspections and monitoring.

- **Purchasing Department.** Although their role in setting quality control standards is not an obvious one, the purchasing department must be involved throughout the entire standards-setting process so that they are fully aware of the needs of the organization in terms of the quality and price of the materials it will purchase. The purchasing department will also be able to provide information on the availability of the requirements needed for the specification proposed and its effect on the overall cost of production, which will ultimately play a large part in determining the sales price.

- **Customers.** Although not an official department of an organization, the customers are indirectly involved in setting quality control standards. For example, if goods produced by the company are inferior to other brands, the customers will not buy them.

While it is important for departments to work together to set quality control standards, there are no guarantees that all of the departments within an organization will always agree. Conflicting interests are not uncommon at this stage and may include: a production department unwilling to be tied to strict standards of output that might result in subsequent delays; a marketing department demanding high quality yet unwilling to accept the increased prices this will bring; or a purchasing department that understands the need for high quality materials but is itself conflicted because it knows it must keep costs down.

INVENTORY CODING

The modern industrial organization is complex and the range and type of items held in its inventory are correspondingly complex. In order to manage this complex range of inventory, an inventory classification system is needed so that individual inventory items can be stored, identified, and issued quickly and efficiently. Common names of items, such as *table* or *pump*, which work well in the everyday world, present difficulties in the world of inventory management.

Common name terms are very limited and often not very descriptive. For example, the word *table* reveals some information about the look and function of the item, but it reveals nothing about its size, color, or composition. Also, an item may have more than one common name, which can lead to confusion and improper issue. This is especially true for global organizations, in which different languages and even variations of the same language may be used across its global operations. For example, what we call a *tractor-trailer truck* or *eighteen-wheeler* in the United States is called an *articulated lorry* in England. Finally, many items used in the production environment are so highly technical that it would require extensive explanation to label them in common language.

Because of these problems encountered with common names and common language, most organizations have developed extensive codes to identify all of the items held in their inventory, without using long, complex, or wordy terminology. These **codes** are usually a homogeneous, concise system of letters, numbers, and/or symbols used across the entire organization, which convey a wealth of necessary information about each item. Even those of us not currently in the inventory management field already use codes in our everyday lives, from UAA for the University of Alaska Anchorage to our library's Library of Congress Numbering System to the label of MP3 for the audio files we listen to on our computers or iPods, which actually means Moving Picture Experts Group Audio Layer 3. Could you imagine having to say all of those words every time you wanted to talk about a music file?

Aside from the advantage of replacing a complex item's time-consuming tongue twister of a common name with only a few numbers or letters, inventory codes and their corresponding classification systems offer most organizations a wealth of advantages including:

- **Advantage #1: Increased Efficiency.** With an inventory coding system, a long and complex requisition no longer needs to be completed. Using only a simple series of numbers or letters, an exact item required can quickly be communicated to warehouse staff, thus saving considerable time and effort. Remember how long it used to take your local grocery store cashier to ring up unusual produce selections, such as papayas, mangoes, and cassavas? First they would have to figure out what the item was and then they would have to look up the price because the prices of infrequently purchased items would not always be the easiest to memorize quickly. Meanwhile, you would begin to regret your yen for papayas! Today, however, papaya shopping is hassle-free because most grocery stores code their produce and place a bar coded sticker on each fruit or vegetable item, making for streamlined efficiency at the cash register.

- **Advantage #2: Improved Accuracy.** When a warehouse receives a correct code for an item required, it may then easily select and issue the item without the fear of issuing the wrong item. This aspect of inventory coding is particularly advantageous when multiple items appear visually similar and their differences are not immediately discernible, such as screws with a 3/4-inch thread versus those with a 7/8-inch thread. A simple code can classify and isolate such differences for immediate and accurate identification.

- **Advantage #3: Error Reduction.** Because of the exact nature of an inventory coding system and its logical approach (which we will explore in greater detail later), it is actually quite difficult to make an error in item identification, unlike the process of using long and complex written inventory requests, which is traditionally an open invitation for issuance mistakes.

- **Advantage #4: Inventory Location and Marking Benefits.** Because of the logical nature of inventory coding, it lends itself well to inventory location planning and marking within a warehouse. In many cases, different types of materials are stored within different sections of a warehouse. A well-devised inventory coding system can be integrated with the actual physical placement of inventory so that an item's code and placement work together in a logical, easily understood system. This combination of inventory placement and coding system can then be used for marking-up storage areas quickly and efficiently. (We take a more in-depth look at coding in inventory location systems in a later chapter.)

- **Advantage #5: Purchasing Department Benefits.** Not only does warehouse staff benefit from an inventory coding system, but the Purchasing department does as well. One of the basic responsibilities of Warehouse management is to keep the Purchasing department informed about inventory levels and goods required for purchase. When the Warehouse and Purchasing departments use an inventory coding system together, greater and more efficient understanding is fostered between the two departments. Using a simple but information-rich code, lengthy and time-consuming requisition requests are no longer needed.

- **Advantage #6: Assistance to Suppliers.** In some cases, a copy of the inventory coding system can be sent to an organization's major suppliers, who would then be able to easily interpret purchase requests completed using the code. This extra use of an inventory coding system would save both time and effort at all stages of an organization's purchasing cycle, and thus reduce the administrative costs of ordering.

- **Advantage #7: Information Technology Benefits.** For a computer system to operate efficiently and effectively, it must be able to locate and identify the files associated with the items held in its inventory so that transactions for inventory records, control, and storage can all be processed as quickly and as accurately as possible. These computer operations are greatly enhanced when a logical inventory coding system is used. Because of the logical way in which computers operate, they are able to immediately identify the item in question and all of its accompanying documentation by its code number.

Different organizations have their own needs and resources, all of which will influence the different coding systems they each develop. The coding systems they choose to employ may be as simple or as complex as the organizations need them to be. There are, however, different basic types of coding systems. An organization may choose to employ one of them, all of them, or any combination in between. A few of these basic coding systems include:

- **Item-Based Coding.** In *item-based coding*, an inventory item is classified and coded with letters, numbers, and/or symbols according to its nature and make-up. For example, an item-based code could first reveal that the item is a pipe and then might reveal its length, diameter, thickness, and composition (copper, plastic, etc.). Because it can hold a great deal of information about an individual item and be universally applied and easily created with infinite variations, item-based coding is the most widely employed coding system in inventory management.

- **End-Use Coding.** In *end-use coding*, an item is coded according to its final use in terms of the operation or product. End-use coding is very similar to item-based coding, but its emphasis and primary classification scheme is based on the final use of the item and not the item itself. For example, in an assembly line operation, items are end-use coded according to a production line. Items heading to a Ford automobile assembly line will be coded first according to their designated production line (i.e., whether the item be used in assembling an Escort or an Explorer), with secondary sections of the code perhaps revealing information about the item itself.

- **Color Coding.** *Color coding* is an identification system based upon using different colors as the primary means of coding and identifying items held in inventory. While it can be a very effective means of immediate identification, color coding has the disadvantage of being limited in its range. A box of crayons may have 164 colors, but, at a distance, how discernible is *brick red* from *burnt sienna*? There are actually a finite and relatively small number of immediately discernible colors. Once the basic colors (red, blue, yellow, black, white, green, orange, and purple) have been used, the color coding system can no longer be used effectively to create new code categories. Therefore, color coding is used primarily in connection with chemical and lumber warehouses.

- **Supplier Coding.** In *supplier coding*, the organization simply uses the codes created and used by the item's supplier. While this system can be an easy one to implement and use when an organization has only one supplier, it can become very confusing when multiple suppliers are involved because each will typically have their own unique coding systems.

- **Location Coding.** In *location coding*, inventory is assigned a code that is based on the item's location, i.e., warehouse, row, bay, shelf, etc. Often a location code will be used in conjunction with one of the other four coding systems, such as item-based coding.

Before a new coding system is introduced into any inventory management system, an organization must consider a range of issues, including the following three factors. First, it must consider the *range and type of inventory* to be coded. The more complex and variegated the items held in inventory, the more complex and flexible the coding system will have to be. It is critical for a newly constructed inventory code to be both logical and flexible enough to accommodate inventory change and growth. Second, it must consider the *staff and resources available* to introduce and update the inventory code. A very complex system will need a great deal of time and skill for its introduction and maintenance. In such a system, warehouse personnel will require specialized training to ensure its success. Finally, in introducing a new coding system, an organization must consider whether or not the system will be *digital or manual* in its operation. Computers now play an integral role in most inventory management systems, especially those of large, widespread organizations. In such systems, numerical coding systems are preferred and even essential for efficient computer data storage and retrieval systems.

Once an organization has established its need for an inventory coding system and the basis upon which it will operate, it must now actually construct its coding system. Let's take a code-building journey as we code an item according to a new item-based coding system! Our coding system, which is numerically based for computerized inventory use, will code the glamorous and exciting item of 1/4 inch copper rods. Our final code will contain six fields, each with a distinct number revealing a different bit information about our item. So that the numbers within our fields don't become confused, they are separated by decimal points. For example, a code within our system might look like: 3.2.10.6.5.24

Let the coding begin!

CREATING AN INVENTORY CODE FOR 1/4 INCH COPPER RODS

FIELD 1: To begin coding our illustrious 1/4 inch copper rod, we determine which number will be assigned to its first field. In our coding system, our first field reveals the following information about the basic nature of the item:

1 = raw material   2 = component part   3 = finished product   4 = electrical

Our item, the 1/4 inch copper rod, is a raw material. We begin by assigning 1 to the first field of our code: 1.

FIELD 2: Now that our code's first field shows that our item is a raw material, we will use the coding system's second field to classify our item's type of raw material, using the following system:

1 = metal   2 = plastic   3 = wood

Our item, the 1/4 inch copper rod, is base metal, so we assign 1 to the second field of our code: 1.1

FIELD 3: Having classified our item's type of raw material, we next assign a number to the third field of our code, which is used to identify type of metal, using the following system:

1 = lead   2 = steel   3 = copper   4 = aluminum

Our 1/4 inch copper rod is obviously copper, so we assign 3 to the third field of our code: 1.1.3

FIELD 4: The fourth field in our coding system will now classify the basic three-dimensional form of our raw material, metal, copper item. We use the following system to code the fourth field:

1 = nuggets   2 = bars   3 = flat sheets   4 = rods

Again, our 1/4 inch copper rod is obviously a rod, so we assign 4 to the fourth field of our code: 1.1.3.4

FIELD 5: Having established the form in which our item is stored, the fifth field in our coding system now provides more refined information about the item's rod shape, i.e., its two-dimensional cross-section shape:

1 = square   2 = hexagonal   3 = round/circular   4 = oval

Our 1/4 inch copper rod is round, so we assign 3 to the fifth field of our code: 1.1.3.4.3

FIELD 6: The sixth field within our coding system provides the final bit of information about our copper rod – its diameter – using the following numeric system:

1 = 1inch   2 = 1/2inch   3 = 1/4inch

Because our copper rod is 1/4 inch in diameter, we assign 3 to the sixth field of our code: 1.1.3.4.3.3

Interpreted, 1.1.3.4.3.3 in our imaginary inventory coding system means: raw material (1), metal (1), copper (3), rod (4), round (3), and 1/4 inch diameter (3).

When organizations create their own inventory coding systems, they may use a series of six fields of numbers separated by decimal points, as we have in the example above, but they may also use any number of fields containing numbers, letters, or a combination of both, separated by any other symbol, such as a dash, slash, asterisk, or whatever else may strike the code designer's fancy. The overall design, however, must be logical, relevant, and easy to use by the organization and all those involved in its inventory management.

Once an organization has devised and introduced an inventory coding system which best meets its needs, the information related to the new system must be stored and made accessible to all of those who will need to know and understand the system. Usually a glossary or catalogue within a book or computer file is created, which contains information on the logic behind the coding and full descriptions for each of the fields of numbers or letters within the code. These explanations of the coding system must be both clear and thorough because they serve as a guide to a multitude of users, including those in the production, inventory control, warehouse, and purchasing departments; suppliers; and anyone involved in accounts and invoice-checking because the inventory code created is also typically used on invoices and delivery documents. Therefore, because so many rely on these coding glossaries or catalogues, they must be updated both frequently and regularly and include coding criteria for all current and planned future items within the organization's inventory.

An inventory coding system will always be judged by its immediate results, i.e., how efficiently and successfully the item sought is identified. When striving to achieve the most efficient and easy-to-use inventory coding system, an organization typically abides by the following five rules of inventory coding:

Rule #1: Be able to cover every item held in inventory. An inventory coding system must be able to provide a corresponding code for all items held in inventory. A system that does not include a means for coding even the most obscure and rarely used items can quickly experience control problems.

Rule #2: Make it flexible! Every year, many new products are created. Design, packaging, and performance changes occur in existing products. All product creations and alterations must be assigned new, logically consistent codes. Therefore, a truly efficient inventory coding system must be flexible and able to expand to accommodate increases in inventory type, range, and scope.

Rule #3: Use consistent and logical formatting. It is absolutely critical that, once the basic logic of an inventory coding system is established (such as 1 = raw materials), it is continued throughout all coding. Some organizations make the mistake of creating a coding system for one part of their warehouse operation and later find that they end up creating several different coding systems, resulting in confusion and errors.

Rule #4: Meet your organization's needs. Every inventory coding systems must meet the needs of the organization using it. While the logic behind their systems may be similar, Ford Motors would use a far more complex inventory coding system than a local auto parts distribution center.

Rule #5: Include other departments. In all organizations, the members of the Inventory Management and Warehouse departments are not the sole users of inventory codes. Other departments, such as Purchasing, Production, Distribution, and Engineering, must also use the newly developed coding system. Therefore, to enhance cross-departmental communications and develop an efficient, fully workable inventory coding system, other departments must understand the logic of the system and its common classifications and headings.

CHAPTER 2 REVIEW QUESTIONS

1. What are the five classifications of inventory? Please provide examples of each.

2. What is decoupling inventory and why might it be important for an organization that manufactures goods?

3. During the inventory receipt cycle process, what is allocated before the goods actually arrive? Why?

4. For an organization receiving goods, how might an Advice Note of Intended Delivery from the supplier help assist the inventory receipt cycle process?

5. Who helps set an organization's quality control standards? What type of input do each of these provide?

6. Why should customers be considered when setting quality control standards?

7. Describe three of the benefits of inventory coding.

8. When might an organization use color coding? When might it be best not to use color coding?

9. When might an organization use supplier coding?

10. What makes an inventory coding system efficient?

CHAPTER 2 CASE EXERCISE

Big Changes at the Fabulous Floating Ferries Company

The story you are about to read is true. The names and places have been changed to protect the innocent (and not-so-innocent).

A European ferry company called Fabulous Floating Ferries currently runs a car ferry between New Winterfell and Narniaville. The ferry crossing time is 8 hours. The ferry leaves New Winterfell at 8am each day and arrives at Narniaville at 4pm, resulting in an eight hour crossing time. The same ferry then leaves Narniaville at 8pm and arrives back at New Winterfell at 4am the next day. As with all Fabulous Floating Ferries ships, the New Winterfell-Narniaville ferry has a full restaurant, buffet bar, lounge, and various snack machines throughout the ship. The ferry's supplies are all ordered from local suppliers and loaded at the port of New Winterfell. It is loaded with enough supplies to cover both the trip to Narniaville and the subsequent return journey to New Winterfell.

The system for resupplying the New Winterfell-Narniaville ferry has been the same for years. On the return journey from Narniaville, the ferry's onboard supply officer contacts a purchasing officer at the Fabulous Floating Ferries headquarters onshore and orders what is needed for the next trip from New Winterfell to Narniaville and back. Many of the same supplies are ordered consistently during each trip, but they must be ordered in small quantities because there is very little room for storage on the ship.

The onshore purchasing officer for Fabulous Floating Ferries then contacts the local suppliers (usually around 10 to 12 suppliers) and orders the ship's requirements for delivery. This takes place while the ship is loading and unloading the cars and people that are traveling at New Winterfell, which is between between the ship's docking time of 4am and its departure time of 8am. Early every morning, there is a line of suppliers waiting on the dock for the ship to arrive.. The ship's storage area is below deck and can be accessed only by a single elevator and a very narrow circular stairway. In the winter months, when fewer people are traveling, this resupplying system works pretty well. In the summertime, however, the volume of cars and people traveling are much higher, which results in a constant state of quayside chaos as all the suppliers try to get their goods unloaded and their documentation signed. For years, this has resulted in far too many late ferry departures from New Winterfell.

The supply officer onboard the New Winterfell-Narniaville ferry is growing weary of this recurring problem and has often complained to the higher-ups at Fabulous Floating Ferries about the lack of time to properly receive and inspect the goods in New Winterfell. Often, because of this tight resupplying schedule, items ordered were not sent or the quantities were short or goods were damaged. The finance department at Fabulous Floating Ferries is also concerned about the price the company is paying for these goods. The process of ordering goods every day and in such small quantities means that they always pay full price and never receive a bulk discount from any of their vendors.

INSTRUCTIONS:

Answer the following questions.

1. **If Fabulous Floating Ferries were to purchase or rent affordable warehouse within 5 minutes of the ferry's New Winterfell docking site:**

2. **What types of goods might be stored in the warehouse?**

3. **What inventory management benefits might Fabulous Floating Ferries experience? Please explain your answer.**

4. **How might the inventory receipt process change from the existing process? Would this change be beneficial or detrimental to Fabulous Floating Ferries. Please explain your answer.**

Bonus Exercise: Inventory Coding Practice!

Look at the example of "Creating an Inventory Code for 1/4 inch Copper Rods" on page ___ of this chapter. Using the fields and coding system provided, create inventory codes for the raw materials listed below. Make sure to use exactly the following format: **1.1.1.1.1.1**

QUESTIONS:

1. What would the inventory code be for 1 inch oval lead nuggets?

2. What would the inventory code be for 1/2 inch hexagonal aluminum rods?

3. What would the inventory code be for 1/4 inch circular sheets of copper?

Chapter 3
Internal Processes: Putaway

INTRODUCING PUTAWAY

In Chapter 2, we tackled the topic of inbound process in warehouse management and the inventory receipt cycle. After goods come in and are inspected, they have to go somewhere. In a standard warehouse, the goods might be put away onto warehouse shelves while at a cross-docking distribution center, goods might be taken from one incoming truck and placed onto ten different outgoing trucks. This internal process of placing goods in their appropriate location after they have been received and inspected, with corresponding paperwork completed and signed, is called *putaway*.

Depending on the size of the warehouse operation and the nature of the goods, the warehouse staff handling putaway may the same people who handled inventory receipt or it many be handled by an entirely different set of people or department. If someone else takes over, they now take responsibility for and ownership over getting the goods to the right place, usually as quickly as possible. An important goal of putaway is to minimize *dock-to-stock time*. Goods need to be cleared from the receiving area quickly to make room for new incoming goods. Incoming goods also need to be put into their warehouse or cross-docking locations as quickly as possible so they can be available for distribution to their users. Imagine a retail warehouse receiving a last minute shipment of sold-out Halloween costumes of this year's favorite reality TV star - just two days

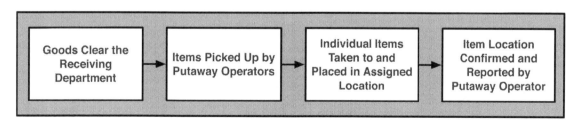

Figure 3.1 - The Putaway Process

before Halloween! If those costumes don't get put away and made available for distribution to end users immediately, chances are that the warehouse will be stuck with pallets of Real Housewives or Duck Dynasty costumes that will be yesterday's news next Halloween.

When the receiving department has signed off on the delivery of incoming goods, the company receiving them now has legal ownership of the goods. Therefore, those handling the putaway process should understand that they are handling the company's potential profits (and their salaries) when they put the goods away. To ensure that goods are handled in a manner in which they are least likely to become damaged, putaway operators check with the receiving department to see if there are any special handling instructions for the goods being put away. For example, some goods may be especially fragile or need temperature-controlled storage and handling conditions. In addition, there may be special handling instructions to keep putaway operators safe while handling the items, including the need for protective clothing, gloves, masks, or lifting belts.

LOCATION AND THE PUTAWAY PROCESS

As shown in Figure 3.1, during the putaway process, goods must not only be put away quickly, but those putting the goods away must also confirm and report each item's new location. When put away in a warehouse, goods are placed in a specific *location*, which could be a designated area of the warehouse floor for larger items or a designated rack, shelf, or storage bin for smaller items. In addition, during the putaway process, goods may be placed in either a *slot* or in a *reserve area*. A specific area designated for specific items to be placed for subsequent order picking is called a *slot*. When determining an inventory's slot, also known as *slotting* or *profiling*, three things are considered: what is being stored (the product, its physical characteristics, any special storage needs it may have, how often it will be needed), the storage location (its shape, its structure, exactly how much of the item it can hold, exactly where it can be found in the warehouse, and the warehouse inventory code used to identify its location), and maintenance requirements (what type of maintenance will be needed to keep the slot in regular working order and keeping track of how often items are taken from slots to see if they need to be moved to areas of items picked less frequently or more frequently).

If goods do not need to be picked immediately, they may instead be placed in a *reserve area* where they are stored until they are needed to be placed for picking. For example, if Kudzoo's Contemporary Kitchens received more hot pink granite countertop material than it might need in a year (the purchasing department got a smoking hot deal on them), it may place 300 square feet of the hot pink granite in a specific hot pink granite slot in the warehouse while placing the remaining 30,000 square feet of the hot pink granite from the incoming order in a reserve area further back in the warehouse, to be placed in the warehouse slot for picking on future dates as needed.

When goods are being put away in a location, they may also be coming from an *internal* or an *external* location. For example, when the hot pink granite is taken from the Groovy Granite delivery truck and placed into Kudzoo's Contemporary Kitchens' warehouse in our previous example, it is coming from an *external location*, which is any location or entity outside of the company receiving the materials. A few weeks later, when the hot pink granite has been picked from its slot in the warehouse and need to be replaced (or *replenished* in warehouse management lingo), it is taken from the warehouse's reserve area, which is an ***internal location***. Other internal locations could include any location from within the company needing the goods, such as another warehouse location or distribution center that belongs to the same organization.

When the putaway process involves taking goods from one internal location and placing them into another internal location, replenishment is often the reason. ***Replenishment*** is the process of moving goods from a reserve area to a ***forward pick location***, which is another term to describe the slot into which goods are placed in a warehouse for subsequent order picking. Items are replenished and placed in their forward pick locations when product levels are running low. The exact quantity level at which items are replenished may be determined by the judgment of the putaway operators or by warehouse management software and inventory control systems, depending on the size of the warehouse and the scope of its operations. When replenishment happens, its it documented by the putaway operator so that the warehouse's inventory systems accurately reflect the new location of the inventory.

But why on earth do warehouses bother to move goods internally from a reserve area to a forward pick location? Wouldn't it just be simpler to put goods in one spot until they are needed, without all this inter to-and-fro? While using a single location for goods may appear to be simple, for many goods and organizations, it is not cost effective. In the world of warehouse management, time is money. The more time it takes to pick an order and the further warehouse workers must travel into the depths of the warehouse on a regular basis, the more it costs an organization in labor and equipment costs. In warehouse management, it is most effective to store inventory according to its ***frequency of usage***, or how often it is used and must be accessed. Materials are usually grouped in three logical sections: ***high usage rate***, ***medium usage rate***, and ***low usage rate***. In most cases, materials that are constantly picked and issued out should be placed near the entrances and exits. This method of placement reduces the handling times of these high usage materials and minimizes traveling time. The same logic is applied to the medium and low usage rate materials, placing the less frequently delivered and issued inventory progressively further away from the inventory yard point of entry.

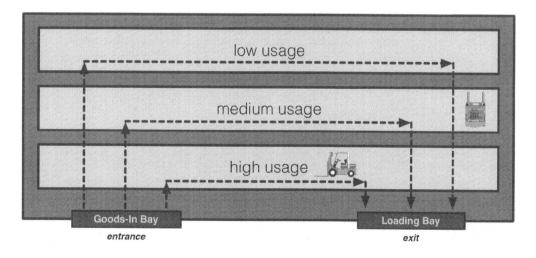

Figure 3.2 - Inventory Location and Frequency of Usage

Similarly, there is a *golden zone* of inventory location on vertical warehouse shelves which is determined by frequency of usage. Those items which are placed into and taken out of inventory most frequently are placed so that they are in slots that are easiest for warehouse workers to reach, which is generally in the area between the shoulders and the knees of the average warehouse worker. Items that have medium and low usage rates are placed in higher or lower locations on the shelves, so that warehouse workers don't have to bend down, stretch up, or use ladders, stools, or lifts as frequently.

Figure 3.3 - The Golden Zone of Inventory Placement. Notice that, in addition to more frequently issued items, lighter items that a warehouse worker could lift are placed in the Golden Zone, between shoulder- and knee-height. Heavier, palletized goods are placed higher, with more frequently used palletized goods placed closer to the floor and less frequently picked goods placed closer to the ceiling.

THE "WHERE" OF THE PUTAWAY PROCESS

Earlier in this book, we mentioned that a *warehouse* is an area in which an organization may receive, inspect, store, select, pack, and issue any of a variety of materials needed for manufacturing, distribution, maintenance, and packaging within the organization. These areas in which warehousing takes place may either be inside buildings or outside in inventory yards. Let's first look at *warehouse buildings*, including their functions, types, construction, and layout, and later explore *external inventory yards*.

Well-designed warehouse buildings are an important element of any successful supply chain. Their design can either help or hinder the efficiency of materials movement. How warehouse buildings are designed, their size, and their scope will all differ based on the: size and complexity of the operation involved, resources and capital available for building and/or conversion, location of existing operations, and future plans and expectations of the organization.

While the functions of a warehouse building may vary with the needs of individual organizations, some of the more common functions of warehouse buildings include:

- Storage for all materials within a company, including work-in-progress, finished inventory, and raw materials

- A large central store within a manufacturing plant, which acts as the distribution and collection point for all inventory

- Central storage for materials for one or more companies, which acts as a regional collection, consolidation, and distribution point

- A location for administrative and management resources for the warehousing function, including offices, issue counters, and delivery bays

- A central location for Quality Control and Inspection operations that are performed within the confines of the warehouse building

- Storage for materials handling equipment used within the warehouse (This storage might also include charging areas for rechargeable electric equipment, such as electric forklifts.)

- Pricing and hand-shelving customers' orders

There are also two basic types of warehouse building design: the *single-story warehouse building* and the *multi-story warehouse building*. The most widely used is the **single-story warehouse building**, which, as the name suggests, is built on one level without stairs or upper floors. Many single-story warehouse buildings use **mezzanines**, smaller stories in a warehouse building with low ceilings built above functioning warehouse areas, to provide additional storage.

Figure 3.4 - Mezzanine at a Household Goods Retailer. This warehouse mezzanine is used for both storage (on the right) and an office (on the left).

Being the most widely-used type of warehouse building, single-story warehouse buildings have several advantages, including:

- **Cost.** They are relatively cheap to construct and maintain because of their simple design and lack of upper floors. (Costly foundation support is needed for the extra weight of upper floors.)

- **Flow.** With a well-designed warehouse building, the logistics of materials handling and the natural flow of materials through the warehouse can occur at maximum efficiency by keeping everything at one level.

- **Convenience.** Ventilation and other basic services (electricity, water, gas, etc.) are easier to install and operate.

- **Weight.** When using only a ground floor, greater weights may be stored without the problems associated with the upper-floor weight limitations of multi-story buildings.

Single-story warehouse buildings sound perfect, so why don't we see only single-story ones in our wonderful world of warehousing? In a word: space. Many organizations operate within a confined area and do not have the ability or resources to purchase large plots of land for single-story warehouse construction. Therefore, in areas of high population density, where land and resources are scarce and expensive, or in situations where an organization is based on a multi-story site, with different floors housing different sections of the organization, the ***multi-story warehouse building*** becomes the design of choice.

In addition to handling space restrictions, multi-story warehouse buildings also have the following advantages:

- **Flexibility.** The multi-floor environment allows for greater flexibility in alternative use of storage space (for offices, production facilities, etc.) should the need arise.

- **Safety and Security.** Separating areas of inventory by floor lends itself more to security and fire safety. For example, a fire outbreak can be contained on one floor without damaging the rest of the inventory located on other floors.

Multi-story buildings are well suited to handling small, light units of high value, such as electronic components. For these organizations, the advantage of having an optimal warehouse building location outweighs the advantage of having warehouse operations all on one floor. The primary disadvantage multi-story warehouse buildings bring is cost, including both the high capital outlay in construction and the subsequent costs of maintaining the building.

When considering new warehouse space, an organization must consider whether they want to construct a new building, refit an existing structure, or rent warehouse space. A ***purpose-built warehouse building*** is a warehouse building that has been designed and constructed according to an organization's individual needs and operational requirements. Purpose-built warehouse buildings are typically associated with large organizations that have the resources to embark on designing and constructing these specialized buildings. Smaller organizations may also acquire purpose-built warehouse buildings on the open market, however, provided the warehouse meets the organization's needs. For example, an organization storing a large amount of heavy palletized materials would require a large, open-plan warehouse building, while another organization holding numerous small, manufactured units my need a multi-story warehouse building with several open and closed shelves.

Designing and constructing a purpose-built warehouse building brings three primary advantages. First, warehouse managers have the opportunity to ensure that the most efficient layout design for materials handling and storage is produced. Also, the latest techniques, innovations, and warehouse developments can be incorporated into the basic design requirements. For example, the use of computerized materials handling systems requires laying down guide tracks, which can best be installed during building construction. Finally, purpose-built warehouse buildings provide the organization with exactly what its needs dictate, leaving no wasted space but instead leaving room for expansion based on the organization's projections of future requirements.

While purpose-built warehouse buildings may sound ideal, they do bring some disadvantages with them, primarily in terms of: expense, conflicting interest, and misjudgment. Designing and constructing a purpose-built warehouse building consumes a great deal of time and money. Because of this expense, conflicting interests can arise between warehousing and other departments in the organization concerning both the design and expense of the building. Finally, any misjudgment during the design phase concerning the real needs of the organization may result in a great waste of resources.

The Importance of the Design Phase in Purpose-Built Construction

A bathroom products wholesaler we knew decided to construct a new purpose-built warehouse. They were in a rush to complete the project because the organization had an immediate need for warehouse space. In their haste, the company executives signed off on the architectural plans and began construction before reviewing them with the warehouse and logistics managers.

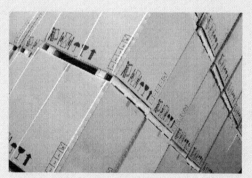

The company used a standard sized pallet load for each of its larger items (toilets, bathtubs, and sinks). When the construction was complete, the warehouse managers were horrified to find that they could stack their larger inventory items into two tiers of pallets loads but that they were just 1" short of being able to stack a third tier of goods. Had the company paid greater attention to its needs and its inventory during the warehouse design phase, the warehouse storage capacity could have been increased by a full fifty percent!

Unlike a purpose-built warehouse building, which is designed and constructed according to individual needs, a **converted warehouse building** is a building which had originally been designed for another purpose but which was converted and is now being used for warehousing purposes. As organizations develop and expand, their need for storage space and handling facilities expand in proportion. Many of these organizations commonly find themselves having to convert buildings into warehouse facilities. These buildings can range from old factories to large residential houses, depending upon the size of the operation and the properties available.

Using the converted warehouse building approach can be quite advantageous because buildings to convert can often be relatively inexpensive to acquire, either by outright purchase or by lease from the owner if the organization lacks the capital to buy. Because relatively less capital has been invested, the organization then has the option to move its inventory to another location in the future should its demands change. With careful planning and layout, converted warehouse buildings can produce very useful and cost-effective storage facilities.

Before converting a building into a warehouse facility, the organization and its warehouse management must consider the possible disadvantages a converted warehouse building may pose. Aside from the obvious disadvantage of not having a purpose-built facility designed with the needs of the organization in mind, environmental conditions needed to store materials may not be correct, making it necessary to install expensive equipment. (This is especially true for frozen foods or materials requiring damp-free storage.) The converted area may not be suitable for the materials handling and storage systems needed by the organization. For example, many buildings available for conversion do not have the doors and loading bay access needed for warehouses and older buildings sometimes do not have the level floors required for many electric trucks. Finally, when using a converted warehouse building, further expansion may be restricted by factors outside the control of the organization, such as local government planning permission.

In some situations, the organization may not want to become involved in either building or conversion projects. It may instead decide to rent a facility to meet its storage needs. Motives for **renting warehouse space** include:

- **Inventory level variations.** When inventory levels fluctuate, storage space may only be needed for a short period of time, making it less cost-effective to build or convert warehouse space. Such inventory level variations are most common in organizations with seasonal products, such as swimming pool supplies, Christmas trees, or Halloween candy.

- **Lack of resources.** When an organization cannot afford to buy or convert warehouse space, it can still continue its warehousing function by renting storage space.

- **Temporary changes in demand.** When a company experiences a drop in sales, its inventory typically increases because it is stuck holding the inventory it hasn't sold. Rather than build or convert another warehouse to house this excess inventory, rented warehouse space can offer the company the most cost-effective solution to its temporary storage needs.

- **Local government planning issues.** When in the process of planning, constructing, or converting warehouse space, organizations often face challenges in gaining required local government planning permissions needed. While ironing out these issues, organizations often turn to temporary rented storage facilities to ensure that warehousing operations begin or continue as scheduled.

- **Future demands.** When an organization is unclear of the future demand of its product, it may decide to rent warehouse space until future demand can be determined, at which time it may then build or convert warehouse space.

Before committing to renting a particular warehouse space, organizations consider a range of factors including: the location of the warehouse in relation to the organization, the transportation links and traveling time between the warehouse and the other links in the logistics chain, the cost of storage, and whether the conditions of storage are suitable for the materials involved. When a company is considering renting, constructing, or converting a warehouse facility, the new facility's location is a tool the company can use to reduce transportation costs and speed up delivery times. Ideal warehouse location can be determined using mathematical formulae and a range of computer software programs.

Before any materials can be stored in a rented warehouse, a contract or agreement is formulated between the organization wishing to rent the warehouse and the warehouse owner. It is absolutely vital that the organization's legal team and warehouse managers examine the contract carefully before it is signed. Factors closely examined in the contract or agreement include:

- **Cost.** The actual cost of storage must be clearly determined and an agreement regarding the nature of the costs should be outlined. For example, does the cost given include the whole storage space, regardless of usage, or only the space used?

- **Termination.** It's important to examine the *notice of termination*, clearly outlining what is required of each party.

- **Inventory Checking.** The contract should also outline the responsibility and access for physical inventory checking. Some warehouses may conduct all inventory checks themselves while others will provide access to the company storing good so it can conduct inventory checks.

- **Damage and Insurance.** Contracts should clearly outline which party should provide which type of insurance and who is responsible for which type of damage to goods.

- **Storage Conditions.** The exact environmental conditions under which the inventory must be handled and stored should be clearly outlined and agreed.

- **Inventory Control and Records.** The contract should also outline the responsibility for physical inventory control and record-keeping. Similar to inventory checking, some warehouses may handle all inventory control themselves and supply records to the company about its goods stored while others may be hands-off and expect the company to control and keep records about its own goods.

- **What's Included.** Contracts should also out line any extras that are included in the terms of service, such as provision of labor and materials handling equipment.

A final type of warehouse worth mentioning is the ***bonded warehouse***. When goods arrive from another country, the company receiving the goods must immediately pay excise taxes and customs duties. If the company secures a bond for potential taxes and duties of future incoming goods, it may then temporarily store foreign inbound goods in a bonded warehouse. The company then may legally defer payment of taxes or duties until the goods are removed from the bonded warehouse. In addition, not only can goods be stored in a bonded warehouse but they may also be assembled or partially assembled.

WAREHOUSE BUILDING CONSTRUCTION AND LAYOUT

You can never have too many chefs in the kitchen when starting a warehouse construction or conversion project. Architects, engineers, and company CEOs alone do not constitute an effective warehouse design team. Any decision related to the design and construction of a new warehouse or converted warehouse space should also be made with the advice and guidance of the warehouse manager and the managers of the organization's additional logistics activities. While *capital* and *land* available form two key factors in warehouse design and construction, warehouse and other logistics activities managers provide invaluable information for design and construction, including information on:

- **Volume of inventory involved,** including both present inventory and future demands.

- **Nature of inventory involved.** In most cases, a wide variety of inventory is to be stored. Special sub-warehouse and storage sections may be required in which specific environment conditions can be maintained.

- **Value of the inventory** and the security systems needed to protect it, including security doors, alarms, motion sensors, CCTV (closed circuit television), and remote monitoring.

- **Materials handling systems** already used by the organization. The new warehouse may then be designed to be compatible with these existing systems. For example, an organization using diesel-powered trucks for outside handling may not be able to operate these trucks within a closed warehouse building.

- **Primary method of transport** used by the organization and its suppliers. These methods of transport must be considered because they will have a direct effect upon the design and construction of new and converted warehouse buildings.

- **Environmental conditions** needed for inventory storage. These include type of ventilation and climate conditions required, along with the heating and lighting systems needed to maintain these conditions.

- **Ancillary services.** Within the warehouse, accommodation will need to be made for ancillary services, thus reducing the overall storage capacity of the space. Such ancillary services include: warehouse offices (inventory records, inventory control, general administration, etc.); computer terminals; washroom and restroom facilities; and employee canteen facilities.

- **Loading bays required** within the new warehouse. Loading bay requirements depend upon the rate of issue from inventory, the method of transport used, and the frequency of delivery to customers.

- **Goods-in bays required.** Good-in bay requirements depend upon the frequency of deliveries, the transport method used by suppliers, and the method of packing. (More on loading bays and goods-in bays in a few short paragraphs.)

When contemplating any warehouse building or conversion project, there are many costs to be considered. Each of these costs must be carefully examined to ensure that the project is economically feasible and that the organization will be financially able to operate the warehouse once construction is completed. Typical costs that warehouse construction projects face are often those related to: construction and labor; materials handling and storage equipment required; and rates levied upon the new building by local authorities.

Once warehouse construction is completed, an organization faces an array on ongoing costs, including those related to: maintenance and depreciation; energy needed for operation (gas, electricity, fuel, etc.); operational labor, administration, and management needed; transportation (i.e., delivery to customers); cleaning (floors, offices, pest control, etc.); and security (hiring outside security firms, alarms, specialized locks, firefighting equipment, and insurance cover premiums).

To meet a company's needs for inventory receipt; inventory storage; and picking, packaging, issue, and dispatch, a standard layout of a company's warehouse typically includes the following areas:

- *good-in bays,* the area into which a warehouse receives incoming inventory, typically from a truck or rail car.. This is also called a *receiving dock*.

- *receiving area,* in which the goods are temporarily held while the order is checked, inspected by the Quality Control department, and classified and labeled for subsequent storage.

- *storage area,* in which goods are held by the organization until an order for them is received. The storage area can include: *floor storage*, where large, bulky items or high volumes of items secured on pallets can be kept; *pallet racks*, where unitized pallets of items are stored; *shelves and bins*, where smaller individual items are kept; and other types of *specialized storage*, such as *carousels*, *refrigerated* storage areas, or *HazMat* (hazardous materials) storage areas.

- *order picking area,* from which goods are selected after an order has been received. The order picking and storage areas may be: 1) exactly the same areas; 2) opposite aisles flanking the same rows of goods; or 3) in the case of automated or live storage systems, a separate area of the warehouse. (We'll cover these in much, much greater detail later in the book!)

- *packaging and unitization area,* in which goods to be issued are packaged and placed into unit loads, such as pallets loads or containers.

- *staging area,* in which the packed and/or unitized goods are labeled for issuance and held until transportation arrives.

- *loading bays,* in which the packaged and unitized goods are transferred from the warehouse onto a transportation vehicle, such as a truck or rail car. This is also called a *shipping dock*. Side note: Loading bays and goods-in bays may look exactly the same, but, in a large warehouse, they are actually very different. Efficiently designed larger warehouses usually have their loading bays and goods-in bays in separate locations to ensure an efficient, one-way movement of inventory.

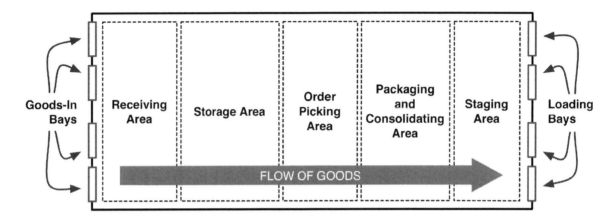

Figure 3.5 - Example of a Warehouse Layout and Flow of Goods

One of the primary design and construction factors that affect the efficiency of the entire warehouse operation is the main building layout. When designing a warehouse layout, the following additional ten factors must be considered to achieve efficient operations overall:

1. **Item Specifications and Handling Requirements.** The range of items to be stored within one warehouse is likely to be quite diverse. Items of similar size and handling requirements tend to be stored together. For example, car tires, light bulbs, and ice cream might all be in the same warehouse but are unlikely to be stored in the same locations.

2. **Frequency of Issue.** Different items and categories of items held in a warehouse are usually issued (i.e., pulled out of storage and given to its requester) at different rates of frequency. If frequency of issue is not considered when considering a warehouse layout, the problem of *honeycombing* can arise, in which slow-moving SKUs are scattered in different places throughout the warehouse, taking up valuable space in an uneven and random manner. When addressed in warehouse layout design, the position of fast-, medium-, and slow-moving inventory should be related to materials handling and inventory issue. Materials that are constantly being delivered and issued out should typically be placed near warehouse entrances and exits. This method of placement reduces the handling times of these high usage materials and minimizes traveling time. The same logic applies to medium and low usage rate materials, with less frequently delivered and issued inventory located progressively further away from the warehouse entrance. When considering the importance of frequency of use, it is important to remember that this issue is related less *volume* (how much of the item is put away and retrieved) and is related much more to *hits* (the number of times an item is requested and how many trips to retrieve it and put it away are are needed).

3. **Space Optimization.** To avoid current and future issues of crowding and congestion, warehouse layout designers must consider how best to use the space available. In addition to considering *frequency of issue* previously discussed, warehouse layout design can optimize valuable floor space by considering use of mezzanines and racking; *ceiling height*, not only for the product, but for stacked pallets of products; and *aisle width*. One thing to keep in

mind about ceiling height is that goods stored at spaces over 30 feet high might not be able to be retrieved using lift trucks and will instead need automated storage/retrieval systems. In addition, many warehouses have traditionally set aisles at fourteen feet wide, but narrower, twelve-foot aisles can be considered because aisles should only be as wide as necessary without taking up unnecessary floor space.

4. **Loading and Goods-In Bays.** Depending upon how frequently inventory is issued and received, the size and number of loading and goods-in bays required will vary across organizations and their warehouses. Smaller warehouses may have only one loading bay and one good-in bay located side by side. Larger, more complex warehouses have multiple loading and good-in bays, often with each handling different types of incoming and outgoing inventory and assigned corresponding specialized materials handling equipment.

5. **Equipment Maneuvering Space Needed.** Layouts for all warehouses must consider the amount of space needed to effective move and maneuver loading/unloading and materials handling equipment. Sufficient space is needed for maneuvering equipment when loaded to maximum capacity while maintaining a safe environment for warehouse pedestrians.

6. **Office Accommodation.** Inclusion of effectively placed office accommodation is a critical but easily overlooked component on any warehouse's layout. The office is the management and information center for the entire warehouse and materials handling operation and thus demands a central location from which almost all operations can be viewed.

7. **Gangways and Access.** In order to keep all who enter and work in the warehouse safe from injury, location and types of gangways and pedestrian access must be considered in warehouse layout, especially as they relate to materials handling equipment and procedures.

8. **Electric Charging Points.** If electrically powered, rechargeable materials handling equipment (such as battery powered lift trucks) is to be used within the newly designed warehouse, strategic placement of maintenance and charging points is essential for efficient operations.

9. **Structural Limitations and Immovable Obstacles.** Although they may keep you from achieving your dream layout, structural limitations and immovable obstacles, such as warehouse floor weight bearing limitations and support pillars, are a reality of both newly constructed and converted warehouse buildings and must be considered in layout design.

10. **Current and Future Automation Needs.** Many larger warehouses are moving toward implementing digital warehouse management systems (more on these in alter chapters) in conjunction with putaway activities partially or fully automated with robotic systems. Much of this automation equipment and warehouse management systems equipment will have specific space and environmental conditions requirements. Therefore, even if a company has not yet automated its warehouse, it must consider future automation possibilities when planning for warehouse layout.

PUTAWAY AND EXTERNAL INVENTORY YARDS

As an addition or alternative to using a warehouse building, many organizations use an *external inventory yard*, an open, outdoor storage area used for storing a variety of nonperishable goods. *Nonperishable goods* are materials that will not deteriorate or perish when exposed to the elements over long periods of time. Depending upon the organization and the nature of its inventory, it may have an external inventory yard, a warehouse building, or both.

Because an external inventory yard is typically exposed to the elements, it provides excellent storage for materials that are destined to spend their working lives in open or exposed conditions, such as concrete paving stones, sand, shingles, etc. An external inventory yard also provides suitable storage for:

- **stoneware**, such as concrete slabs and bricks;

- **heavy iron and steel casting**, such as drains, piping, bridge units, and lamp posts;

- **heavy duty electrical cable**, such as the type used to carry high voltage electricity in underground conditions;

- **outdoor machinery**, such as tractors, cars, tractor-trailer trucks, drilling equipment, and cranes;

- **scrap and waste materials**, such as filings, turnings, obsolescent inventory, chemical waste, and byproducts;

- **coal, coke, and other fuels**, typically stored in drums; and

- **garden materials and supplies**, such as topsoil, plant seedlings, and fertilizer.

Inventory yards are often set aside from the rest of the organization's warehouse installations and are connected by a link road. In some cases, inventory yards may be located miles from the primary warehouse building and instead be part of the organization's distribution system, acting as a constant source of inventory to outlets in the area. Small unit warehouses and retail organizations may have inventory yards as an extension of their main buildings. For example, to handle their large quantities of extra gardening inventory every summer, many Walmart stores fence off part of their parking lot. When an organization is deciding where to locate its external inventory yard, specialist advice is typically sought from warehouse managers. Five factors that influence location decisions include:

1. **Cost of land.** The cost of land in the immediate area or surrounding districts directly affects whether or not the external inventory yard is set up close to the organization's present warehouse buildings or retail locations. In the case of high local land prices, it may have to be located at some distance away.

2. **Space available.** If space is not available near the organization itself, the external inventory yard may again have to be located some distance away.

3. **Transportation connections.** Depending upon the requirements of the organization, its product, its suppliers, and its distributors, the inventory yard may need to be located near a major transportation link.

4. **Size needed.** Typically, the larger the inventory yard needed, the more likely it will be set up outside an inner-city area.

5. **Materials stored.** The type and character of materials to be stored also influences inventory yard location. For example, highly dangerous materials would have to be stored away from population centers and the rest of the organization's installations in case of accident.

Similar to warehouse location, a company may determine its external inventory yard location in an effort to reduce transportation costs and time. Factors such as those listed above can be placed into computer models to determine optimal external inventory yard locations.

Compared to warehouse buildings, external inventory yards offer low construction and running costs in exchange for large storage capacity. Inventory yard construction costs are far less expensive because only a sound base, secure fencing, and strong gates are required, unlike complex warehouse buildings, which require foundations, walls, roofing, ventilation, and heating. There are four basic methods of external inventory yard construction based on flooring type: *open ground*, *gravel surface*, *asphalt surface*, and *concrete surface*. The construction method used is determined by both the cost of construction and the material to be stored.

Open ground is the cheapest form of inventory yard because it needs no outlay for a base. This type of inventory yard consists of standard ground with no additional surface construction and often includes a surrounding fence. It provides basic security, requires no maintenance, and it can easily be removed and set up in another location when desired. Because it is difficult to manage and locate inventory in open ground yards, they are often limited to storing scrap or obsolete materials. Using open ground inventory yards also restricts pallet loads because materials handling equipment tends to sink on unsupported surfaces, especially when faced with heavy loads or adverse (wet) weather conditions.

Gravel surface inventory yards are popular with many organizations, especially when storing low value inventory in large quantities when limited resources are available. These yards support more weight than open ground inventory yards, remain relatively inexpensive to install, and can be relocated easily. Gravel surface inventory yards still tend to become waterlogged in adverse weather conditions and do not support heavily laden equipment and pallets.

Asphalt surface inventory yards are, by far, the most popular of the inventory yard flooring types. The asphalt surface is very strong and will support most heavy loads in all weather conditions. Because asphalt surface inventory yards offer excellent storage, can easily be laid out and marked for a location system, and can be easily maintained and repaired, many organizations make them their permanent inventory yard of choice. Asphalt surface construction is more expensive than open ground or gravel surface construction, however, and is subject to damage in very hot weather, with heavy loads creating indentations and holes in the surface.

Concrete surface inventory yards are the strongest and most stable of the four inventory yard flooring construction types. They are able to handle the heaviest loads, remain operable all year round regardless of weather conditions, and can easily be laid out and marked for efficient location and selection. Concrete surface inventory yards, however, are relatively very expensive to construct and even more expensive to relocate, typically limiting their use to organizations with materials that have very heavy storage loads, such as heavy cables or construction equipment, which need corresponding heavy materials handling equipment.

Figure 3.6 - Flooring Types for External Inventory Yards: an open ground lumber storage area in Boston, Massachusetts; a refrigerated container storage area for a fish processor in Nuuk, Greenland; an asphalt surface external inventory yard for a flour factory in Reykjavik, Iceland; and a concrete surface external inventory yard for a concrete slab company in Lerwick, Scotland.

As previously mentioned, external inventory yards do have a few advantages over warehouse buildings as a means of storage. They are relatively inexpensive to set up and surface. They also offer an ideal set-up for storing non-perishable, unusually bulky and heavy materials at a very low cost per unit stored. External inventory yards also allow for the use of heavy, diesel-powered inventory handling equipment without the problems of ventilation associated with using such equipment in an enclosed warehouse building. Finally, external inventory yards consume less energy (e.g., in lighting and heating) and have lower maintenance costs (e.g., in repairs and replacement of fittings) when compared to typical warehouse buildings.

Despite all of these advantages, external inventory yards often have a variety of constraints or faults. Most of these disadvantages can be avoided in the early stages of inventory yard design, however, with proper planning and expert advice. Such design and planning faults include:

- **Incorrect surface.** Organizations may sometimes choose an external inventory yard surface that does not match the materials being stored and handled, especially when they select the cheapest rather than the most appropriate material available. Such organizations create a false sense of savings, however, because they must later pay to have the lesser surface pulled up and replaced with the more appropriate surface needed to cope with their heavy loads in adverse conditions.

- **Waterlogged surfaces.** When drainage designs and facilities fail, waterlogged surfaces result. Working in the inventory yard is then more difficult and more dangerous, especially in the winter when surface water can turn to ice. In addition, even the most highly resistant surface materials can deteriorate when left in constant contact with water.

- **Inadequate lighting systems.** In the hours of poor daytime light or nighttime darkness, adequate lighting with floodlights and spotlights is essential. Such lighting makes accurate materials selection possible and reduces the accident rate, especially in inventory yards in which materials are handled 24 hours per day and 365 days per year.

- **Inadequate security.** When fencing and alarm systems are inadequate (or worse yet — nonexistent), external inventory yards may experience all too frequent visits from a variety of unauthorized personnel.

- **Poor location and marking system.** Inventory yards are often used as a dumping area for all types of materials. In such situations, goods are typically stored anywhere, without any thought given to utilization of space or the frequency of materials usage.

- **Inefficient and neglected control centers.** *Inventory yard control centers*, such as the gatehouse, should be centers for documentation, control, and location plans. When there is a lack of supervisory control, these centers are often neglected, leading to loss of control over storage and inventory selection.

- **Inadequate transportation links.** Many organizations make the mistake of providing resources for an excellent inventory yard while failing to ensure that links to the main transportation system, such as rail or highway systems, are adequate. As a result, these inventory yards can become isolated from the rest of the organization's storage system in adverse weather conditions.

For an external inventory yard to operate efficiently and effectively, a logical, workable yard layout must be designed and implemented. Exactly as we discussed in a considerations for warehouse layout design, external inventory yards must also consider frequency of usage of the inventory stored, with the most highly used items put away and stored closest to the entrances and exits of the inventory yard. Other factors to consider in inventory yard layout include: *entrances and exits, control centers,* and *location systems.*

When considering inventory yard layout design, ***entrances and exits*** must be placed so that a one-way traffic flow system can be implemented. Such one-way systems are essential for reducing inventory yard delays and traffic accidents, especially because fork lifts and other heavy machinery equipment are involved. In many large external inventory yards, the entrance and exit gates are side by side with the control center or gatehouse situated between them, enabling materials to be easily recorded on delivery and issue. Furthermore, in a well-designed inventory yard, the entrance and exit gates are secure, lockable, and wide enough and high enough to allow the largest vehicle used in the yard to pass through.

The ***control center*** (or ***gatehouse***) is also an important element of inventory yard layout design. The control center must be located in a position of central control and thus be able to function as an observation center for the main areas of activity within the external inventory yard. The control center must also have the resources needed to control and record the movement of inventory into and out of the yard.

Finally, to ensure that inventory can be stored in and selected from the external inventory yard as quickly and efficiently as possible, a logical and workable ***inventory location system*** is required. With a well-designed location system, the external inventory yard controller is able to locate any item in the yard at any time and thus direct materials handling resources in the right direction. In such a system, a master copy of the yard location plan is kept in the control center, often on a large board-type visual aid that can easily be used as an immediate reference. In the external inventory yards of larger companies, there are often computerized inventory location systems, with those in the control center or gatehouse able to pinpoint exact locations of inventory within massive inventory yards with only a few keystrokes.

In addition to considering layout design, industrial external inventory yards also need to consider the basic equipment needed for efficient operations. The type and amount of equipment required will depend upon the size of the yard and the materials being handled. Five types of equipment essential for most external inventory yards are:

- **Mechanical handling devices.** Mechanical handling devices, such as forklift or pallet trucks, are used primarily in the external inventory yard itself for bulk inventory storage and issue.

- **Manual handling equipment.** When small loads or orders must be moved or when mechanical devices fail, external inventory yards used manual handling equipment, such as pump lifts and hand trucks.

- **Security equipment.** No matter how large or small, all external inventory yards should have security equipment. This equipment may range from locks and chains to keys to complex, multi-zone alarm systems.

- **Firefighting equipment.** Another necessity for all external inventory yards is firefighting equipment, such as fire extinguishers, fire blankets, hose reels, and the organization's fire instructions with details on how to deal with the kinds of fires their inventory might produce (e.g., chemical or petroleum fires).

- **Racking equipment.** Except in the case of very large, bulky, or oddly shaped inventory, racking equipment is another common find in external inventory yards. Such equipment allows items on pallets or other standardized platforms to be stored vertically, thus maximizing the inventory yard's storage capacity.

Figure 3.7 - Control Center at a canned vegetable processor and distribution center in Newport, Tennessee; Security Equipment in the form of high fencing, armed and locked gates, and lighting at an external inventory yard for a home improvement store in Anchorage, Alaska; and Racking Equipment at construction supply storage area in Vancouver, Canada

Because they often hold the organization's finished product, external inventory yards play a vital role in the physical distribution system. By ***distribution***, we mean the process of getting the organization's product from the place of production to the point of consumption. In the physical distribution system, external inventory yards can be used as a "topping-up" center, where goods are stored in bulk from the place of production and distributed to customers in the local area. In addition, small external inventory yards with an emergency inventory of goods can be located up and down the distribution network to be used in the event of sudden high demand or emergencies, such as adverse weather conditions that make movement over long distances impossible. Finally, external inventory yards can be used as ***marshaling areas*** where goods are collected from various parts of the productive system, sorted into customers' requirements, and dispatched to various centers of demand.

In order to play a full part in the physical distribution process, external inventory yards must be fully integrated with warehouses and depots throughout the distribution system. Coding systems, location codes, warehouse procedures, and materials handling equipment must be uniform to ensure that the inventory yard, despite its open construction, will be managed the same way as the warehouses and depots in the system.

Finally, external inventory yards must be carefully and professionally controlled and managed to provide their organizations with full potential storage capacity at the minimum cost per unit. A vast amount of capacity is wasted in many external inventory yards due to poor management, with organizations using the yard as a dumping ground, leaving it to its own devices, and not integrating it into the organization's larger warehouse management system. To avoid waste and ensure full use of resources, the following factors should be considered when managing the inventory yard:

- **Placement.** Overall placement of pallets, bins, and drums must be neat and logical to avoid accidents and wasted space.

- **Staff.** The staff who are involved in running and supervising the external inventory yard must not be isolated from the rest of the warehouse staff. Such isolation leads to slack control and low morale. Both training and staff rotation are useful means of avoiding warehouse isolation.

- **Management.** Management involvement and resources must be provided to ensure adequate control of inventory and operations and to ensure full integration into the logistics management system as a whole.

- **Equipment.** Up-to-date and well-maintained equipment is vital for an external inventory yard to operate efficiently.

- **Location system.** As previously mentioned, a sound and logical inventory location system is vital to the efficient operation of any external inventory yard.

- **Security.** Security systems provided to protect an organization's main warehouse and other installations must also be extended to cover the external inventory yard.

- **Delivery and issuance supervision.** Diligent supervision of inventory delivery and issuance is vital if storage control is to be established and dumping of materials is to be prevented. This is possible only with a policy and management backing of constant manning of the inventory yard and control center.

WAREHOUSE INVENTORY LOCATION CODES

Warehouses vary greatly in size, layout, and types of specialized equipment used within them. Some warehouses can be as large as several football fields, while others may be no larger than the refrigerated section of your local 7-Eleven convenience store. While their sizes and the items they store may differ, warehouses all have one thing in common: they must have an inventory location coding system. An *inventory location coding system*, whether it is complex and digital or basic and manual, lets those working in the receiving area of the warehouse know where to store goods. It also lets those completing order picking and issuing tasks know where to find goods after they have been stored.

In an inventory location coding system, an item is given a code that indicates where the item is to be stored and found. This code has been given a variety of names, but the two most common names are the **warehouse inventory location code** and the **warehouse inventory address code**. No matter what name a company uses, the objectives of this code remain the same: to provide an efficient and effective means of putting goods away within the warehouse and to provide an easy means of finding them again.

There are two principle approaches to allocating space to incoming inventory: *fixed* and *random*. In the **fixed approach** to allocating space for incoming inventory, each item in inventory has a pre-assigned location. These pre-planned location assignments may be based on item quantity, weight, or frequency of use. The advantage of a fixed location system is that it allows warehouse staff to become familiar with the location of an item. Such location familiarity can save considerable time when goods are stored or picked for issue. One drawback of a fixed location system, however, is that more space is required to facilitate the greatest possible item quantity. For example, Cycles-R-Us might store 60 days inventory of an item such as the Road Rage Racing Tricycle (also called the Triple-R Trike). After 30 days, half of the space allocated for the Triple-R Trike is empty and not being used but must remain unoccupied until the Cycles-R-Us warehouse receives its next shipment of the popular tricycle.

Figure 3.8 - Alaska Communications, a telecommunications and business technology service provider, uses a fixed approach to allocating space for incoming inventory (left) because its technicians often pick their own orders and knowing where certain items are always located speeds up their picking process. Their labor hours are best spent if they are out doing complicated line repairs and not in the warehouse looking for supplies. Alaska Communications also has a generously sized warehouse and is less concerned with the extra space required for this approach. Sam's Club, like many other large warehouse-style retail stores, uses a random approach to allocating space for incoming inventory (right) because large quantities of inventory come in and go out with customers. Storage space in the retail environment is also at a premium and companies like Sam's Club also have the information technology systems to help record and find inventory locations with a random approach.

Unlike fixed location, in the **random approach** to allocating space for incoming inventory, goods are stored in the first available space in the warehouse. This system makes greater use of space, but for it to work effectively, there must be a highly effective set of warehouse inventory location codes and typically a corresponding digital inventory location coding system. At the enormous Amazon.com distribution centers around the U.S., goods are put away based on the random approach to space allocation. Inventory management is based on highly specific scannable codes and goods are stored in places to maximize space and facilitate the speedy flow of goods. With this random approach, you find goods that are not at all similar or related in the same storage bins or in adjacent slots, such as the most recent action film on Blu-Ray in the same bin as bicycle parts and boxes of Irish lace handkerchiefs.

While warehouses may differ in their use of fixed or random space allocation systems, they share the need for an inventory location coding system, unless they are a small "Mom and Pop" operation who enjoy the thrill of the hunt when "Pop" invariably forgets where he placed the light bulbs. The complexity of an inventory location coding system, however, will depend upon the size of its warehousing network and the volume, variety, and complexity of items to be stored.

When an organization begins to construct a new inventory location coding system, it typically works from the outside and moves inward, starting at the level of geographic location of one warehouse with a network of company warehouses moving eventually to a specific location on a specified shelf. Let's again take a code-building journey, this time as we assign a warehouse inventory location code to an item according to an organization's inventory location system! Let the coding begin!

The warehouse inventory location code format for our company, We-Do-Food, is based on six fields and it written within six sequential boxes:

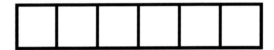

The first field of the We-Do-Food warehouse inventory location code tells us in which warehouse our item, papayas, is located. The We-Do-Food Company has five warehouses throughout Alaska and the codes for each warehouse by geographic location are:

Eagle River: 1   Anchorage: 2   Fairbanks: 3   Juneau: 4   Soldotna: 5

Our papayas happen to be located in the Soldotna warehouse, which means that we can fill in the first field of our warehouse inventory location code:

The second field of the We-Do-Food warehouse inventory location code tells us in which sector of a warehouse our item is located. We-Do-Foods uses only single-story warehouses, but companies with multi-story warehouses might use this field to indicate which floor within the warehouse an item is located. The sectors of the We-Do-Foods Soldotna warehouse are:

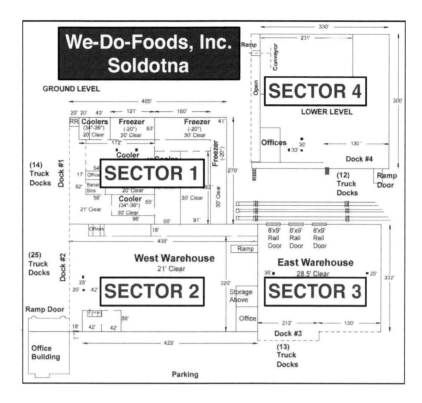

Because our delicate papayas must be refrigerated, they are located in the coolers within Sector 1 of the Soldotna warehouse, which means that we can fill in the second field of our warehouse inventory location code:

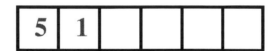

The third field of the We-Do-Food warehouse inventory location code tells us the aisle or row of the specified warehouse section in which our item is located. For Sector 1 of the Soldotna We-Do-Foods warehouse, the aisle/row numbers are:

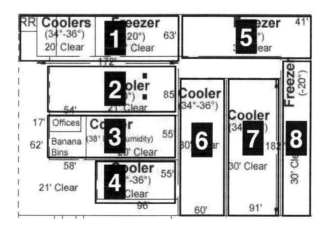

Our refrigerated papayas are located within the cooler in Aisle 7 of the of Sector 1 of the Soldotna We-Do-Foods warehouse, which means that we may now fill in the third field of our papaya warehouse inventory location code:

The fourth field of the We-Do-Food warehouse inventory location code tells us in which bay of the specified aisle/row our item is located. Within warehousing, a bay is a compartment of a building or section used for a specific purpose. In the We-Do-Foods warehouse, the bays are the vertically divided cooler subsections of each row or aisle. For Aisle 7 of Sector 1 of the Soldotna, the cooler bays are numbered as follows:

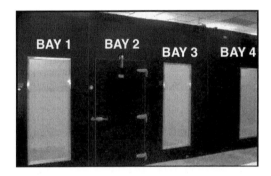

Our We-Do-Foods papayas are located within Bay 2 of Aisle 7 of Sector 1 of the Soldotna warehouse, making the papaya warehouse inventory location code now read:

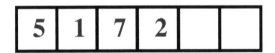

The fifth field of the We-Do-Food warehouse inventory location code tells us on which shelf within Bay 2 our delicious papayas are located. The shelves in Bay 2 are labeled as:

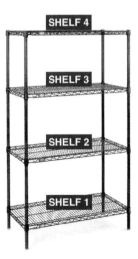

Our papayas are located on the third shelf, which means that our warehouse inventory location code now reads:

The sixth and final field of the We-Do-Foods papaya warehouse inventory location code reveals the section on the third shelf in which the papayas are located. The sections on Shelf 3 are divided as follows:

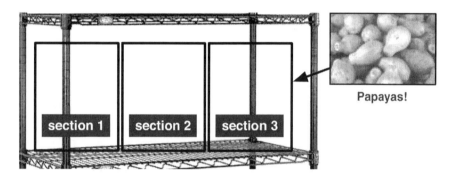

Lo and behold, our delectable papayas appear to be in Section 3 on Shelf 3 of Bay 2 within Aisle 7 of Sector 1 of the Soldotna We-Do-Foods warehouse. Therefore, our completed warehouse inventory location code reads:

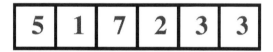

Inventory location codes for different companies will be different because they are based on the needs of that company, its products, and the layout of its warehouses and external inventory yards. No matter what company or what warehouse, developing a inventory location coding system and making sure all warehouse staff understand the system is essential to quick and accurate putaway and inventory picking.

Figure 3.9 - Efficient and effective use of inventory location codes help to make sure putaway and picking are fast and accurate. They also help to keep warehouses tidy and organized, like this one owned by Alaska gift and memorabilia retailer, Once in a Blue Moose.

CHAPTER 3 REVIEW QUESTIONS

1. What is slotting? When and how is it used?

2. If an item in a warehouse is one that is frequently picked, where should it be located within the warehouse? Where should it be located on a shelving system and in what situations might it not be located in this area of the shelving system?

3. When might a company want to use a converted warehouse building? When might it want to rent warehouse space?

4. What is an external inventory yard? For what types of goods is it used?

5. What must a company consider when selecting a location for an external inventory yard?

6. Under what circumstances might a company choose to use open ground flooring in their inventory yard? Under what circumstances might a company choose to use a concrete surface inventory yard?

7. In a typical inventory yard layout, where are items delivered and issued frequently located?

8. What are some examples of equipment required for an external inventory yard?

9. Why might a one-way flow of traffic be important to an external inventory yard?

10. What is an inventory location system? How might one be used in an external inventory yard setting?

CHAPTER 3 CASE EXERCISE

External Inventory Yard Construction... You Decide!

You're the expert! You must figure out which type of external inventory yard construction to use for six different situations. Remember, the four different types of external inventory yard construction are:

open ground, **gravel surface**, **asphalt surface**, and **concrete surface**

Read each of the following six scenarios and decide which type of external inventory yard construction would be the most effective and cost effective for each. In the space below each scenario, write which of the four construction types you have selected and explain why that is the best choice.

1. **A Christmas tree company needs a place to store its freshly cut trees before bundling them and taking them to individual lots across the northeastern United States.**

2. **A bridge building company in Florida needs to create a permanent inventory yard for its finished bridge parts, including 2-story-high concrete pillars and 15-foot wide coils of steel cable.**

3. **A sailboat manufacturer needs a place to store its meticulously handcrafted finished inventory, 250 sailboats of different sizes, each on small 2-wheeled trailers.**

4. **A log home building supplier in rainy Seattle needs a temporary location to store freshly cut and debarked logs for 5 nearby new homes. The lot must be able to handle some vehicular traffic.**

5. **Sand and Gravel America, Inc. needs a permanent inventory yard that will be a receiving and distribution center for palletized loads of cultured stone (lightweight stone used on house exteriors). The stone comes in 125 varieties and sizes.**

6. **Sub-Sub-Z, Inc., the premier refrigerator manufacturer in central Asia, has had to recall its MegaFreeze refrigerator because it was found to spontaneously combust when placed next to a microwave. The company needs a temporary place in which to store its recalled MegaFreeze refrigerators before they are dismantled and hauled away for destruction.**

Chapter 4

Internal Processes: Materials Handling

You are now on your way to becoming a superstar of warehouse management! You now know about warehouse buildings, and external inventory yards. What more could you possible need to know? Imagine that you are the regional warehouse manager of We-Do-Food, a grocery retail company catering to the cost conscious customer. You have the perfectly designed warehouse. You have a perfect place for everything and everything is in its place — a stupendous warehouse for a static world! What more could you possibly need?

Apples, frozen crab legs, and potato chips are coming in. Trucks are waiting at the dock for sodas, cheese, and our beloved papayas (more on this later) to go out. Meanwhile, more delivery trucks arrive. The inevitable has come: goods must move in and other goods must move out! Our perfectly designed static warehouse has entered the reality of our dynamic world. We must now physically handle the goods coming in as we enter the big, wide world of *materials handling*.

Figure 4.1 - The Materials of Materials Handling: raw materials, such as lumber, metal, or plastic (*pictured left, lumber transported via barge in Venice, Italy*); work-in-process, such as partially assembled or semi-finished goods (*pictured center, raw milk from the Swiss Alps ready for transport to a pasteurization facility*), and finished goods, such as goods fully assembled and ready to be delivered to the customer (*pictured right, washing machines in a retail warehouse in Alaska*).

A First Look at Materials Handling

We know we need to move things into, within, and out of our warehouse, but where do we begin? With the discipline of materials handling, of course! The Materials Handling Industry of America (MHIA) defines **materials handling** as *the art and science associated with the movement, storage, control, and protection of goods and materials throughout the process of their manufacture, distribution, consumption, and disposal.* In a nutshell, it is a focus on materials and how they are handled (moved and stored) in the logistics chain. The *materials* being handled in materials handling are typically **raw materials**, such as limber, metal, or plastic; **work-in-process**, such as partially-assembled or semi-finished goods; or **finished goods**, such as goods fully assembled and ready to be delivered to the customer.

When addressing materials handling, organizations have at least one of the following objectives in mind:

- **Space.** How goods are handled when moved and stored has a direct impact on warehouse space needed. If the objective of an organization is to design a new warehouse, it will plan for the appropriate amount of warehouse floor space needed for the materials handling equipment to be used. For example, if materials are to be stored and retrieved using a large forklift, more aisle space will be allocated in the warehouse design than if materials are to be stored and retrieved using a small hand truck.

  Conversely, if the objective of an organization is to work within existing warehouse space limitations, materials handling equipment and methods chosen will be those which fit and work within the existing space constraints. For example, in an inner-city warehouse with no room for expansion, a company may decide to use small hand trucks instead of forklifts for materials storage and retrieval.

- **Labor.** Put in simplest terms, labor equals people and people equal money. The longer and harder warehouse employees must work, the more they are likely to have to be paid. Organizations then look to materials handling to reduce labor cost by designing and utilizing materials handling systems which allow people to work more effectively and smarter – not harder

- **Service.** Unless a company has absolutely no competition in our ever-growing vast, global marketplace, it is almost certain to place a high premium on the ability to provide outstanding customer service. The way in which a company addresses its materials handling can allow it to enhance the levels of customer service it provides. For example, the We-Do-Food regional grocery warehouse might revamp its materials handling system, which would get fresh produce onto delivery trucks 50% quicker in the middle of a sub-zero Alaskan February, allowing less freezing damage to set in, resulting in a fresher papaya for the grocery store customer!

The way in which a company handles its goods during their movement and storage can dramatically increase or decrease warehousing costs. While an organization may incur significant set-up costs for a well-designed materials handling system, it can reap substantial cost-saving benefits for many years to come. Thus, when considering the array of materials handling systems covered throughout the remainder of this chapter, companies are ever mindful of the system set-up costs, their long-term cost saving benefits, and the positive impact it could have on internal and external customer satisfaction.

BENEFITS OF MATERIALS HANDLING

As a discipline, materials handling has continued to gain increasing momentum across the world into the 21st century. MHIA reports that, in the United States alone, the annual expenditure on the materials handling industry had grown from $34.5 billion in 1990 to $64 billion in 2000 to a whopping $156 billion in 2015. Organizations invest money and time into materials handling because of the significant benefits it can bring, which include:

- **Enhanced output and distribution.** Materials handling addresses the movement of materials from storage in the physical warehouse system, through the production process, into storage again, and, finally, to the final distribution system. When companies focus on this movement and attempt to make materials flow quick, efficient, and seamless, output becomes more efficient and distribution can begin seamlessly, with reduced delays and product shortages.

- **Employee health and safety.** The quality of a company's materials handling system, including the equipment used and the training received by equipment operators, can have an enormous impact on the health and safety of employees within its warehouse, production, and distribution facilities. For example, a faulty system or a poorly trained driver can lead to serious or even fatal accidents.

- **Reduced operating cost.** A poorly operated or designed materials handling system is not only dangerous to people and products, but it can also increase logistics cost by as much as 600%! When materials are handled unnecessarily or inefficiently, materials handling equipment, plant, time, and labor costs all increase. Conversely, when materials are moved and stored quickly and more efficiently, the cost per unit moved reduces.

- **Reduced damage.** Poor or careless materials handling can result in damage and premature stock deterioration, not to mention the associated exorbitant increases in cost! Careful and consistent materials handling can reduce the risk of such costly damage.

MATERIALS HANDLING SYSTEMS

In order to reap the potential benefits of materials handling, organizations look to the design and efficiency of their materials handling systems. A materials handling system is the network of equipment, methodologies, procedures, and rules used by an organization for the movement, storage, control, retrieval, and protection of goods. A materials handling system may be as simple as a small refrigerated storeroom at the back of a restaurant into which food is delivered by a small hand truck, stored on shelves, and retrieved by hand by restaurant kitchen staff or it may be as complicated as the computerized system of containers, trains, cranes, and forklifts found at many sea ports.

When selecting or designing a materials handling system, an organization will typically seek input from corporate strategic planners and logistics managers, but specifically, those leading the warehousing, production, and physical distribution departments. This cross-departmental team will then consider a variety of factors when selecting, planning, and/or designing a materials handling system, such as:

- **Materials Center Locations.** *Materials centers* are simply where an organization's materials are located. These include warehouses, external inventory yards, production facilities, and distribution areas. For most organizations, these materials centers are separated by barriers, such as roads, railroad tracks, or pure distance. The presence of such physical barriers often creates a need for a combination of various forms of materials handling systems and devices, e.g., a forklift-gravity conveyor-tow truck- pallet truck system.

- **Nature of Materials Handled.** Different materials, especially those with different weight, size, and shape characteristics, will require different materials handling methods. (This may sound like common sense, but we can't tell you how many new business owners we've met who are both shocked and dismayed to learn that, despite the salesman's assurances, their one forklift does not lift all!) For example, large, bulky materials tend to be handled best by a large number of small devices with a limited weight range while dense and heavy materials, such as steel, tend to be handled best by very large and powerful trucks or cranes.

- **Capital Resources.** When an organization has meager funds allotted for a materials handling system, they will often end up with a materials handling system with meager capabilities. No matter how much is available in capital resources, the materials handling planning and design team has as one of its primary goals to find the most effective and most suitable system and equipment available for the organization's budget.

- **Future Needs.** Very few organizations will remain exactly the same size throughout the useable lifespan of their materials handling system. Materials handling systems planners must consider the future growth or contraction of logistics and warehousing needs by creating a flexible system which can be easily adjusted to meet the changing needs of the organization. Imagine that a We-Do-Food warehouse purchases $1 million in special handling equipment, which will handle only large volumes of oranges and grapefruit. The following year, a severe drought occurs in Florida and California, resulting in We-Do-Food receiving 70% fewer oranges and grapefruit, which, in turn, results in the special handling equipment sitting idle and the portion of warehouse space it takes up being unused 70% of the time.

- **Total Cost.** It may seem obvious that a materials handling system planning and design team would consider the total cost of a potential new systems, but less obvious, however, are what comprises the total cost. Not only must the planning and design team consider the actual cost of the pieces of equipment they will purchase, but they must also consider system operating costs, such as fuel, power, maintenance, labor, spares, and depreciation costs.

- **Equipment Compatibility.** Unless a company is building an entirely new warehouse and materials handling facility from the ground up, the materials handling system planning and design team will have to consider the nature of the existing equipment and facilities. For example, a warehouse with primarily small shelf storage and narrow aisles would be unsuitable for forklift trucks or palletized materials.

- **Devices Available.** There are many materials handling system devices and equipment available on the market. Before a hasty decision based on which equipment looks the best, which system is used successfully by a competitor, or which salesperson seemed the friendliest, the materials handling system design and planning team must consider the wide range of devices and equipment available, while remaining mindful of their company's unique needs and any cross-device or cross-system compatibility issues.

- **Packaging Used.** The forms of packaging used by both the organization and its suppliers and distributors often play a defining role in the types of materials handling equipment ultimately used. Later sections of this text highlight different forms of packaging and the handling methods required for each.

PRINCIPLES OF MATERIALS HANDLING

Before looking at types of materials handling systems in depth, we must first dig a bit deeper into the world of materials handling. As was mentioned at the beginning of this chapter, the Materials Handling Institute of America (MHIA) defines materials handling as "the art and science associated with the movement, storage, control, and protection of goods and materials throughout the process of their manufacture, distribution, consumption, and disposal." But what exactly are the "art" and "science" of materials handling? We can begin to discover these by looking at some of the guiding principles of materials handling!

The three primary principles of materials handling to are:

- *Manage for efficiency.*

- *Avoid the curse of double handling!*

- *Look at your flow.*

For students or professionals in the world of warehousing and materials handling, invaluable industry-related tools and information are available on the Internet from professional organizations such as the Material Handling Industry of America (MHIA), which can be found on the web at www.mhia.org.

MANAGEMENT FOR EFFICIENCY

One of the most significant benefits that can be reaped from materials handling is increased efficiency. Materials handling efficiency requires careful and professional management by senior logistics professionals. Many organizations have adopted the practice of appointing a senior member of the logistics management team as Materials Handling Manager, with overall responsibility and authority for all materials handling. This offers many efficiency advantages, including:

- *Centralization of authority with a logistics manager, who has a holistic view of total requirements, should result in better utilization of materials handling resources.*

- *A skilled and specialized logistics professional will be able to recommend and employ the best and most efficient system in line with his/her own knowledge and experience.*

- *Central control of materials handling within logistics will help reduce the bottlenecks and holdups that plague many organizations.*

The Materials Handling Manager can also follow set procedures to continue to dramatically increase efficiency, including:

- **Using only the correct equipment** for each task and never allowing materials handling devices to be misused, which can result in accidents and stock damage.

- **Properly training and testing all materials handling operators** in the use of relevant materials handling equipment. Many larger producers of materials handling equipment provide in-plant training schemes as part of their purchase and service packages.

- **Ensuring that the materials handling system employed truly meets the needs** of the organization. For example, a small company with a simple materials flow will require only a simple system. Managers must resist the temptation to use overly elaborate systems, no matter how attractive all the "whistles and bells" may be.

- **Ensuring that all other departments concerned are fully aware** of the problems and limitations of the materials handling system employed. This will reduce system bottlenecks by reducing unreasonable demands placed on the system.

THE CURSE OF DOUBLE HANDLING

While management practices and procedures can be used to enhance materials handling efficiency, *double handling* can be one of the greatest hindrances and must be addressed to achieve a truly efficient system. ***Double handling*** is the term used to describe the practice of handling materials more times than necessary, primarily due to inefficiencies within the entire logistics management system.

When materials are delivered to a warehouse, they should, in theory, make only a limited number of journeys, such as: from the delivery vehicle to the place of storage; selection from the place of storage; or from the storage or selection area to delivery vehicle or production.

In many organizations, however, this simple flow is not maintained and materials are handled too many times. The real cost of handling, especially in fuel, warehouse space, and labor, is greatly increased, accompanied by an increase in accident risk and stock damage. We once knew of a top automobile spare parts store in Ireland that received goods into its warehouse area loading bay, then transferred the goods to a "to-be-shelved" area, then moved them to a temporary shelving area which divided the goods/parts into model number categories, then moved the goods to the primary storage/shelving area, and finally, moved the goods into the store. In this case, goods were not only "double handled," but triple- and quadruple-handled as well! When this excess handling was eliminated, labor costs fell dramatically, warehouse shelving space was freed up, and stock damage decreased by 300%!

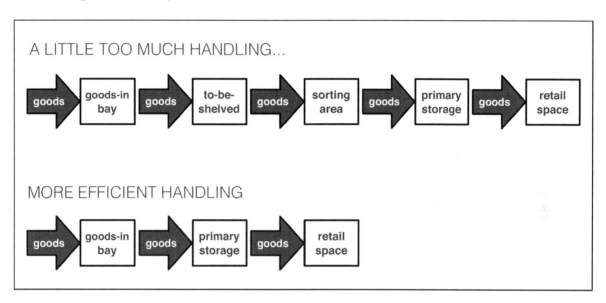

Figure 4.2 - Efficient Materials Handling

As will be discussed in later chapters, when inventory location systems are not used, warehouse personnel may spend an entire day looking for that last box of papayas or the last Road Rage Racing Tricycle.

- **Poor Communications.** Good communications between the departments involved in materials handling is essential. For example, materials should only be supplied to retail or production departments when they can be accommodated. Retail or factory floor space can become clogged with materials when there is poor communication between those in materials handling and those in retail or production.

- **Incorrect Materials Handling Device Use.** When the wrong device is used for the job, the job may need to be duplicated, resulting in double handling. For example, a small capacity truck will need to make several journeys to unload a vehicle with very heavy units, while a large device could perform the task in one movement. Think also of a large warehouse-style store, such as Costco, Sam's Club, or BJ's, which uses forklift trucks to move large quantities of a product straight from the delivery truck to the store aisle, instead of using smaller hand-trucks to move lesser quantities of the product. Definitely a labor- and cost-saving avoidance of double handling – as long as you avoid the speeding forklifts!

- **Lack of Space.** The most common cause of double handling is lack of space. This often happens when an organization has grown over time and its warehousing and materials handling space has not grown accordingly. When there is a lack of space and a need to unload delivery vehicles as quickly as possible, materials tend to be placed temporarily in the nearest available space, resulting in a sure-fire-recipe for double handling!

One strategy used by most contemporary companies to minimize the scourge of double handling is computer control of materials handling. For most companies, their materials that are handled are valuable and important to the operation as a whole. As such, many companies have developed complex computerized materials handling systems. For example, central control boards displaying the position of every materials handling device can feed data into a warehouse management system program, which can then analyze the current situation and direct the most efficient use of materials handling resources.

Materials handling can become almost total automated with the aid of computers, thus eliminating excess human-error resulting in double handling. Organizations may also choose to have their materials handling equipment radio-controlled, especially in situations where operations are spread over a wide area and a great deal of outdoor handling is performed. This enables central control be in constant touch with every truck, allowing them to minimize double handling by overseeing and controlling the flow of the entire operation from a central point.

EXPLORING MATERIALS FLOW

In order to ensure that materials handled throughout with maximum efficiency and that all unnecessary double handling is eliminated, materials handling experts examine the flow of materials within the organization. For example, one item is selected and its movement is examined and documented from the time an organization received it to the time the item is either consumed or leaves the organization. Materials handling practitioners and analysts use *flow process charts* to document and examine this flow of goods. Materials flow process charts document both existing and proposed methods or stages of materials flow.

In flow process charts, standard symbols are used to represent action within the flow of goods. For example, a circle represents an operation, an upside-down triangle represents storage, a block arrow represents transportation, a "D" represents an unnecessary delay in process, and a square represents an inspection activity. Symbols may also be superimposed when actions occur

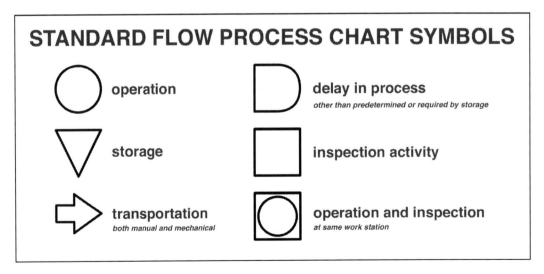

Figure 4.3 - Standard Flow Process Chart Symbols

simultaneously at the same place, such as a circle inside a square for when an operation and inspection occur at the same workstation.

Flow process charts may also take many forms, depending on the needs of the organization. For examining and documenting materials flow in relation to physical space and location of goods, a flow process chart can be superimposed on an actual facility layout map, documenting a spatial materials flow, as shown in the sample below. More often, however, materials flow is documented on a tabulated flow process chart, which highlights the actual number of times a material is handled within an organization. These charts are often used for efficiency analysis, with reducing the number of times a material is handled as the ultimate goal.

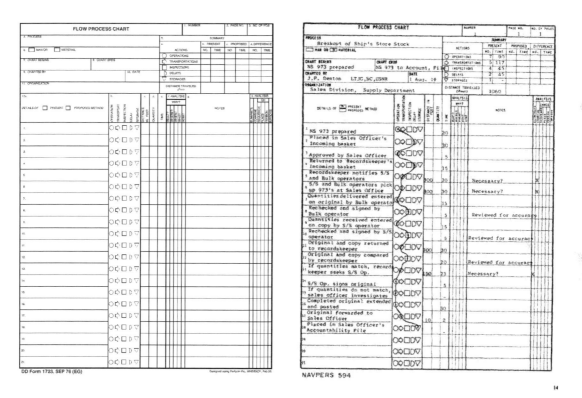

Figure 4.4 - Flow Process Charts. A blank flow process chart used by the U.S. Department of Defense (left) and a completed chart (right) used to analyze materials flow.

MATERIALS HANDLING EQUIPMENT

Now that you understand the principles of materials handling, think you're ready to make a move away from the wide and wonderful world of materials handling? Not so fast! It's now time to delve into the nitty-gritty of *materials handling equipment*! Any static (stationary) or dynamic (moving) manual or mechanical device used to move or store a material during any segment of its logistics chain falls under the broad spectrum of **materials handling equipment**. Aside from its obvious role in moving and storing goods, why else might today's materials handler want to use materials handling equipment? In three words: *cost*, *quality*, and *service*.

Effective use of materials handling equipment can help an organization reduce its materials handling or warehousing costs. For example, forklifts allow an organization to store palletized materials far higher than human arms can reach. Using vertical storage space effectively in a warehouse means that less of the costly, horizontal floor space is needed. Materials handling equipment also helps to ensure that a high quality standard can be attained and maintained for company goods and operations. For example, in an ice cream factory, conveyors zipping from production floor to refrigerated trucks can ensure that precious tubs of its frozen gold can stay frozen, with no hot little human hands melting the Rocky Road! Finally, effective use of materials handling equipment can increase service levels to an organization's internal and external customers. For example, although unheard of forty years ago, grocery store customers in cold and snowy Alaska now have the same selection of tropical produce available in sunny California, thanks to containers and dockside cranes which allow tropical fruits to be delivered quickly before freezing or spoiling. This allows the Alaskan shopper to enjoy papayas all year long!

According to the online *Material Handing Taxonomy* of the College-Industry Council on Material Handling Education (CIC/MHE), materials handling equipment falls within one of five categories:

- *transport equipment*, which is used to move goods from one place to another;

- *positioning equipment*, which is used to reposition goods in place so that they are in the correct location and alignment for subsequent handling;

- *storage equipment*, which is used to hold materials statically (shelving) or dynamically (carousels), from temporary holding to long-term storage timeframes;

- *unit load formation equipment*, which is used to restrain goods and form them into a single unit load, such as on a pallet or in a container, for subsequent transport and storage; and

- *automatic identification and communication equipment*, which is used to identify goods to assist with inventory control and materials flow.

In the sections to follow, we will examine the first three of these five categories. We will look at unit load formation equipment in the next chapter when we discuss *the unit load*. Also, because its use is far more product-specific than its four counterpart, we'll leave discussions on positioning equipment for more detailed, industry-specific materials handling texts.

After reading about these five categories of materials handling equipment, you may be interested in hoping on the nearest forklift or tiger piece of equipment and trying it out. If you are so inclined for that exciting bit of warehouse adventure, STOP! The U.S. Department of Labor's Occupational Safety and Health Administration (OSHA) requires all operators of materials handling equipment to be formally trained in the equipment they plan to operate.

TRANSPORT EQUIPMENT

As previously mentioned, **transport equipment** is used to move goods from one place to another, typically within a specific facility or location. Thus, our definition of transport equipment within the context of materials handling equipment does not include transportation vehicles that move goods from one facility to another, such as trains, planes, and tractor-trailer trucks. Within the world of materials handling equipment, there are three primary types of transportation equipment: *industrial trucks*, *cranes*, and *conveyors*.

When many of us think of materials handling equipment, especially those of us who spend a little too much time in Costco or Home Depot, our minds first wander to industrial trucks. **Industrial trucks** include hand-trucks, forklift trucks, automatic guided vehicles, and any other transport device with maneuvering as its primary function and carrying, stacking, loading, and/or unloading as additional functions. Industrial trucks typically operate by picking up loads from underneath. (Think of a forklift placing its forks underneath a palletized load before lifting and moving it.) They can also maneuver goods of different sizes and types over variable paths at varying speeds. They can go almost anywhere, carrying almost anything, at almost any speed! These superheroes of the materials handling world do have their limitations, however. They can function effectively only on suitable flat, level surfaces, such as asphalt or concrete. Because they need sufficient maneuvering room, they also don't handle well in confined or congested areas.

While there is a wide range of industrial truck types, they all fall into one of the following three categories: *non-palletized trucks*, *palletized trucks*, and *automatic guided vehicles*. **Non-palletized trucks** are built to maneuver and carry items and unit loads other than those secured to a pallet. Because of their adaptability in the types of items and loads they can handle, non-palletized trucks typically cannot stack their loads or lift them more than a few inches. Manual (people-powered) non- palletized trucks include hand trucks and dollies. Powered non-palletized trucks include platform trucks, in both their **walkie** (operator walks to push and steer) and **rider** (operator rides and steers) versions.

Figure 4.5 - Non-Palletized Trucks. A walkie platform truck in Pike's Place Market in Seattle, Washington (*left*); a rider platform truck in a Sears distribution center in Anchorage, Alaska (*center*); and a UPS rider platform truck on the Isle of Capri, Italy (*right*).

Figure 4.6 - Inventive Non-Palletized Truck Solution. At Once in a Blue Moose, after experimenting with a variety of non-palletized truck options, the owners discovered that traditional shopping carts, with hand baskets secured with zip ties to use for smaller goods, were the most effective solution for both order picking and inventory putaway. Tags representing each of the organization's retail locations were also created to easily be attached to the front of the carts using velcro.

Palletized trucks, as their name suggests, are built to maneuver and carry palletized unit loads. (In the next chapter, we'll cover pallets and palletization in greater detail.) The simplest palletized trucks can be manually or power operated, can lift loads only a few inches high, and can either be *pallet jacks*, which are pushed, or *pallet trucks*, which are ridden on by the operator.

Figure 4.7 - Pallet Jacks in Lucern, Switzerland (*left*) and Anchorage, Alaska (*right*).

For many palletized trucks, however, palletized unit loads can not only be maneuvered and carried, but can also be lifted several feet and stacked. These, too, may be pushed by a walking operator, as with manual or powered *walkie stackers*, or ridden on and steered by an operator, as with *forklift trucks*. Forklift trucks come in a variety of styles based on the function they are intended to perform, including:

- *counterbalanced lift trucks*, which are used for standard maneuvering, carrying, lifting, and stacking palletized loads up to 13 feet;

- *narrow aisle trucks*, which are specially constructed for narrow aisle maneuvering;

- *turret trucks* and *swing mast trucks,* which are designed to lift and stack palletized loads in narrow aisles up to 40 feet high, far above what is humanly possible without such equipment; and

- *pallet jacks* and *pallet trucks*, which are designed to lift palletized goods only high enough to clear the floor so that it can be moved across the warehouse without dragging on the floor.

Figure 4.8 - Turret truck (*left*), counterbalanced lift truck, also called a forklift truck (*center*), and an automatic guided vehicle (*right*)

Automated guided vehicles (AGVs) are purpose-built to handle either palletized or non-palletized loads of varying weights over fixed or variable paths. Unlike the previous two categories of industrial trucks, however, AGVs do not require a hands-on operator. Because they are very expensive to purchase and require little to no direct labor, AGVs are typically used in environmentally sensitive (e.g. sterile medical equipment manufacture) or hazardous (e.g. sub-zero refrigeration warehouses) environments.

Cranes, the second category of transport equipment within the world of materials handling, are characterized by their ability to move individual items or unit loads of varying weights over a variable horizontal and vertical path within a fixed area. Their movement is less adaptable than that of the industrial trucks previously discussed, but they can often carry heavier loads, such as stacked containers. The primary function of a crane is to lift and carry or to place into a specific position. Cranes typically lift loads from above, can be used indoors or outdoors, and are useful in dangerous or congested areas. The four most common types of cranes are:

- *jib crane*, which uses a 360-degree pivoting arm extended out from a vertical support structure or a wall, in which case it pivots 180 degrees;

- *bridge crane*, which enables items to be moved to any location within an entire facility. Tracks are mounted on opposite walls of a facility with a perpendicular moving beam placed on these tracks and a moving hoist placed on the beam;

- *gantry cranes*, which are similar to bridge cranes but have floor-based support tracks, rather than wall- based ones. They are typically used outside, where there are no walls, or when less facility floor space is needed for crane operations; and

- *stacker cranes,* which are also similar to bridge cranes but have a fork- or container-based apparatus suspended from its tracks instead of a beam with a hoist. Stacker cranes are primarily used for pallet load and container applications, especially when storage and retrieval needs exceed 40 feet.

Figure 4.9 - Jib crane (*upper left*), bridge crane (*upper right*),
gantry crane (*lower left*), and stacker crane (*lower right*)

Conveyors, our third and final category of transport equipment, move individual items and unit loads across a fixed path. An item is placed onto or attached to a conveyor at a fixed point and, with no human accompaniment, the item is transported to a different fixed point. The primary function of conveyors is to move goods. Unlike industrial trucks and cranes, which may have maneuvering, lifting, and positioning as additional functions, conveyors focus almost entirely on movement. Also unlike industrial trucks and cranes, conveyors work continuously and, as such, need items or loads of relatively uniform weight and size for them to function effectively. (While the same crane could be used to lift an elephant and a snow pea, placing an elephant on a conveyor you use everyday to move snow peas might cause a bit of damage.) Like the other forms of transport equipment, conveyors may also be purpose- built for indoor or outdoor use.

Although there are many types of conveyors built for a wide range of materials and transport needs, most fall into one of three major categories:

- *gravity conveyors*. Most gravity conveyors are based on a downward slope and use chutes, wheels, or rollers onto which items are placed. Following the rules of gravity, the items slide or roll downward to their ultimate destination. Gravity conveyors are the most inexpensive type of conveyor system, but a decline is essential for them to work and, because of their lack of control over individual items, they are not recommended for fragile or breakable goods.

- *powered conveyors*. These types of conveyors operated on electrical power and are typically based on a system of rollers, belts, and/or chains. (The next time you're collecting your luggage after your sun-soaked Hawaiian vacation, check out your airport's luggage conveyor belt to see if it operates using rollers, belts, and/or chains.) Some powered conveyors include vertical lift components, allowing items to be carried to higher or lower floors of a facility. They may also include an automated sorting component, which use sensors to identify items or loads and sorts them onto one of multiple divergent paths.

- *overhead conveyors*. Overhead conveyors may be powered or non- powered and operate using ceiling- mounted tracks, chains, or monorails. Items or unit loads are suspended onto these conveyors from overhead, making this type of conveyor extremely useful when floor space is unavailable.

Figure 4.10 - Gravity conveyor (*left*) and powered conveyor (*right*)

STORAGE EQUIPMENT

Along with transport and unitization equipment, **storage equipment** is another important category of materials handling equipment. The primary purpose of storage equipment is to store or hold items or unit loads for a specific period of time, ranging from temporary, 2-hour storage of papayas in the We- Do-Foods distribution center to indefinite storage of hazardous chemical waste at a remote government facility. Most storage equipment is very straightforward and not nearly as complex or as expensive as other types of materials handling equipment. In the next chapter, you will become acquainted with one of the most common forms of storage equipment: *pallet racking*. Additional types of storage equipment for non-palletized goods come in a range of *static* and *dynamic* forms.

With **static storage equipment**, the items or loads being stored remain stationary. The most common forms include standard shelves and drawers. **Static shelving** is typically 12' to 24" deep and products may be placed directly onto the shelves or into bins placed on the shelves. Another popular form of static storage is the **mezzanine**, a storage system, which can add a second layer of storage or office space to a warehouse. Because they are not a permanent part of a warehouse facility's structure, mezzanines are somewhat adaptable and can be moved or readjusted to suit an organization's needs.

Figure 4.11 - Storage carousel, *pictured left* (Photo credit: Wiese USA) and automatic storage/retrieval system, *pictured right* (Photo credit: "Miniload ASRS" by Thomas Philippi - TGW Mechanics GmbH, Wels, Austria.)

With **dynamic storage equipment**, the items or loads stored move, typically by power-operated means. The three most common forms of non-palletized dynamic storage equipment are *flow racks*, *storage carousels*, and *automatic storage/retrieval systems (AS/RS)*. **Flow racks** are like static shelving, but goods are loaded onto the racks from the back and flow or move forward as goods are taken from the front. These racks are angled downward from the back to the front and goods flow forward by letting gravity do all the work!

Storage carousels are made up of a set of bins or shelves that revolve either vertically or horizontally. Because they bring bins/shelves to the end of the aisle for an operator to pick or place items, storage carousels maximize floor space by allowing for extremely narrow aisles. Storage carousels also allow for high pick rates, allowing warehouse workers to pick orders quicker because they don't have to move all over the warehouse. The items come to them instead. *Automatic storage/retrieval systems*, also known as *AS/RS*, are systems of rows of racks, with each row able to move vertically and horizontally to get goods to the person picking an order in the warehouse. AS/RS maximizes floor space by allowing for narrow aisles that are up to 100 feet high. This type of storage is also fully automated throughout the retrieval, picking, and placement process. As a result, AS/RS is more efficient, controlled, secure, and expensive than carousels and other forms of storage equipment.

AUTOMATIC IDENTIFICATION AND COMMUNICATION EQUIPMENT

Our final major category of materials handling equipment is *automatic identification and communication equipment*. Its primary purpose is to identify items or unit loads and then store or transmit this information, which will then be used to coordinate and control the flow of goods. While item identification and communication can be performed manually with our eyes and mouths, these functions can be performed far more efficiently and effectively when specialized equipment and systems are used. The two most frequently used systems upon which this identification and communication equipment is based are: *barcodes* and *RFID*.

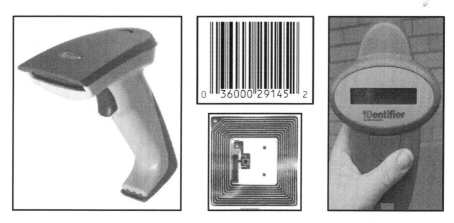

Figure 4.12 - Automatic Identification and Communication Equipment. Barcode scanner (*left*), barcode (*upper center*), RFID tag (*lower center*), and RFID reader (*right*)

Barcodes, the most widely used technology-based form of item identification, consist of a series of bars and spaces printed by a *barcode printer* onto a label, which is then adhered to an item or a unit load. The barcode label is read by a *barcode scanner*, also called a *barcode reader*, which then communicates the newly read information to a central inventory control system. Barcode scanners vary in cost and application and include: handheld scanners, fixed mount scanners, laser scanners, and image scanners.

With *radio frequency identification (RFID)*, a programmed transponder tag is attached to an item or unit load. The tag sends out information about the item or load via radio waves. An *RFID reader* with an antenna reads this information and, like a barcode reader, transmits it to a central inventory control system. While more expensive than bar coding, RFID technology is gaining immense popularity because of its many advantages. Unlike barcode labels, RFID tags can be read when not in the line of sight, at distances of 90 feet or more, and at high speeds. In addition, active RFID tags can be programmed with additional information, unlike barcode labels and static RFID tags.

CHAPTER 4 REVIEW QUESTIONS

1. What is materials handling? What is its role in the supply chain?

2. When an organization invests in its materials handling, what benefits might it obtain?

3. What is a materials handling system? What must a company consider when designing one?

4. What are the three primary principles of materials handing?

5. What can a company do to achieve materials handling efficiency?

6. What is double handling? What are some of its causes? What implications might it have for an organization?

7. Why do materials handling managers use flow process charts? What do each of the following flow process symbols mean: circle, upside down triangle, arrow, D, and square?

8. What are the five categories of materials handling equipment? What is the task of each?

9. When might a warehouse use an industrial truck? When might it use a conveyor?

10. What type of automatic identification technology would you select if you needed to transmit and read information about containers on a moving train? Why?

FLOW PROCESS CHART	1. NUMBER	2. PAGE NO.	3. NO. OF PGS

4. PROCESS

6. ☐ MAN OR ☐ MATERIAL

7. CHART BEGINS   **8. CHART ENDS**

9. CHARTED BY   **10. DATE**

11. ORGANIZATION

5. SUMMARY

a. ACTIONS	b. PRESENT		c. PROPOSED		d. DIFFERENCE	
	NO.	TIME	NO.	TIME	NO.	TIME
◯ OPERATIONS						
⇨ TRANSPORTATIONS						
☐ INSPECTIONS						
D DELAYS						
▽ STORAGES						
DISTANCE TRAVELED (Feet)						

12a. DETAILS OF ☐ PRESENT ☐ PROPOSED METHOD

b. OPERATION | TRANSPORT | INSPECTION | DELAY | STORAGE
c. DISTANCE IN FEET
d. QUANTITY
e. TIME
f. ANALYSIS — WHY? — WHAT? WHERE? WHEN? WHO? HOW?
g. NOTES
h. ANALYSIS — CH — ELIMINATE COMBINE SEQUENCE PLACE PERSON IMPROVE

#	b. ◯ ⇨ ☐ D ▽
1.	◯ ⇨ ☐ D ▽
2.	◯ ⇨ ☐ D ▽
3.	◯ ⇨ ☐ D ▽
4.	◯ ⇨ ☐ D ▽
5.	◯ ⇨ ☐ D ▽
6.	◯ ⇨ ☐ D ▽
7.	◯ ⇨ ☐ D ▽
8.	◯ ⇨ ☐ D ▽
9.	◯ ⇨ ☐ D ▽
10.	◯ ⇨ ☐ D ▽
11.	◯ ⇨ ☐ D ▽
12.	◯ ⇨ ☐ D ▽
13.	◯ ⇨ ☐ D ▽
14.	◯ ⇨ ☐ D ▽
15.	◯ ⇨ ☐ D ▽
16.	◯ ⇨ ☐ D ▽
17.	◯ ⇨ ☐ D ▽
18.	◯ ⇨ ☐ D ▽
19.	◯ ⇨ ☐ D ▽
20.	◯ ⇨ ☐ D ▽
21.	◯ ⇨ ☐ D ▽

DD Form 1723, SEP 76 (EG)   Designed using Perform Pro, WHS/DIOR, Feb 95

CHAPTER 4 CASE EXERCISES

Examining and Improving the Flow of Papayas at We-Do-Foods

Using the scenario below, please create a flow process chart documenting and analyzing the current exotic fruits receipt process at the We-Do-Foods central distribution warehouse. Please use the Flow Process Chart worksheet provided on the previous page (form DD-1723 available from www.dod.gov). When you have finished, please create a new flow process chart for an improved flow process for exotic fruits receipt at the We-Do-Foods warehouse.

At We-Do-Foods, we receive exotic fruits into our warehouse every day. These exotic fruits, which include mangoes, pomegranates, plantains, kiwis, passion fruit, and papayas, come in 2'x2' cushioned boxes. Shipments of 20 to 50 of these boxes arrive twice a day at approximately 7am and 3pm.

Before the boxes are unloaded from the delivery truck, the Receipt Supervisor checks to make sure that the documentation matches the shipment. Assuming there are no discrepancies, the boxes are unloaded from the delivery trucks, placed onto hand trucks at the dock, and taken 15' to the Receipt Holding Area by warehouse staff. The boxes are unloaded from the hand trucks and placed onto shelves labeled "To-Be-Inspected".

The boxes remain in the Receipt Holding Area until the Receipt Supervisor gets a call from the Quality Control Department, headed by the imperious and somewhat un-clever nephew of the owner of We-Do-Foods, summoning the Receipt Supervisor to bring the boxes to the Quality Control Room. The Receipt Supervisor instructs her staff to load the boxes onto hand trucks again and wheel them 250' to the Quality Control Room. The warehouse staff unloads the boxes onto the Inspection Tables. The Quality Control Staff open each of the boxes and inspect each individual piece of fruit for damage. They discard and make a note of damaged pieces. When they have finished, they place the fruit back into their boxes, mark the outside of the boxes as having been inspected, and write the quantity of post-inspection fruit on the outside of each box.

The warehouse staff then load the boxes back onto the hand trucks and wheel them 250' back to the spacious Receipt Holding Area, where the boxes are taken off of the hand carts and placed on shelves labeled "Approved by Quality Control." The Receipt Supervisor then counts and looks over the boxes to ensure the same quantity of boxes were received back into the Receipt Holding Area as were originally sent to the Quality Control Room. When this has been completed, the warehouse staff then loads the boxes onto hand trucks and wheels them 50' to the storage area and places them on shelves within pre-assigned refrigerated bays.

Bonus Exercise: Fun with Cranes!

Identify each of the three cranes pictured below. Under what circumstances would each be used? Is there another type of cranes not pictured? If so, what is it and under what circumstances might it be used?

1. 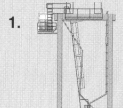   2.    3.

Chapter 5
Internal Processes: The Unit Load

MANUAL VERSUS MECHANICAL HANDLING

When you think of materials handling systems, you may first have grand visions of complex conveyor systems zipping goods across the production floor or forklift drivers racing pallets of goods piled three stories high from section to section of an intricately laid- out warehouse with the skill, speed, and agility of a Le Mans race car driver. Materials handling systems, however, may be as complex as the computerized conveyor systems of the mammoth warehouses of Amazon.com or as simple as two guys and a hand- truck in a restaurant's refrigerated storeroom. Both of these represent the two methods of materials handling: *manual handling* and *mechanical handling*.

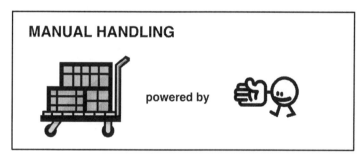

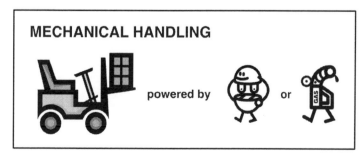

Figure 5.1 - Manual versus Mechanical Handling

Manual handling occurs when materials are handled by hand or by hand- operated devices. For example, moving a box from one end of a warehouse to another by carrying it in your arms, pushing it on a dolly, or wheeling it along on a hand-operated pallet-truck are all forms of manual handling.

Although many of us love to shop for mechanized gadgets with "all the bells and whistles," materials handling system designers and planners must always first seriously consider manual handling as an option for materials handling systems. Manual handling equipment, such as hand-trucks and hand-operated pallet trucks, are: relatively *inexpensive* to purchase; relatively *easier* and less expensive to maintain and repair than mechanized equipment; easily used in *confined spaces*, such as older warehouses built without modern mechanical devices in mind; and *efficient* in relation to the loads that can be handled, especially when equipment with hydraulic jacks are used.

Despite its advantages, manual handling is not always feasible or efficient. For example, loads may be too large (such as a ten-person hot-tub), too heavy (a crate of concrete birdbaths, perhaps), or too cumbersome (such as your garden- variety garden shed) to be handled manually. In these cases, materials are handled using mechanized devices, resulting in **mechanical handling**. Using mechanical devices for materials handling can be extremely advantageous for many situations because they:

- **Are able to handle extremely heavy loads**, typically far in excess of a person's carrying capacity, and are able to move these materials quickly. For example, you could buy a personal forklift with a lift capacity of 500 pounds on E-Bay for moving around those heavy items in your home and garden or you could spend a little bit more and get an industrial forklift with a lift capacity of up to 8000 pounds or more!

- **Can be used in almost any environmental condition** for up to twenty-four hours per day. For example, many forklift trucks are constantly in use, with their drivers rotating according to work shift.

- **Have been developed to cope with many dangerous and difficult handling** problems safely. Even Fred Flintstone used heavy machinery to move boulders around the quarry!

- **Can not only transport heavy loads, but also can lift and store them** as well. For example, you might be able to carry a large load of cotton balls across a warehouse, but could you lift them to be stored on a shelf 12 feet above you?

As wonderful as mechanical handling is, mechanical handling devices do offer some distinct disadvantages, which must be considered and minimized as much as possible. Such disadvantages include: the *high cost* of mechanical handling devices; the *high running cost* of these devices, especially in terms of fuel, power, maintenance, and service; the necessary cost of properly *training and employing staff* to operate the devices; and the *possibility of machine failure*, which can significantly delay an entire operation.

While neither is the perfect solution for every situation, manual handling and mechanical handling must both be considered when designing and planning a materials handling system.

Most systems use a combination of manual and mechanical handling methods and devices. Go to any medium to large sized warehouse and you're more than likely to find both a forklift *(mechanical)* and a hand-truck *(manual)* as commonly used materials handling devices.

Figure 5.2 - Manual and Mechanical Handling. It is common to see both manual and mechanical handling being used in warehouse facilities. This Sears distribution center uses both hand trucks (manual handling) for smaller, non-palletized goods and forklift trucks (mechanical handling) for larger, heavier, or palletized goods.

Figure 5.3 - The Unit Load. Palletized and stretch wrapped goods stacked on the upper shelves in a warehouse and are stored and retrieved using forklift trucks. Lighter, non-palletized goods are placed loosely on pallets on the floor for manual handling during storage and picking, using either hand trucks or pallet jacks.

A LOOK AT UNIT LOAD

One of the core concepts of materials handling in practice is that of the ***unit load***. A unit load is any quantity of a material, either multiple or individual items, assembled and restrained to permit it to be handled, moved, stored, and stacked as a single object. The next time you are in a warehouse-style wholesale store, walk down an aisle and take a look up. Stacked about 12 feet above the ground, you may see one hundred packs of toilet paper, stretch wrapped together onto a single wooden pallet. This pallet of toilet paper is an example of a unit load.

The process of using unit loads within materials handling is called ***unitization***. While developed in the first half of the twentieth century, unitization truly revolutionized the world of materials handling in the second half of the twentieth century because of its undeniably remarkable benefits. Some of these benefits unitization offers include:

- **reduced handling.** When bound together as one unit, individual items are handled less, reducing the risk of damage or deterioration.

- **load stability.** Because of the brick-like way in which items are layered onto a pallet or within a container, the single load is stable because the items' weight is evenly distributed within the unit load.

- **reduced surface area.** Because many items in a unit load are typically enclosed within an outer layer of items, they are protected from possible damage.

- **efficient storage.** When multiple items are bound together as a single, large block, they may be stacked many layers high within storage facilities, resulting in a very efficient use of space.

- **reduced packaging costs.** Before unitization, packaging materials for shipment and internal movement of goods were different. With unit loads, a uniform packaging is used for external and internal goods movement.

Although the idea of unitization may seem like a perfectly logical one that has been around for centuries, unitization as we know it today was born less than 100 years ago in the mid-twentieth century. In New Jersey sometime in the 1930s, a truck owner/operator named Malcolm McLean sat watching as cotton bales were unloaded from his truck and reloaded onto a freight ship. McLean thought about how much simpler and more efficient the process would be if a single unit container of cotton were transferred, container and all, from his truck onto the ship. McLean's not-so-idle thoughts then led to an idea which would revolutionize the world of logistics and materials handling - *containerization*! He took this revolutionary idea and, a few years later, founded the Sea-Land Corporation, which, in 1956, saw its first container ship set sail from Newark, New Jersey bound for Houston, Texas, carrying 58 container trailers. Today, more than 90% of the world's non-bulk cargo spends at least some of its life in a container.

While the container was taking the world suddenly by storm in the middle of the 20th century, another longer, quieter revolution had taken place just a few years earlier and, had it not been for war, might have gone almost unnoticed in the world of materials handling. With the introduction of the lift truck in the late 19th century came the introduction of the pallet. *Palletization* and palletized unit loads quietly and very slowly grew in prominence and popularity for 50 years. During World War II, however, palletization was a revolutionary force which allowed the U.S. military to do more with less - fewer troops could be used to move and handle much larger quantities of goods and less warehouse space could be used to store far more goods before moving them to the front. The military's reliance on the pallet load then led to the world's reliance on palletization, with more than 2 billion pallets in use today in the U.S. alone!

As you may have guessed from our history lesson, two primary types of unitization are *palletization*, in which goods are contained and transported on pallets, and *containerization*, in which goods are contained and transported in standardized containers.

PALLETIZATION

One of the two core structures that form the basis of a typical unit load is the *pallet*. (The other is the *container*, but we'll tackle that one in the next section.) A *pallet* is a flat, wooden, plastic, metal, or even paper structure used to support goods for stable transportation and storage. Goods are placed on top of a pallet and then strapped or shrink wrapped to form a secure unit load. This palletized unit load can then be raised, transported, and handled using forklifts or other jacking devices. The main function of the pallet is to maintain a gap between the floor and the load to be handled so that a lifting device may place its "forks" under the load without affecting its stability or security.

Figure 5.4 - Pallets and Pallet-less. Most goods are placed on a pallet and secured before being transported, like these pallets at the Black Falcon Cruise Terminal in Boston, Massachusetts (*left*). As wonderful and widespread as palletization is, not all goods can be palletized into a unit load. Examples of such "pallet-less" packaging and materials include: drums; large rolls of carpets or textiles; bricks and concrete blocks; tubs; bottled goods; soft loads, such as cotton or wool; and bulk materials, such as grains. In order to overcome the problems posed by pallet-less handling, a wide variety of materials handling devices have been developed, including devices with a range of attachments for different handling needs, such as these drums containing life rafts on specialized loading and deployment devices on a ferry in Greece (*right*).

With almost two billion in use right now in the U.S. alone, pallets are perhaps the most widely used tools of modern materials handlers. 500 million pallets are constructed in the U.S. every year and most of these made from wood. Wooden pallet construction consumes almost 40% of all U.S. hardwood lumber, second only to new home construction. The popularity of wooden pallets can be attributed to the fact that they are not only inexpensive to build and maintain, but that they can also be built to have a relatively long usable life.

Despite their profusion across the world of materials handling and their seemingly similar appearance, not all wooden pallets are created equal. Many are ***single-use wooden pallets***, which are made of softwood, can only be lifted from one of two opposite positions, and are built to be discarded once the unit load has reached its final destination. Others are ***multiple-use wooden pallets***, which are made of hardwood, can sometimes be lifted from any of their four sides, and can be reused or returned to their senders for reuse. Because of the cost of multiple-use pallet construction, organizations must take great care to ensure that these valuable pallets are neither lost nor damaged due to misuse. Pallet collection and control systems can help organizations achieve greater pallet reuse and efficiency.

Figure 5.5 - Single Use and Multiple Use Wooden Pallets. Notice the differences in construction between the single use (*left*) and multiple use (*right*) wooden pallets at this apple orchard warehouse in Cosby, Tennessee.

Not only do wooden pallets differ according to the number of times of their intended use, but they may also have slight to extreme variations based on a wide range of countless variables. For example, both single-use and multiple- use pallet construction may vary based on the unit load to be carried and its expected: *weight*; *type* (i.e., chemical/hazardous, food/perishable, storage, etc.); and type of *fastening* material to be used.

In addition to wood, pallets may also be made from plastic, metal, or paper. Of the 1.9 billion pallets used every year in the U.S., 95% are made from wood, 2% are made from plastic, 2% are made from wood composite, and less than 1% are made from cardboard and other paper materials. **Plastic pallets**, **wood composite pallets**, and their less commonly used counterpart, **metal pallets,** like multiple-use wooden pallets, can carry very heavy loads. They are reusable and can typically be lifted from any of their four sides. Because wooden pallets are difficult to keep clean, *plastic pallets* offer distinct advantages for handling foodstuffs and other potentially messy, perishable items. *Metal pallets*, on the other hand, cannot easily be damaged when under duress, unlike their wooden counterparts, and are thus more advantageous for handling extremely heavy loads. On the other side of the pallet spectrum are ***paper pallets*** and ***cardboard pallets***, which are typically used to carry lighter loads and be disposed of or recycled after a single use.

  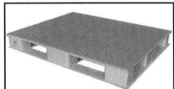

Figure 5.6 - Plastic (*left*), metal (*center*), and cardboard (*right*) pallets.

Pallets can come in a variety of sizes, depending on their function. However, there are six standard pallet sizes across the world that are recognized by the ISO, the International Organization for Standardization, which promotes worldwide standardization of industrial and commercial standards. Four of the more commonly used sizes of the six ISO sanctioned standard pallet are:

- the **North American Pallet**, also called the GMA Pallet or Grocery Pallet, measures 40 inches x 48 inches and is the most commonly used pallet size in the U.S., representing 30% of the pallets constructed every year

- the **ISO Standard Pallet**, which is used in the U.S. and across most of the world, measures 1000mm x 1200mm and typically weighs 15-21kg alone so that it can carry loads of up to 1000kg

- the **EUR Standard Pallet**, also known as the CEN pallet, is still commonly used in Europe and measures 800mm x 1200mm, narrower than other pallets because it is used primarily in the retail industry and is built to match European delivery truck and doorway dimensions.

- the **Australian Pallet** measures 1165mm x 1165mm and is used primarily in Australia

Because reusable pallets can be expensive to purchase and maintain, **pallet pool** businesses have arisen. These businesses, like ORBIS Reusable Packaging Management in the U.S. and Mexico and Nippon Pallet Pool Co. in Japan, rent out and distribute reusable wooden, plastic, and metal pallets to companies that need pallets and collect them when they no longer need them. For example, ORBIS has 14 service centers across North America that ship out and haul back pallets, while using a specially developed software system to keep track of the locations of all of their many pallets. When a pallet is brought back to an ORBIS service center, it is immediately cleaned and prepared to be placed back into service so that there is always a pool of pallets, ready for use.

So, now that your goods are safely secured as a unit load onto a pallet, you can lift them and move them around with a forklift. Now what do you do until you need them? You store them, of course! And, at the heart of every palletized unit load storage system is **pallet racking**. Pallet racking is a shelving system used for storing palletized unit loads to maximize available horizontal and vertical storage space. The type of pallet racking used within a materials handling system will vary according to: available *floor space*; *handling equipment* to be used; goods *safety requirements*; and stock variability, rotation, and order picking *requirements*.

The five most commonly used types of pallet racking are: *adjustable pallet racking, narrow aisle racking, drive-in racking, powered mobile racking,* and *live storage.* **Adjustable pallet racking** is the most widely used system for storing palletized unit loads. This flexible racking system is made of a system of vertical frames and horizontal beams which can be adjusted in height, both to make the most effective use of building/warehouse height and to accommodate changes in the height of unit loads. Because of its adaptability, this racking system is suitable for most types of storage applications.

Narrow aisle racking may also have an adjustable height system, but its hallmark is narrow aisles between racks or shelves. Narrow aisles allow for more floor space to be used and allow or goods to be stored higher with more security than with other racking systems, meaning that more goods can be stored in a given space. Specialized materials handling equipment is required for narrow aisle pallet racking, however. For example, specially designed trucks are used which do not need to turn 90 degrees, but instead run on a fixed path between the racks. This type of racking system is typically used in tall buildings in which underemployed space can be effectively transformed into safe, high- density warehouse storage.

Figure 5.7 - Adjustable Pallet Racking (*left*), Narrow Aisle Racking (*center*), and Drive-In Racking (*right*)

Drive-in racking is a racking system in which palletized unit loads are driven onto racks, pushed back on the rack, and additional unit loads are placed in front of them. This racking system uses a minimum of floor space but, because loads are aligned into lanes with only the loads on each end of the lane exposed, stock variability would be restricted to each lane carrying only one product. Drive-in racking is widely used in cold store conditions where floor space costs are high and refrigeration costs can be reduced by keeping cold products blocked together.

Powered mobile pallet racking is made of units of conventional/adjustable pallet racking, each mounted on a steel-framed base fitted with electrically- driven wheels, which run on a track set into the floor. Individual racking units may then be wheeled together and "closed up," allowing up to 80% of warehouse floor space to be used for storage, as opposed to the 30% used for conventional racking systems. To store or access goods, the wheel-mounted racking units can be wheeled aside to create an aisle next to the desired rack. Because of the increased storage density it offers, powered mobile pallet racking can often be found in higher rental premises or in warehouses feeling the need for expansion but not yet ready to move to larger premises.

Live storage is a unique type of racking system, which may be used for palletized unit loads or other types of non-palletized contained storage, such as cartons or drums. In a live storage system, a contained unit load is supported on inclined roller or gravity wheel tracks so that the goods travel automatically from the loading side of a facility to the unloading side. This system maximizes space utilization by reducing the amount of access aisles needed and ensures automatic stock rotation. Similar to drive-in racking, live storage systems do limit each moving lane to be filled only with the same stock. Thus, live storage systems tend to be used for perishable goods requiring failsafe stock rotation, unpalletized goods, and fast- moving multi-product ranges, particularly where small quantities of different items must be collated quickly.

Figure 5.8 - Powered Mobile Pallet Racking (*left*) and Live Storage (*right*). In the powered mobile pallet racking picture on the left, at least three sets of shelves are shown wheeled together, allowing for the warehouse to use more of its floor space. In the live storage picture on the right, the shelves are made up of rollers and sloped downward, letting gravity move the goods from one side of the shelving to another.

For storage of palletized unit loads, racking is not always necessary, however. Many palletized loads are stabilized so that they can be placed on the floor and stacked, one load on top of another. For increased stability, a ***block stacking*** technique is used in which palletized loads are stacked into rows which are placed side by side to form blocks. While this is a very inexpensive means of storage, it is advantageous only for temporary storage, lighter loads, and when additional vertical storage space is not needed. For safest storage conditions, block stacking should rarely be more than 2 to 4 pallet-loads high, depending on the height of your load.

Figure 5.9 - Block Stacking. Pallets of flour block stacked 2 to 3 pallet-loads high at a warehouse in Christiansand, Norway (*left*) and pallets of cement tiles block stacked 2 to 4 pallet-loads high in an external inventory yard in Lerwick, Scotland (*right*).

CONTAINERIZATION

As we have covered in the previous section, the first of the two core structures that forms the basis of a typical unit load is the *pallet*. The second of the two core structures that forms the basis of a typical unit load is the *container*. In the world of materials handling, a **container** is a standard large unit load structure, which can be used for **intermodal transport** (transport using multiple modes of conveyance, such as road and rail or air and water) of goods with reduced handling of individual items. Basically, containers are large, oblong, rectangular boxes of a standard size into which goods can be placed and then transported interchangeably using a wide range of transportation vehicles, including trucks, railroad cars, ferries, deep sea vessels, and aircraft.

Figure 5.10 - Intermodal Transport and Containerization. At the Port of Vancouver, British Columbia, containers are transferred from ship (*top left corner*) to rail (*bottom right corner*).

Containerization is the materials handling practice based on using a system of unit load containers and a variety of modes of transportation, which has led to a high degree of integration between transport systems. For example, a standard 40ft container is loaded with finished goods and sealed at the factory. A truck transports the sealed container to the docks. The container is then stored dockside until the ship is ready to be loaded. Once the ship has been loaded and has reached its final destination, the container is loaded onto a vehicle and delivered to its customer to be unsealed and opened.

Since its conception in the first half of the twentieth century, containerization has revolutionized the world of materials handling and logistics. Containerization has become the transportation and materials handling system of choice during the past sixty years with more than 90% of the world's non-bulk cargo having spent some of its life in a container. According to the website of the World Shipping Council, in 2013 there were approximately 120 million containers around the world packed with cargo, totaling an estimated value of $4 trillion. Given that just one container can hold 500 computer monitors, 6,000 pairs of shoes, or 20,000 dolls, that's a lot of goods worth a lot of money!

But why has the world so quickly become reliant on containers? Containerization has brought a slew of benefits to the world of materials handling, including:

- **Reduced handling of individual items**, thus reducing damage, deterioration, and theft (It's very difficult for someone dockside to "relieve" a sealed container of a single Gucci handbag…);

- **Improved turnaround time** for transport vehicles because containers can be handled dockside quickly with specialized equipment and, when needed, can easily be stored and stacked;

- **Vastly improved efficiency** and time savings in vessel loading, thus reducing freight tariffs;

- **Reduced insurance rates** as a side benefit of the reduced risk of damage, deterioration, and theft; and

- **Increased transport mode integration** because, as the world has moved to standard container sizes, standardization of container transport vehicles and systems has followed, leading to seamlessly integrated modes of container transportation worldwide.

Over the course of the past fifty years, globalization of trade has pushed container sizes to become increasingly standard worldwide. When pillows are stuffed and sewn in the Xi'an Province of China, they are sealed into a container. This container must be transported by a Chinese truck to the port of Shanghai; loaded onto a Dutch container ship; travel by sea to the port of Los Angeles; unloaded from the container ship to a rail car; transported by railroad to Chicago; unloaded from the rail car onto an American truck; and driven to a Walmart in Wabash. During this entire process, the pillows will never leave the sealed container until it is unloaded at the Wabash Walmart, which means that only the container is handled. Thus, the same size container travels from Xian, to Shanghai, onto a Dutch ship, to Los Angeles, across the U.S., to Wabash, Indiana. All of the handling and transportation equipment used during this process must all be standardized to handle this container size. Because millions of similar movements of containerized goods occur around the world at any (and every) given moment, standardization of equipment and containers is essential to prevent containerization from being cost prohibitive.

For intercontinental shipping, as with our Xi'an to Wabash example, containers are typically 20 or 40 feet long. Containers of these lengths are so common that the ***twenty-foot equivalent unit*** or ***TEU*** has become a standard measure of container capacity and traffic flow of ships and ports. For example, TEU comparisons show how the 2014 container traffic flow of the world's largest port, Hong Kong (22.2 million TEUs), truly dwarfs those of North America's and Europe's largest ports — Los Angeles (7.9 million TEUs) and Rotterdam (11.9 million TEUs).

Figure 5.11 - Container Sizes. A 10' container port-side in St. John's, Newfoundland (*left*); a 20' container rolling down the streets of Boston (*center*); and a 40' container waiting for transport in St. John's, Newfoundland (*right*).

Although the majority of the world's containers are 40 or 20 feet long, containers may also be 10, 30, 45, 48, and 53 feet long, with 10ft containers more common for European domestic use and 48 and 53ft containers more typical of North American domestic use. Despite some variation in length, the standard container width worldwide is 8 feet. Containers are also typically 8ft 6in high. For especially tall cargo, however, there are **high cube containers** or **hicubes**, which are 9ft 6in high and, for especially dense, heavy cargo, such as steel rods, there are **half-height containers**, which are 4ft 3in high.

Figure 5.12 - 40' and 53' Containers. Most cargo containers transporting goods across the globe are 40 feet long, like these 40' containers on a barge near Rotterdam, the Netherlands (*left*). However, the containers most commonly used for U.S. domestic transport of goods measure 53'. These large containers can easily be identified by the "53 written on them, as circled above (*right*).

In addition to containers coming in a small variety of sizes, they also come in a variety of types based on the type of goods that they will transport. The wide world of container types, along with the goods they are intended to carry, includes:

- **Standard** or **Dry Van Containers** for all types of dry cargo. This is, by far, the most common type of container. Stand by any railroad track long enough and you are likely to see 100 or more standard containers zoom by...

- **Open Top Containers** for especially heavy cargo and cargo that needs to be packed and unpacked from above

- *Flat Rack Containers* for overly heavy, tall, and/or wide cargo

- *Flatbed* or *Platform Containers* for oversized and very heavy cargo

- *Ventilated Containers* for cargo that must be ventilated in transit, such as green coffee beans

- *Refrigerated Containers* or *Reefers* for perishable goods that must be kept at a constant temperature

- *Bulk Containers* or *Bulktainers* for dry, bulk cargo, such as grains or spices

- *Tank Containers* for liquid goods as innocuous as fruit juice or as dangerous as chemical waste

- *Swapbodies*, which are not true containers because they lack upper support and cannot be stacked, but are common in Europe for road-rail connections a

Figure 5.13 - Types of Containers. An open top container being moved dockside at the port of Reykjavík, Iceland (*top left*); reefers plugged into electricity to keep them cold as they are being loaded at a fish processor in Kodiak, Alaska (*top right*); a flat rack container leaving the port of Nuuk, Greenland (*bottom left*); and a swap body waiting for transport in Norway (*bottom right*).

Figure 5.14 - More Types of Containers. Although they appear similar , tank containers (left) and bulk containers (right) are built for uniquely different purposes and are generally not interchangeable.

An interesting thing about containers, especially standard containers, in that people have begun to use them for a range of multiple purposes, such as for small homes, doomsday shelters, or in-ground and above-ground swimming pools. Many organizations have begun to use containers as small warehouses themselves. When some companies do not have enough room in its warehouse, especially for reserve area or seasonal items, they use containers parked outside their warehouse facility as additional storage space because they are a cost effective means of keeping goods temporarily dry, safe, and secure.

Like pallets, containers are expensive to purchase and maintain. Also like pallets pools, there are **container pools**, businesses that rent out, deliver, and collect shipping containers so that companies only use and hold containers as needed. One examples is TTX Company, which is the leading provider of railcar containers in North America. TTX is owned by multiple North American railroads and has a pool of 220,000 railcars that are rented out to companies wishing to move their goods in a container by rail.

UNITIZATION EQUIPMENT

As mentioned in the previous chapter, **unitization equipment** is one of the five major categories of materials handling equipment. Unitization equipment is used to restrain goods and form them onto a single unit load from subsequent transportation and storage. We know that a unit load is any quantity of a material, either multiple or individual items, assembled and restrained to permit it to be handled, moved, stored, and stacked as a single object. Pallets, containers, and a variety of other packaging materials may form the basis of a unit load. Within the materials handling environment, specific equipment may be used to either form these unit loads or to stabilize them.

Palletizers, which assist in placing individual items into palletized loads, are one example of **unit load formation equipment**. They may be manually operated or automated, with some even having a robotic arm that picks items and places them into the unit load.

Stretch wrap and strapping machines, on the other hand, are examples of **unit load stabilization equipment**, i.e., their primary purpose is to make the load stable, thus preventing item damage and hazardous transport conditions. **Stretch wrap machines**, which may range from predominantly manual to fully automated equipment, are used to bind the load with protective layers of plastic film. A unit load is placed onto a pedestal, which swivels as a sheet of plastic film from a stationary roll is stretched and adheres to it. Stretch wrap machines are beginning to replace their former counterpart, *shrink wrap machines*, which uses heat to shrink plastic film onto a unit load, making it more expensive and labor intensive than stretch wrapping.

Strapping machines, which may also range from predominantly manual to fully automated equipment, are used to place straps around unit loads to secure them. While stretch wrapping is more useful for lighter loads and for those requiring outside storage, strapping is the preferred unit load stabilization technique for heavy or bulky loads, items which need to be compressed, or for materials with sharp edges which would tear the stretch wrap. Both stretch- wrapping and strapping may also be used together on the same unit load. Strapping is often used to secure a load to a pallet while stretch wrapping is then used on the same load to provide additional security and protect it from the elements.

Figure 5.15 - Unitization (*from left to right*): stretch Wrap Machine sold by ITW Muller; palletized and stretch wrapped load of produce; palletized and shrink wrapped load of flour; and a flat rack container with strapping to secure pipes

PACKAGING

Another core concept of materials handling and unitization in practice is *packaging*. Packaging plays a large role in the formation of unit loads. Containers and pallets are two types of packaging frameworks. Packaging is a critical component of the materials handling process because it:

- **minimizes damage.** When goods are packed well with the proper materials, potential transportation- and handling-related damage can be reduced or even eliminated. Although packaging is not a materials handling activity that adds value, it can certainly keep value from being lost.

- **influences equipment choice.** How an item is packaged, especially the packaging materials used and its packaged dimensions, directly influences which types of materials handling equipment can be used, especially the types of transport and storage equipment. The table below highlights different forms of packaging and the handling equipment required for each.

PACKAGING	HANDLING EQUIPMENT NEEDED
palletized loads	forklift truck
sacks and bags	conveyor system
bulk grains	conveyor system
bulk liquids	pipeline and tanker
unit stores	containers
smail units	manual handling
drums	forklift truck

Figure 5.16 - Types of Packaging with the Handling Equipment
Needed to Move Their Corresponding Goods

- **can provide additional customer service.** Just as packaging influences equipment choice, existing materials handling equipment can influence the packaging materials used. In order to provide additional service to customers, many companies select their products' packaging style and materials based on which are best suited for their primary customers' materials handling equipment. For example, wholesale-style retailers such as Costco rely heavily on pallet/forklift-based materials handling equipment. Therefore, companies selling their wares to Costco tend to provide the added customer service of providing their products wrapped onto standard-sized pallets.

Figure 5.17 - Specialized Packaging. Goods are shrink- wrapped onto specially sized pallets (*left*) for delivery via cogwheel train (*right*) up Mt. Pilatus in Switzerland.

Now that we understand the impact and influence of packaging, what exactly is packaging? For many industries, there are two categories of packaging: *individual item packaging* and *unit load packaging*. The **individual item packaging** (also called **consumer packaging**) is that which the end user sees, such as a Raisin Bran cereal box or a Campbell's soup can. While it may have some influence on materials handling matters, individual item packaging is of more interest to marketers wishing to create or enhance a unique, distinct, and recognizable brand.

Unit load packaging (also called ***industrial packaging***), however, is of great interest within the world of materials handling because it comes directly into contact with materials handling equipment. Basically, how a unit load is packaged determines how it will be handled. Unit load packaging has one or more of the following purposes: *cushioning*, *containing*, or *restraining*. Bubble wrap, foam, polystyrene peanuts, and pieces of corrugated cardboard are a few examples of ***cushioning materials***; pallets, skids, pallet boxes, cartons, containers, and bags are ***containing materials***; and tape, bands, straps, glue, and stretch wrap are ***restraining material***s. For most products, combinations of all three of these types of packaging materials offer the safest and most secure protection.

CHAPTER 5 REVIEW QUESTIONS

1. What is the difference between manual handling and mechanical handling? When might an organization select manual handling?

2. What are some of the basic advantages of mechanical handling?

3. What is a unit load? Why is unitization so popular in materials handling today? What are two common forms of unitization?

4. How does palletization work?

5. What is the most common type of pallet? Under what circumstances might a paper pallet be used instead?

6. What is block stacking? Why is it used?

7. How does containerization work?

8. What is the standard size system for containers used for intercontinental shipping?

9. What is the relationship between packaging and handling equipment?

10. What is the primary function of unitization equipment? What are some examples of this type of equipment?

CHAPTER 5 CASE EXERCISE

FIND THE CONTAINERS!

Examine the photos below and identify as many containers by type and size as possible. The container types include: **standard containers**, **open top containers**, **flat rack containers**, **refrigerated containers**, **bulk containers**, and **tank containers**. Container sizes include: **10'**, **20'**, **40'** and **53'**.

Chapter 6

Internal Processes: Inventory Management and Control Systems

In the early chapters of this text, we defined *inventory* as the collection of goods, materials, and physical resources held by an organization, typically in warehouse facilities, distribution centers, or external inventory yards. Some warehouses have large ranges of SKUs and many thousands of individual items within each range. Each of these individual items in inventory represents a financial investment. Too much unnecessary inventory can tie up a lot of money for an organization, sometimes it's not even money that the company has and they then have to borrow money to purchase inventory. Companies also face the cost of holding inventory, such as warehousing and insurance costs. Even in the fortunate situation of a company having surplus money, in most situations the money could be put to better use elsewhere in the organization; the extra cost of unnecessary inventory becomes a lost opportunity cost. In this chapter, we will discuss the principles of *inventory management and control systems* and how they strive to minimize the financial investment in inventory while at the same time ensuring that the needs of internal and external customers are met.

To truly master an understanding of inventory, we must explore not only its mechanics but its management! Why and under which circumstances is inventory held? How are the levels of inventory held determined? What information must be gathered to make these decisions? The answers to all these questions and more lie within the realm of *inventory control*! The essential objective of efficient and effective inventory control is simply ensuring that the right inventory of the right quantity is available at the right time and at the right place. A system that controls inventory and its levels to achieve this objective, i.e., the *inventory control system*, is designed to meet the needs of a particular organization. Although they may differ from organization to organization, effective inventory control systems share the following qualities:

- **accuracy and speed**, with the ability to react successfully to situations influencing inventory, such as incorrect quantities received due to transportation problems, raw materials shortages, or just plain old human error.

- **open communication** between departments within the organization. For example, when an inventory control system has determined the correct quantity level of inventory to hold, the system must communicate this information immediately and openly with the purchasing department, so that it may purchase the correct quantities needed, and with the warehousing department, so that it may prepare the warehouse for receiving, inspecting, and holding the determined quantity of inventory. (Imagine a top class inventory control system determining absolutely the most effective and efficient levels of inventory of tricycles and bicycles the organization should hold and not communicating this information to the purchasing department, who orders too many bicycles, too few tricycles, and a plethora of unexpected unicycles!)

- **economy in operation** and demand upon capital and human resources. Without an effective inventory control system, our We-Do-Foods grocery warehouse may think that it needs to hold three weeks worth of watermelon for all of south-central Alaska when it is indeed more efficient to hold only three-days-worth. As a result, a lot more labor and precious temperature- controlled warehouse space is needed to manage this extra inventory.

- **centralized control** of inventory. Inventory is definitely an area in which there can be too many chefs in the kitchen! Final decisions for when and what to order are ultimately handled by the purchasing department but are based on critical information from an inventory control system.

- **access to the inventory control system**, i.e., various organizational functions and departments should be able to operate and access information in the inventory control system. For example, marketing should be able to access information on finished goods in stock, manufacturing should be able to access information on the availability of production inputs, and maintenance should be able to access information on the availability of spare parts.

- **flexibility** so that all items held within a warehouse or other facility are controlled and new additions are covered automatically. Although you may have the absolute perfect level of papaya inventory for optimum efficiency and effectiveness, this level will not remain static. As crates of papayas are issued, new ones, perhaps even different varieties, will come in and must be accounted for within the inventory control system. The system must be flexible enough to facilitate constant dynamic changes in customer demand.

INTRODUCTION TO INVENTORY CONTROL

No matter how you look at it, holding inventory is an expensive endeavor. When an organization builds up its inventory, it first must purchase that inventory from suppliers. In many cases, an organization must pay the supplier for the goods long before any profit can be earned on them. This gap of time between when an organization pays for inventory, then processes it to develop its finished goods, and finally sells the finished goods forces an organization to commit a great deal of its resources, which equals money that can not earn any interest and resources that cannot be used for any other purpose until the goods are sold. When this process takes a long time, it can be very costly and lead to cash flow problems for the organization.

Figure 6.1 - Inventory Control of Food for a 1200 Passenger Cruise Ship:
Handling (*left*), Housing (*center*), and Administration (*right*)

In addition, when inventory is held, it must also be:

- **handled.** Inventory held must be handled by the warehouse staff. In addition to these labor costs incurred, inventory handling equipment is also typically used, which can be expensive to purchase and maintain.

- **housed.** Inventory held is kept within a warehouse or other facility. Inventory may also require specific handling conditions, such as dry, warm, or refrigerated settings. If these special environmental needs are not met, inventory may rapidly deteriorate and become unusable. Therefore, specialized warehouses or warehouse areas with specific heating, cooling, ventilation, and/or lighting systems are needed, all of which can be very expensive.

- **administered.** When goods are held in inventory, a great deal of administrative work is involved, including control of inventory receipts, issues, inventory records, and other documentation. This all consumes valuable space, labor, and skills resources.

- **insured.** As stated a few times before, inventory is money. Because an organization has so much of its financial assets tied up in its inventory, insurance coverage becomes vital. In the event of fire, flood, or accident, an organization must be able to replace lost inventory.

Therefore, the greater the amount of inventory kept, the higher the costly insurance premiums.

- **kept secure.** Because inventory represents some of the largest assets of many companies, it must be protected from theft with costly security systems. If security systems are not used or should they fail, the organization faces the added item replacement costs resulting from theft.

Seeing that holding inventory is so expensive, why do organizations bother to hold any at all? Why not operate solely under just-in-time style conditions in which inventory is received from the supplier only when it is needed and only in the exact quantities needed? Believe it or not, when done properly with an inventory control system, holding inventory can be extremely advantageous and even cost effective. Some of the many reasons organizations choose to hold inventory include:

1. **Unreliable inventory deliveries.** Organizations often find it difficult to rely on all of their suppliers to deliver every order exactly on time every time an order is placed. Few suppliers could claim (and I might doubt the veracity of those making such claims) that they have never had shipments delayed by strikes, transportation difficulties, bad weather, or administrative errors. Therefore, holding inventory ensures that an organization will have adequate inventory to maintain operations, even when a supplier's shipment has been delayed.

2. **Bulk discounts.** By holding more inventory than is needed for one manufacturing period (such as a week), an organization is able to buy goods in larger quantities. Thus, the Purchasing department can "buy bulk" and obtain a lower per unit price. In a company that spends millions of dollars every year on inventory, such discounts can have a significant impact on overall profit levels.

3. **Reduced purchase order processes.** Before an item is delivered to inventory from the supplier, one process that must occur is the purchase order process. When an organization holds very little inventory, it must perform this process frequently, resulting in higher time and labor costs for the Purchasing and Warehouse (Receiving) departments. When an organization holds greater amounts of inventory, however, it performs the purchase order process less frequently, resulting often in significant cost savings.

4. **Reduced risk to manufacturing operations.** When extra inventory is not held, the risk of a "nil inventory" situation increases, in which inventory of an item runs out and manufacturing is halted until more inventory can be delivered. The cost of halting manufacturing operations can be very high because, in addition to fixed costs, it creates a loss of profit, a loss of sales, a diminished reputation among customers, and an increased labor cost of employees waiting around and doing nothing until the inventory arrives.

5. **Inventory value appreciation.** When higher quantities of goods are held in inventory, an organization can deflect the burden of price inflation for those goods. For example, an automobile manufacturer buys six-months-worth of tires and, suddenly, there is a shortage of rubber worldwide, causing tires to double in price. Because it is holding such a

large tire inventory, the manufacturer has successfully deflected the current drastic tire price hike for six months!

6. **Increased output flexibility.** When an organization holds higher levels of inventory in reserve, it is better able to increase production output levels should the need or demand arise.

7. **Low seasonal prices.** Some products, especially agriculturally based raw materials, are more readily available at some times of the year than at others. If an organization purchases its annual needs of such products when their prices are the lowest, it can reap substantial price savings benefits.

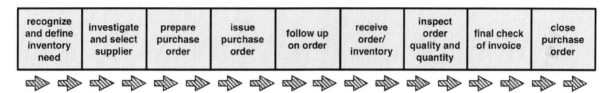

Figure 6.2 -The Purchase Order Process

When an organization has determined that it is advantageous to hold inventory, it then uses an inventory control system to establish the most efficient and effective inventory levels for each item, i.e., how much inventory to hold of each item. These inventory levels vary from item to item based on a variety of needs, including:

- **Operational Needs.** Operational needs refer to the amount of inventory of an item needed by various departments, including Manufacturing, Sales, Distribution, and Maintenance, for the organization's core operations over a set period of time. These inventory levels are typically affected by demand and sales forecasts based on information about past inventory usage.

- **Shelf Life.** Shelf life refers to the salable life of a product, i.e., how long it has until it will begin to deteriorate and can no longer be sold. If an item has a very short or restricted shelf life (such as fresh fruit or dairy products), the amount of inventory of that item held will be smaller because it is dictated by its shelf life.

- **Delivery Period.** The delivery period is the time it takes for the supplier to manufacture, dispatch, and transport the goods needed. An item's delivery period has a significant impact on its inventory levels. Sufficient quantities of inventory must be purchased to last from one delivery to the next. Typically, items with longer delivery periods are held in larger quantities in inventory.

- **Buffer Inventory.** Buffer inventory, also called *safety inventory*, is the extra inventory held by a warehouse to cover any unforeseen delays in delivery or sudden changes in demand. The size of an item's buffer inventory varies according to delivery reliability and operational risks. For example, an organization might decide that 25% of the minimum inventory level is considered a necessary buffer or emergency inventory level.

- **Capital Available.** Capital available, or the financial resources available to spend on inventory, is an important factor for establishing the levels of inventory held. If funds are not available to finance the most efficient and effective inventory levels, the inventory levels must be reduced.

- **Warehouse Capacity.** An organization's warehouse capacity is the cubic footage of its warehouse and other storage facilities. The amount of inventory an organization can hold will be restricted by the physical capacity of its warehouse facilities. In some cases in which items require specialized warehousing, e.g., refrigerated or frozen storage, the actual limited space in these high cost facilities available will restrict inventory levels even more.

Given that, in most cases, at least some inventory must be held, what are the organizing principles and core objectives of inventory control and inventory control systems? First, **inventory control supplies a constant flow of inventory to the operation.** As stated earlier (actually, this can't be stated enough), the primary aim of inventory control is to ensure that the correct quantity of items needed for manufacturing, maintenance, distribution, and other activities are in inventory and ready for issue when and where required.

Second, **inventory control ensures that the appropriate quality of inventory is available.** The correct quality and type of inventory, as established by the user and the purchasing and quality control departments, must be available in sufficient levels. If only substandard quality items are available, organizations must make the painful decision to either halt operations until quality items can be delivered or proceed with lesser quality inventory, perhaps resulting in disappointed and even angry customers.

Third, **inventory control supplies information for manufacturing management and control.** Inventory control information advises manufacturing planners about what to produce and within what timeframe in order to keep up with established levels of the organization's finished inventory. In addition, inventory control information about the levels of working inventory held is also critical for manufacturing, maintenance, and distribution operations.

Fourth, **inventory control controls obsolescence and obsolete inventory.** Inventory control is responsible for ensuring that all inventory being held by an organization is being used at a regular rate and that an item held in inventory has not already been superseded by a new or redesigned item. (Imagine an electronics store's warehouse still holding an inventory of beta VCRs and eight- track cassette players.) Holding an excess inventory of obsolete items is an easy mistake for an organization to make, as changes in design, technology, and the law can quickly make items and finished products obsolete. Inventory control must work hard to ensure that such obsolete inventory within the system is kept to a bare minimum so that it does not occupy valuable warehouse space and needlessly consume the organization's resources.

The fifth and final objective of inventory control is to **control inventory rotation**, the process by which inventory with the shortest shelf life or closest expiration date is used first. With the guiding help of inventory control, warehouses typically operate under the "First In, First Out" principle, in which those goods arriving into the warehouse first are the first to leave when it is time to distribute items to a user.

> ## WORDS IN THE WORLD OF INVENTORY CONTROL
>
> *FIFO* and *LIFO* are two accounting terms commonly heard in the world of warehousing and inventory control.
>
> **FIFO**, an acronym for *First In, First Out*, is the practice of issuing or using the oldest items in storage, i.e., the ones that arrived into storage first.
>
> **LIFO**, an acronym for *Last In, First Out*, is the practice of issuing or using the newest items in storage, i.e., the ones that arrived into storage most recently.

At the heart of inventory control is a system that helps organization make decisions about inventory levels, which, in turn, affects many departments and elements of the organization's operations. To enable such important decisions to be made efficiently and effectively, the inventory control system must be supplied with a constant flow of relevant and up-to-date information on:

- **Corporate manufacturing schedules.** Perhaps most critical to establishing inventory levels of raw materials and in-process goods is manufacturing information, i.e., information related to what items the organization intends to manufacture along with their desired amount, type, and quality.

- **Sales forecasts.** Perhaps most critical to establishing inventory levels of finished goods are sales forecasts, i.e., what the Sales department predicts regarding how many of which items the organization will sell, where, and to whom. This information is needed to establish levels of finished inventory as well as pre-manufacturing inventory. Inventory control must ensure that inventory is available to meet present and future demands.

- **Distribution plans.** Information on inventory distribution, especially that related to transportation and depot capacity and demand, is also vital for inventory control. This information, which is usually supplied by the Sales, Transportation, and Warehouse departments, is used to ensure that inventory is in the correct location at the correct time.

- **Maintenance and engineering schedules.** The basic function of the Maintenance department is to service and maintain the manufacturing plant and other equipment used by the organization. This function is typically conducted according to a predetermined program, meaning that specific maintenance items (spare tire, new machinery parts, etc.) will be needed at set times. With current maintenance and engineering schedules, inventory control can ensure that adequate quantities of needed maintenance and engineering items are held in inventory.

- **Manufacturing planning.** Almost all manufacturing activities follow a schedule of operations. Using this schedule, inventory control can ensure that all related inventory (raw materials, work-in-process, component parts, packaging, etc.) are controlled and supplied to the correct area within the manufacturing plant at the right quality, in the right quantity, and at the right time and place.

The Nitty-Gritty of Inventory Control Systems

No matter how you look at it, holding inventory is an expensive endeavor. Thus, efficiency-minded organizations turn to *inventory control systems* to help them manage the cost of inventory holding by determining the most efficient and effective inventory levels to maintain for individual items. In order to manage and control inventory levels of even the most basic inventory operations effectively, organizations must determine two key factors for each item held in inventory: *how much to order/reorder* and *when to order/reorder*.

In more complex inventory operations, especially those involving multiple warehouses or distribution facilities, the factor of where (i.e., the location of inventory order and delivery) also becomes important. As inventory circumstances become increasing complex, so do the systems and techniques used to manage and control them. In this section, we cover a range of inventory control systems, but they may also be described as *inventory management systems* or as *inventory control/management tools*, *techniques*, or *approaches*. It is not important how you choose to label the series of ideas you will encounter in the remainder of this section, but it is important that you understand how and under what circumstances each are used.

Before we delve more deeply into the world of inventory control systems, we must first cover a few basic definitions and mathematical formulae, which are central to the principles of inventory control systems and techniques. These definitions are:

- *Lead time*. Lead time is the length of time it takes from the moment it is decided that an item must be reordered until the item has been received and ready for issue in the warehouse. Lead time is often thought of as an item's average delivery time from the supplier.

- *Buffer inventory*. Also known as safety inventory, safety stock, or minimum inventory, buffer inventory is the inventory held to cover unforeseen usage increases and delays during an item's lead time. Buffer inventory is held in case of such unforeseen events, not for regular use.

    formula: To calculate the *buffer inventory* needed in terms of weeks, the number of weeks coverage desired is multiplied by the weekly item usage.

    buffer inventory = weeks coverage desired x weekly usage of item

- *Reorder point*. An item's reorder point is the level of inventory or predetermined quantity of an item at which a new order is placed to replenish the item's inventory.

    formula: To calculate the *reorder point* for an item, the number of units used within the item's lead time is added to the buffer inventory.

    reorder point = units used per lead time + buffer inventory

- *Order quantity.* In its most basic terms, the order quantity is the amount of inventory to order. This may be predetermined using historical data and personal judgment, such as when an organization takes looks at the quantity of an item used the previous year and divides by twelve to determine the quantity for months orders. However, more commonly used today is the economic order quantity (EOQ) mathematical formula, as will be described later in this chapter..

  formula: Most commonly used to calculate *order quantity* is the EOQ formula, as will be described later in this chapter. Organizations also sometimes calculate an item's order quantity by dividing the annual units of the item used by the number of orders to be placed within the year.

  order quantity (non EOQ) = units used per year/# orders placed yearly

- *Progress level.* When an item's inventory on hand falls to the progress level, the organization checks with the item's supplier on the status of the outstanding order.

  formula: To calculate the *progress level*, half of the number of units used within the item's lead time is added to the buffer inventory.

  progress level = units used per lead time/2 + buffer inventory

- *Maximum inventory.* An item's maximum inventory is the quantity of an item above which its inventory should never rise.

  formula: To calculate the *maximum inventory*, the order quantity is added to the buffer inventory

  maximum inventory = order quantity + buffer inventory

USING THE EOQ TO GET THE REORDER QUANTITY

When warehouse managers want to minimize an organization's investment in inventory, one formula used commonly within inventory control systems and techniques is the ***economic order quantity (EOQ)***. The most widely used of these EOQ inventory control techniques is the *fixed order quantity (FOQ)* technique, also called the fixed order point system and the fixed reorder model. When using the FOQ technique, an optimal reorder quantity is determined, i.e., what is the most efficient size of order for this item. This reorder quantity then remains constant (thus the name fixed order quantity) while the time interval between reorders varies depending upon the demand and subsequent issuance of the item. The FOQ is then used to determine the most efficient minimum inventory level at which the item should be reordered to replenish its inventory. This minimum inventory level for reorder is called the ***reorder point***. When the reorder point is reached, the fixed order quantity is automatically ordered.

INVENTORY CONTROL FORMULAE IN ACTION!

Using the definitions and formula provided, let's do some number crunching! Let's say that a local pizzeria, Leaning Towers of Pizza, uses 40 cases of mozzarella cheese every week. The lead-time it takes from Leaning Towers to receive the cheese from its discount supplier, Wisconsin Wonders, is 4 weeks. Based on past experience, Leaning Towers has set its buffer inventory coverage of all items at one week of units. Finally, because Leaning Towers is not a large operation, they do not like to receive too many deliveries. Therefore, they place only 10 orders per year.

Using all of this information, how can we determine the buffer inventory, reorder level, order quantity, progress level, and maximum inventory for Leaning Towers' mozzarella cheese inventory?

Lead time   = 4 weeks

Buffer inventory   = 1 week x 40 units/week = 40 units

Reorder level   = (4 weeks x 40 units/week) + 40 units = 200 units

Order quantity (non-EOQ)
                             = (52 weeks x 40 units/week) / (10 orders) = 208 units/order

Progress level   = (4 weeks x 40 units/week) / 2 + 40 units = 120 units

Maximum inventory   = 208 units + 40 units = 248 units

Thus, Leaning Towers of Pizza holds 40 units as buffer inventory or safety stock in case there are lead-time delays. When the level of mozzarella cheese reaches 200 cases, the pizzeria places a new order for 208 cases. When its inventory of mozzarella falls to 120 cases, Leaning Towers calls its cheese supplier, Wisconsin Wonders, to check on the status of the cheese order. If its inventory of mozzarella exceeds 248 cases, it investigates why it is holding excess inventory and then determines if this was a single occurrence or if a new weekly cheese usage level must be determined and if new calculations must be made.

The static amount of inventory that is ordered, i.e., the **fixed order quantity,** is determined based on the item's demand and cost and the inventory holding and reorder costs. The number of units of an item held in inventory which triggers a new order, i.e., the *reorder point,* is determined by how long it takes to receive a new order from the item's supplier and the general demand or sales rate for that item at the time. The basic formula used to determine the reorder point is:

reorder point = lead time length x daily item demand (in units)

For example, when your local neighborhood We-Do-Foods store orders Glossy Glam Purely Pink lipstick from Glam Products, Inc., it takes 5 days for the order to arrive. In your neighborhood, Glossy Glam Purely Pink lipstick is in high demand with the local pre-teen population and your nearby We-Do-Foods store sells approximately 143 tubes of this lipstick per day. Therefore, the reorder point for Glossy Glam Purely Pink lipstick at your local We-Do-Foods store is 715 units (or 5 days x 143 units/day).

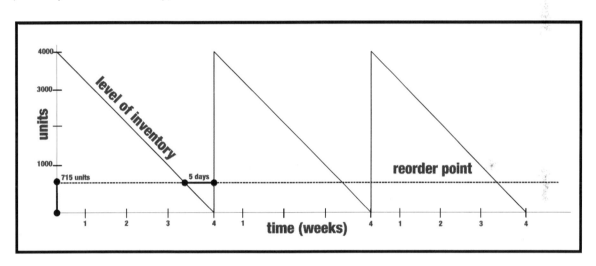

Figure 6.3 -Fixed Order Quantity and the Reorder Point

To determine the fixed order quantity, we will first examine the **simple EOQ model**, which can be used when the following conditions exist:

- *the rate of demand is constant (not changing), known, and continuous*

- *the inventory replenishment or lead time (how long it takes for the supplier to deliver the items ordered) is constant and known*

- *the item price is constant and not dependent on the order quantity or time (i.e., no bulk order discounts or rush delivery payments)*

- *the EOQ model is being used for one item of inventory, which has no interaction with other items*

- *there is no limit on the organization's available capital*

In order to determine the optimal fixed quantity of inventory to order when an item's reorder point is reached, the simple EOQ model takes into account the trade-off between the item's inventory holding cost (how much its costs to store or keep the goods in inventory) and its order/set-up cost (how much it costs to place and set up the order). As shown in Figure 6.4 below, the point at which the inventory holding costs and order and/or set-up costs intersect, the total cost is the lowest, thus indicating the item's optimal inventory order size or *fixed order quantity*.

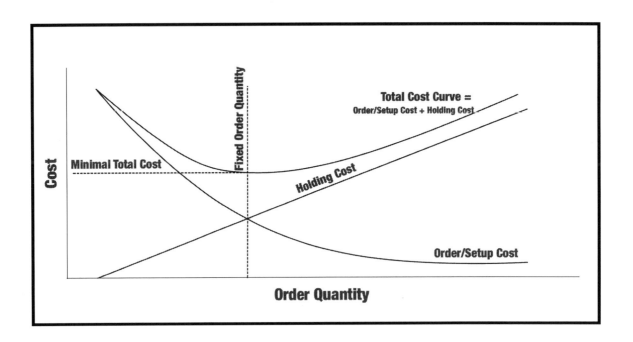

Figure 6.4 -Finding the Fixed Order Quantity.

Adding the inventory holding cost and the order/setup cost allows us to find the point of lowest total cost, revealing the optimal inventory order size, or *fixed order quantity*.

To better understand the fixed order quantity concept, let's look at what happens as we add inventory holding costs and order costs as order quantities vary. Continuing on with our Glossy Glam Purely Pink lipstick example, let's assume that the Smalltown location of We-Do-Foods doesn't sell quite as much lipstick as your local store. At the Smalltown We-Do-Foods, 3600 tubes of Glossy Glam Purely Pink lipstick are sold each year. The value of each tube of lipstick is $5. It costs the Smalltown We-Do-Foods $0.40 to hold each tube of lipstick in inventory per year and $100 to set up a new order with Glam Products, Inc. Therefore, as we increase the number of annual orders of Purely Pink lipstick We-Do-Foods places with Glam Products from one to ten, the following figures result, as shown in Figure 6.5.

Number of Orders	Cost of Orders (Inventory Order Cost) $100 x number of orders	Quantity of Lipstick per Order 3600 / number of orders	Dollar Value of Lipstick per Order quantity of lipstick per order x $5	Cost of Holding Inventory dollar value of lipstick per order/2 x $0.40	Total Cost cost of orders + cost of holding inventory
1	$100	3600	$18,000	$3,600	$3,700
2	$200	1800	$9,000	$1,800	$2,000
3	$300	1200	$6,000	$1,200	$1,500
4	$400	900	$4,500	$900	$1,300
5	$500	720	$3,600	$720	$1,220
6	$600	600	$3,000	$600	$1,200
7	$700	514	$2,570	$514	$1,214
8	$800	450	$2,250	$450	$1,250
9	$900	400	$2,000	$400	$1,300
10	$1000	360	$1,800	$360	$1,360

Figure 6.5 -Illustrating the Fixed Order Quantity Concept

As the table above shows, the lowest total cost, $1200, is achieved when six orders are placed for 600 tubes of lipstick each. Therefore, the optimal inventory order size (or *fixed order quantity*) is 600. Rather than rely on the long-hand method above, the following formula for the simple EOQ is used to determine the fixed order quantity:

$$Q = \sqrt{\frac{2RA}{VW}} \quad \text{or} \quad Q = \sqrt{\frac{2RA}{S}} \quad \text{where}$$

Q = *optimal order quantity*

R = *units used per year*

A = *order/set-up cost (per order)*

V = *value of one unit of inventory*

W = *inventory holding cost (per unit per year)*

$S = VW$ = *the storage cost per unit per year*

Using the same figures from the Glossy Glam Purely Pink lipstick example above, remember that the Smalltown We-Do-Foods sells 3600 tubes of Glossy Glam Purely Pink lipstick annually. The value of each tube of lipstick is $5. It costs the Smalltown We-Do-Foods $0.40 to hold each tube of lipstick in inventory per year and $100 to set up a new order with Glam Products, Inc. Therefore, using the simple EOQ formula:

$$R = 3600 \; units/year \qquad\qquad A = \$100/order$$

$$V = \$5/unit \qquad\qquad\qquad W = \$0.40/unit/year$$

$$Q = \sqrt{\frac{2RA}{VW}} = \sqrt{\frac{(2)(3600)(100)}{(5)(0.4)}} = 600 \; units/order$$

Our world is one of change and the unknown. Because the model above assumes many constant and known conditions, it may seem limited in its applications. Organizations can adjust this simple EOQ model, however, based on the complexity of their individual situations. There are currently more than 200 variations of this model used to assist a wide range of inventory decision makers. One example is the *fixed order quantity under uncertain conditions*.

In our previous simple EOQ model, the item usage or sales rate was assumed to be constant (i.e., always staying the same). This is not the reality for most organizations, however. In the real world, demand varies from season to season, week to week, and even day to day based on customers' changing needs, the weather, or even flash-in-the-pan trends. Also, replenishment or lead times can also vary as a result of production delays, traffic hold-ups, transportation strikes, and human error. How, then, can inventory management and control models assist in these situations in which flux and uncertainty, rather than constant demand and lead times, are the norm?

Although a variety of approaches may be used depending on the situation, at the core of each is a consideration of the level of safety or buffer stock needed to handle variations in demand and lead times. Previously, we defined *safety stock* as inventory that is held and used as supply and demand dictate, i.e., the extra quantities of items held to protect an organization from losses that might be incurred from fluctuating supply availability and customer and market demands. Safety stock becomes critical in an uncertain environment because if too much safety stock is held, excess inventory costs result. If too little safety stock is held, the organization may experience very costly stock outages and work stoppage situations.

Although the fixed order quantity is the most commonly used EOQ technique for inventory control, also worthy of mention is the *fixed order interval (FOI) technique*, also called the *fixed time period (FTP)* or the *periodic review system*. The FOI technique is used when inventory must be ordered at fixed or constant time intervals. The quantity ordered and reordered is not fixed and is based on how much of an item remains in stock at the end of the order cycle or near the time of reorder. While not as common as FOQ, the FOI technique is useful when deliveries or vendor sales visits occur only at set times, such as in the retail food industry or in remote locations which experience transportation limitations.

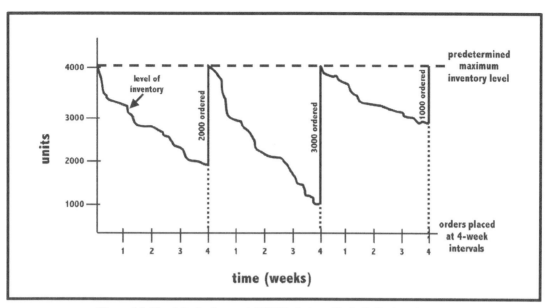

Figure 6.6 -Fixed Order Interval (FOI) Technique (Periodic Review System)

DEMAND ENVIRONMENTS

As previously mentioned, there is a range of inventory control systems, each with its own range of variations. All inventory control systems are not suited for all situations, however. To determine which is the most efficient and effective system or technique to use, the logistics, inventory, or warehousing manager examines key criteria such as the situation's **dynamic demand environment**.

There are two specific demand environments for items held in inventory: one of *dependent demand* and the other of *independent demand*. An item is one of **dependent demand** if its orders for issue from inventory depend on those for another product. For example, refrigerator handles would exist in a dependent demand environment because their inventory levels and orders are dependent upon the numbers of another product, refrigerators, desired by the customers or user. Raw materials, work-in-process goods, and component parts are generally those of dependent demand because their orders and subsequent inventory levels depend on the demand or desired quantity of another finished product and often a manufacturing or assembly timeframe.

An item is one of ***independent demand*** when its orders for issue from inventory do not depend on those of another product. For example, while the handle and other components of the refrigerator in our example are of dependent demand, the refrigerator itself is of independent demand. Finished goods that are end-use items and not component parts are of independent demand. As a side note, let's consider whether or not a single product can be of both dependent and independent demand. Some products may exist in both dependent and independent demand environments. For example, an inventory of automobile tires in a tire manufacturers warehouse may experience dependent and independent demand simultaneously. Tire inventory orders may be dependent on orders from automobile manufacturers and subsequently, the consumer demand for automobiles that use their tires. Conversely, tire orders from tire sales departments in Sears and Costco are independent of demands for another finished product, such as new automobiles.

When the inventory demand environment is one of *independent demand*, demand forecasting is needed (i.e., how many refrigerators can we predict customers will need for the next three months). One inventory control technique used in independent demand environments is **distribution resource planning (DRP)**. When the inventory demand environment is one of *dependent demand*, demand forecasting for the item is not needed because its demand depends upon the demand for the end product (of which it is a raw material, in-process good, or component part). In this dependent demand environment, *just-in-time (JIT)* and *materials requirement planning (MRP)* are inventory control systems/techniques often used. For inventory which exists in a dependent demand environment, many organizations use the **just-in-time (JIT)** inventory control system. At its core, JIT is both a philosophy and practice, which aims to ensure that the right item of inventory is at the right place and time and that no unnecessary inventory is held.

Historically, traditional approaches to meeting manufacturing requirements rested heavily in holding extra safety inventory **just-in-case (JIC)** something went wrong. While the JIC idea provided a buffer against inefficiencies in the manufacturing process, high financial investment levels of inventory were required. From the 1950s through the 1980s, Japanese manufacturers developed the inventory management and control approach we now call Just-in-Time (JIT). The JIT approach sees inventory as wasteful and seeks to eliminate it and anything else held that does not add value to the product. The JIT philosophy calls for a gradual reduction of buffer inventory and for the delivery of raw inventory to the manufacturing function and finished goods to the user just in time for use. In JIT systems, inventory can be reduced by: reducing transits times, reducing manufacturing machine set-up times, creating a more effective manufacturing plant layout, and introducing more automatic or automated equipment. All requirements (i.e., items which were previously held in inventory) are thus produced just-in-time instead of just-in-case.

For JIT systems to become effective, an organization and its suppliers must work seamlessly and to the same JIT standards. Not only does an organization use a JIT system to reduce its inventory of raw materials, work-in-process, and finished goods within its own facility and distribution chain, but it must insist on similar reductions in its suppliers as well. With JIT, suppliers are seen as an extension of an organization's own plant and thus part of its manufacturing team. Suppliers receive special requests and special containers and are expected to make several deliveries per day. Suppliers must also guarantee the quality of their products so that goods may be delivered directly to the manufacturing plant with no quality control inspections carried out. Because of this close, interdependent relationship with suppliers, organizations with successful JIT systems tend to use single source purchasing, i.e., purchasing specific items or a range of items from a single supplier.

JIT systems have garnered much attention over the past few decades for their ability to drastically reduce inventory holding levels, create better relationships with suppliers, highlight potential problems in manufacturing efficiencies, increase manufacturing efficiency as a result of fewer defective products from suppliers,. Although it is very useful for inventory reduction and control in single facility, dependent demand environments, JIT does present a range of challenges, including: problems resulting from late, incorrect, or insufficient deliveries; difficulties posed by single-sourcing relationships; and shortages of skilled JIT staff. Despite its challenges, JIT has grown to become one of the most effective and popular inventory control techniques worldwide.

Six rules for a successful manufacturer-supplier relationship within a JIT system are:

1. *Establish and nurture long-term relationships.*

2. *The relationship must be mutually beneficial.*

3. *The supplier must be able to guarantee its product's quality with zero defects!*

4. *Technical competence of both the manufacturer and supplier must be continually examined.*

5. *Both the manufacturer and supplier must be located within the same geographic area.*

6. *Price guarantees from the supplier are essential!*

In a manufacturing organization, the demand for a majority of items in inventory is dependent on the quantity of finished products required. The timeframe in which these products must be finished is also known. This allows the organization to schedule inventory ordering and receipt into the manufacturing cycle in the exact quantities needed at the time and place required. *Materials requirement planning (MRP)* is an information technology, time-phased requirement planning system to help an organization to minimize inventory holding costs. It is used to determine the timing (when) and quantities (how many at that point in time) when purchasing goods. It also coordinates the when and how many of the purchase with the needs of the production or manufacturing schedule, all to ensure that the organization isn't holding more inventory than it needs at any time.

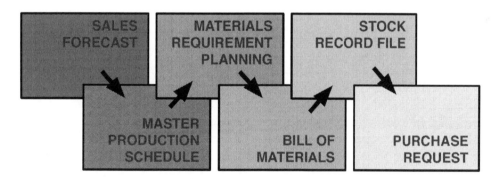

Figure 6.7 - Stages in Materials Requirement Planning

Information on the inventory needs of the organization is taken from the *master production schedule (MPS)*, which details the required outputs of the manufacturing systems, generally by week or month, and is derived from either order books or sales forecasts. The MRP system converts the output needs information in the MPS into a time-phased *report of materials requirements (RMR)*, which is also called the *bill of materials (BOM)*. The RMR or BOM is a structured directory that lists all the items of inventory or parts required to manufacture a finished product. For example, a BOM for an automobile would list one complete engine, four wheels, five tires, one front windshield, two windshield wiper blades, and so on. Before a production run, the MRP system calculates the total quantity of each item that needs to be ordered along with their lead times and supplies the Purchasing department with information on: which items need to be ordered, how many of each must be ordered, and when they must be ordered to meet the production schedule. MRP is taken a stage further with **MRP II** or **manufacturing resource planning**, which integrates system-wide manufacturing, inventory, and finance operations to achieve optimum financial results in inventory and manufacturing resource control. MRP II begins with MRP (as described above), but extends it into a more holistic planning approach involving many departments. As a result, MRP II can help minimize inventory holding costs, reduce production stoppages, and increase flexibility in system-wide planning.

Finally, another inventory control technique worthy of mention is **distribution resource planning (DRP)**. The focus of DRP, a computer-based system like MRP, is receiving, warehousing, and holding goods at the lowest cost possible within the distribution system while still meeting customers' inventory needs through efficient distribution activities, such as transportation scheduling. In a DRP system, a wide variety of factors of inventory holding within the distribution system are considered, including warehouse and external inventory yard space, distribution centers, labor and capital used, and transportation equipment used. The DRP system, at its core, is very useful in using its distribution data to forecast demand and then send that information back to the Manufacturing department to help with production scheduling and the Distribution department to help with transportation planning.

DRP and MRP systems are often used in conjunction with one another at the same organization. For example, a company uses MRP to reduce its incoming inventory for production to highly efficient and effective levels. It then uses MRP and DRP to inform manufacturing production scheduling to produce the most efficient levels of finished products to minimize finished product inventory. Finally, the company then uses DRP to achieve the most efficient and effective levels of outgoing inventory within the distribution chain. Combining these techniques leads not only to drastic reductions in inventory levels, but also to increased levels of customer service by using DRP to more accurately predict customer demand. As with DRP and MRP, JIT and MRP II systems are often used together and are often referred to collectively as MRP III. Used together, JIT and MRP II drastically reduce inventory holding levels, as greater efficiency is achieved in the inbound flow of materials, internally within the manufacturing process, and across the organization as a whole.

THE ROLE OF ABC ANALYSIS IN INVENTORY CONTROL

In many of the previous sections, we explored systems and techniques for controlling and managing the inventory of individual items. Another technique common within the world of inventory control is **ABC analysis**. ABC analysis is not used to manage individual items of inventory, but is instead used to help an organization place its range of inventory into categories based on which items are issued most frequently. Such analysis is useful because it can help an organization determine the most cost effective inventory control techniques and buffer stock levels for an item based on its ABC classification.

ABC analysis is based on the ideas on a nineteenth century Italian economist, Vilfredo Pareto, who posited that a small portion or percentage of something may account for a large portion or percentage of its value or impact. For example, under Pareto's Law, also commonly called the 80-20 Rule, 20% of a company's product lines accounts for 80% of its overall sales. At a grocery store for example, of its hundred and even thousands of types of items sold, its core staples, which include milk, cheese, and bread, typically comprise only 20% of the store's overall types of inventory but account for 80% of the products sold. The remaining 80% of the store's inventory, which would include shrimp, mustard, and our beloved papayas, then only comprise 20% of the products actually sold. Highlighting these high sale items allow a company to focus more attention on their inventory levels to ensure that they always have these items in stock. These 20% of items that make up 80% of a company's sales are its *A* items, according to the following three categories of the BCS analysis:

Products that equal...	And generate...	Are called...
20% of the overall inventory	80% of the company's revenue/ inventory investment	**A products**
30% of the overall inventory	15% of the company's revenue/ inventory investment	**B products**
50% of the overall inventory	5% of the company's revenue/ inventory investment	**C products**

To perform an ABC analysis of types of inventory, an organization first needs a table with all of its items in inventory with the criteria by which they will be classified or ranked, typically annual sales. Also included in the table might be what percentage of total inventory is comprised of each item. An example for such a table for the cheese manufacturer Wisconsin Wonders is:

ITEM CODE	DESCRIPTION	ANNUAL SALES($)	% OF TOTAL INVENTORY
05209BC	blue cheese	$1,000	10%
05806BR	brie	$800	10%
05742CH	cheddar	$55,000	10%
05339ED	edam	$3,000	10%
04991GC	goat cheese	$900	10%
05820GD	gouda	$1,100	10%
05993HV	havarti	$7,000	10%
05103MZ	mozzarella	$25,000	10%
05994SH	spicy havarti	$1,200	10%
05190SW	Swiss	$5,000	10%
TOTAL:		$100,000	100%

To complete the ABC analysis, the items in the table are now sorted in order annual sales, from highest to lowest, and by adding columns showing each item's percentage of annual sales, cumulative percentage of annual sales, and cumulative percentage of total inventory. According to the cumulative percentage of annual sales, the A, B, or C inventory classifications are then assigned.

Item Code	Description	Annual Sales ($)	Percentage of Annual Sales	Cumulative Percentage of Annual Sales	Percentage of Total Inventory	Cumulative Percentage of Inventory	ABC Category
05742CH	cheddar	$55,000	55%	55%	10%	10%	A
05103MZ	mozzarella	$25,000	25%	80%	10%	20%	A
05993HV	havarti	$7,000	7%	87%	10%	30%	B
05190SW	Swiss	$5,000	5%	92%	10%	40%	B
05339ED	edam	$3,000	3%	95%	10%	50%	B
05994SH	spicy havarti	$1,200	1.20%	96.20%	10%	60%	C
05820GD	gouda	$1,100	1.10%	97.30%	10%	70%	C
05209BC	blue cheese	$1,000	1%	98.30%	10%	80%	C
04991GC	goat cheese	$900	0.90%	99.30%	10%	90%	C
05806BR	brie	$800	0.80%	100%	10%	100%	C
TOTAL:		$100,000			100%		

From our ABC analysis of our cheese SKUs, we found that cheddar and mozzarella account for only 20% of our stocked items but 80% of our sales. Therefore, we must make sure to not run out of cheddar or mozzarella. However, a total loss of brie cheese would have little effect on our profits.

LEAN AND STANDARDIZATION

Because of the unnecessary expense of holding unneeded inventory, companies try to reduce inventory quantity through many of the techniques we covered earlier in this chapter, including EOQ, JIT, MRP, and ABC analysis. In a further effort to reduce inventory held and save on warehousing costs, companies now try to reduce warehouse waste through a mode of thinking called *lean*. **Lean** is a focus on examining every step in a business process and eliminating the waste, i.e., the steps that do not add value to the customer. This idea of looking at a work flow and ensuring that it moved through streamlined, standardized processes without unnecessary steps originated with Henry Ford and his development of assembly line processes. The concept of *lean* then got its start in Japan just after World War II with Toyota Motor Company when the company developed the Toyota Production System (TPS). TPS focused on eliminating *muda*

(Japanese for "waste") by manufacturing only what was needed when it was needed and in the exact quantity needed. To eliminate waste, which included overproduction, unnecessary inventory, and excess motion, TPS embraced the concept of *kaizen*, or continuous improvement.

The lean way of thinking gained popularity in global companies in the early twentieth century with multiple expected and unexpected positive results. For example. Goodyear Tire's lean initiatives resulted in $5 million savings, zero landfill waste, and a reduction in OSHA incident rates to less than 33% of the national average. Part of lean's success has been the way in which an organization's employees are invested in the process. Employees are all involved in identifying waste and the companies monitor and celebrate their successes from the waste identified and eliminated.

Lean had now come to mean a way of thinking that involves concepts including:

- **5S**, which refers to the mindset that all work areas are neat and tidy, with everything in its place, and focuses on sorting, setting in order, shining, standardizing, and sustaining

- **total employee involvement**, which means that everyone in a company is involved in the lean way of thinking and part of the continuous improvement process

- **standard work**, which is a focus on standardization of processes and documentation of this standardization to be shared with everyone involved

- **management walkabouts**, in which managers wander around the workplace and ask employees for their suggestions for improvements or what could be done better

- **visual management**, which shows the results of lean and performance scores to all employees in wall charts and other highly visible formats

- **value stream mapping**, which involves mapping processes to see which add value and which do not and should be eliminated

While lean had its origins in manufacturing, it has become popular in the world of warehousing and inventory management. Many warehouse operations have adopted a lean mindset and examined unnecessary processes. A significant part of bringing lean to warehouse management has been inventory *standardization*. **Standardization** is the process of reducing similar items held in inventory, thus reducing the overall inventory holding of the organization.

When it comes to inventory management, variety is not always the spice of life. In most warehouses, inventory variety can increase over time and, without investigation, may remain long undetected. When it is not an absolute necessity, holding a variety of similar items is an undesirable situation for warehouse managers because such duplicate stocking reduces the holding capacity of the warehouse. Thinking back to your own personal warehouse, i.e., your refrigerator, would you stock it with gallon jugs of a variety of milk products (1%, 2%, skim, regular, buttermilk, soy milk, etc.)? Unless you have a gourmet-sized refrigerator, you most likely standardize the milk you stock to include only one or two types.

Through the process of standardization, similar items held in inventory are reduced to one standard item. Each standard item is also called a stock-keeping unit (SKU), each of which is assigned a unique inventory code. When necessary item variety exists due to different sizes, colors, or styles of an item, each unique combination of item size, color, and style would be a different SKU, For example, two gallons of the same brand of milk in a grocery store warehouse would be two different SKUs if one was whole milk and the other was 2% milk.

In the warehouse setting, a variety of factors can lead to unwanted inventory variety. For example, say that Tricycle America, Inc. merged with Unicycle Global, LLC to form a new company, Cycles-R-Us. Some of the warehouse staff of the Unicycle Global must now move to the Tricycle America warehouse. At the Tricycle America warehouse, they maintain a stock of Brand A tire pumps. The new staff from the Unicycle Global, however, are accustomed to working with Brand B tire pumps, so they decide to keep a stock of these pumps as well, leading to unnecessary duplication and unneeded inventory variety.

Unwanted inventory variety may also arise from the personal preferences of the heads of a company's departments, who each demand that an inventory of their preferred items be purchased and stored. For example, because it a global company, the headquarters of Cycles-R-Us generates a lot paperwork. For internal communications, the head of the Marketing department prefers to use only high quality 28lb Hewlett-Packard brand paper, while the head of the IT department prefers to use only Xerox paper because she believes it creates fewer jams in their Xerox printers and copiers. The head of the Accounting department strongly disagrees with both and believes that, for maximum cost effectiveness, only 20lb Office Depot brand paper should be used for internal communications. As a result, a lot of unnecessary space is taken up at the Cycles-R-Us Headquarters supply warehouse because an unnecessary variety of paper is held in inventory.

In addition, unwanted inventory variety may also be caused by a *one-off demand* for a certain variety of item. This item is purchased for one occasion but unwittingly maintained in inventory thereafter. For example, as a cross- promotion with the re-release of the 1982 classic family movie, E.T., Cycles-R- Us sold their children's bicycles and tricycles with a handlebar basket and E.T. plush figure. After the cross-promotion was over, Cycles-R-Us continued to hold and maintain a stock of handlebar baskets and E.T. plush figures, wasting valuable warehouse space and maintenance costs.

Finally, changes in availability at certain times may encourage organizations to hold more than one variety of an item to safeguard against a nil-inventory situation. For example, the executives at Cycles-R-Us really like the bicycle seats manufactured by companies in the Eastern European country of Belarus. The seats are very durable, comfortable, made with high quality leather, and cost one third less than all of their competitors. While there are three competing bicycle seat manufacturers in Belarus, none of them are able to provide a consistently high volume of seats. Therefore, Cycles-R-Us maintains a stock of the three varieties of seats from these three manufacturers in Belarus in addition to a stock of seats from another company in Taiwan to accommodate for the sporadic availability of supply from the Belorussian companies.

As it happened with Cycles-R-Us, staff turnover, personal preferences, one-off- demand, and changes in availability can all lead to unwanted inventory variety in any company. The goal of the warehouse or inventory manager is to reduce this variety and its corresponding high levels of duplicated stock through initiating a process of *standardization*.

Because the warehouse department is primarily concerned with receiving, storing, and issuing inventory, items that have a high degree of variety can be easily spotted and eliminated, or **standardized**, by a diligent warehouse professional. This standardization of inventory yields great rewards for an organization, including:

- **Reduced storage space used.** When the variety of items is reduced, less overall inventory is held and, thus, less storage space is needed.

- **Reduced warehouse administration.** With a reduced variety of inventory, fewer administrative staff and hours are required to handle inventory records, control, inspection, checking and issue, computer time, and documentation.

- **Improved inventory control.** When varieties are reduced, greater attention can be paid to inventory control because there are fewer varieties to inspect, maintain, and manage.

- **Reduced inventory cost through bulk buying.** When the number or varieties of an item is reduced, a greater number of items of a single variety are purchased. Therefore, organizations can reduce inventory cost when they purchase in bulk from the suppliers. This practice can be repeated throughout the whole inventory holding of an entire organization, resulting in vast savings in capital, which was previously tied up in unnecessary inventory.

ARGUMENT OR OVERSTOCK? STANDARDIZE AND BUY BULK!

Remember Cycles-R-Us and its problem with an unnecessary variety of paper types due to the personal preferences of its department heads? Let's look at the monthly cost of purchasing 1000 reams of paper with the current situation and how costs can be reduced using standardization and bulk buying...

DEPARTMENT/Paper	Reams Needed	Cost/Ream	Total Cost
MARKETING/HP 28lb	40	$12	$4800
IT/Xerox 24lb	200	$10	$2000
FINANCE/Office Depot 20lb	400	$ 8	$3200
		TOTAL:	$10,000

If the paper choice is standardized to the mid-range paper (i.e., the 24lb Xerox paper preferred by the IT department), Xerox will offer Cycles-R-Us a 15% discount because they have agreed to more than double their original purchase agreement. Therefore, 1000 reams of paper/month purchased at $10/ream – with a 15% discount – is $8,500/month, a whopping $1,500/month or $18,000/year in savings!

- **Improved service from suppliers.** When standardizing inventory and reducing the varieties of one item produced by competing suppliers, a competition between these suppliers often results, translating to both better service and lower prices for the purchasing organization. In the Cycles-R-Us example, standardization of paper inventory to only one supplier could lead to improved service from suppliers, such as free delivery and paper upgrades.

- **Improved standards establishment.** After the items in a warehouse's inventory have been standardized, the process of setting standards in the organization improves greatly. Both the Warehouse and Quality Control departments now have only one standard to set and monitor for each item held, rather than having a system of standards for each variety, which might lead to a lack of conformity in implementation.

While standardization seems an ideal solution for inventory management, it sometimes brings disadvantages that must be considered. Standardization does bring reduced flexibility and sudden shortages of a particular line may cause supply problems. Because standardization also brings reduced choice for the user, some users may feel shortchanged because they believe that a variety phased out may have been the best for the job. It is up to each individual company to decide whether or not the benefits of item standardization outweigh the potential difficulties it may bring.

When an organization decides that the benefits of standardization outweigh its disadvantages, they partake in the *standardization process*. First, duplicate varieties in the inventory are identified. This is often achieved when warehouse coding has been completed and similar code numbers warrant investigation. Once the duplication has been discovered, the organization then selects the best *standard item* from the variety of items based on usage, price, performance, or other relevant factors. The newly selected standard item must be able to meet all of the needs of the present inventory variety. In these instances, the universal or all-purpose item tends to be selected in an effort to meet all the requirements placed upon the item involved.

Figure 6.8 - The Standardization Process

Finally, the organization calculates the new total inventory requirements and establishes the revised level of inventory for the item involved. The total usage of the variety of previously held items, and not the individual item itself, will indicate the overall level of demand for the newly chosen standard item.

Throughout the standardization process, the warehouse department is in a unique position to assist and prevent excess variety from being created in the inventory held. First, the warehouse can discourage users from ordering non-standard issue items whenever possible. This can be accomplished by recommending and even actively promoting the standard inventory item. Next, Warehouse management can inform the users of the cost involved in holding a wide variety of inventory and its effect on the organization's profitability. The Warehouse department can also constantly review the inventory records to locate possible sources of inventory standardization. Finally, Warehouse management can work with the Purchasing department to discuss the subject of standardization and the possible items on the market which could be made standard items and thus reduce inventory variety.

PHYSICAL INVENTORY CHECKING

Remember Glossy Glam, Inc., the lipstick manufacturer mentioned not too long ago? Glossy Glam used a DRP system to streamline its pipeline inventory and forecast customer demand. It has also nearly perfected its MRP systems for incoming inventory. Things were running along smoothly for Glossy Glam until last June, when its inventory of finished products fell short by a whopping 33%! Glossy Glam execs' heads were spinning, utterly confused as to why their streamlined MRP and DRP inventory control systems might have let them down and scared of what they must now report to their stockholders.

Glossy Glam's MRP and DRP systems had indeed not let them down. The fault for Glossy Glam's inventory shortages lies instead in the company's shortsighted belief that these computer-based systems were all it needed to manage its inventory. Had Glossy Glam regularly conducted physical inventory checks, the company might have realized that it had not begun recording quantities of free samples taken from inventory for the new Visiting Student Scholars program and that, since hiring "Light Fingers" Louie to work in the warehouse, more than 30% of the finished product stock had mysteriously vanished. In addition to the inventory control systems outlined in the earlier parts of this chapter, *physical inventory checking* is a critical component to effective inventory management.

The security and accountability for all inventory and equipment held within the warehouse system is the direct responsibility of the warehouse manager and staff. As we've mentioned throughout a few of the previous chapters, inventory represents a substantial financial asset on an organization's balance sheet. This enormous responsibility demands that the warehouse manager and staff perform continuous physical checks of all the items held in inventory and verify their item counts with the balances shown on the inventory control and recording systems. This process is called **physical inventory checking**. For most organizations, a full physical check must be carried out at least once a year to provide validated inventory figures for the organization's yearly final accounts.

The cost of physical inventory checking, i.e., physically verifying inventory held by an organization in a warehouse or other holding facilities, is considerable. Many valuable warehouse labor hours are needed to arrange and conduct an inventory check and, when discrepancies are found, many more inventory and quality control labor hours are needed to investigate. The many benefits of physical inventory checking far outweigh these costs, however.

First, the physical counts of inventory checking both test and verify inventory recording and control systems, financial reports and systems, and a variety of additional computerized systems by acting as a performance check form which adjustments can be made to further enhance the efficiency and effectiveness of these systems. Furthermore, financial reports produced by an organization's auditors, including the company's ever-important balance sheet, demand some form of physical inventory verification to support the value of the inventory indicated within the balance sheet. Inventory valuations that are not backed up by physical inventory counts have little relevance and value to an organization's internal accountants and internal and external auditors, especially those at tax revenue agencies such as the IRS!

Another benefit of physical inventory checking is the enhanced inventory security it provides. Within any warehouse, regular physical checks of inventory help ensure that possible fraud and theft is detected quickly so that immediate investigations may be conducted. Conversely, such regular inventory checking and immediate investigations into inventory inconsistencies can act as a deterrent to those contemplating fraud and theft within the warehouse.

Finally, physical inventory checking acts as an indicator of overall warehouse efficiency and control. The number and size of inventory check discrepancies are good indications of the efficiency of the receipt, issue, and storage processes. A high incidence of inventory discrepancies, for example, would typically warrant a close look at the system and personnel involved. Furthermore, accurate inventory levels, backed up by a regular physical count, will ensure that all users' requirements are covered by existing inventory and will be physically available to be issued promptly and efficiently. This helps organizations avoid the all-too-common occurrence of inventory shown as being available within the inventory records system, but not actually being physically present.

Because organizations are all different with very different inventory receipt, storage, and issuing needs, they may choose one of many methods for conducting a physical inventory check. However, the three most common methods of physical inventory checking are: *periodic physical inventory checks*, *continuous physical inventory checks*, and *physical spot-checking*. In a ***periodic physical inventory check***, a complete physical inventory check is performed at regular intervals, usually quarterly or at the end of the organization's fiscal (financial) year. This most common method of inventory counting and checking must be carried out on a non-working day when the warehouse is completely closed to allow the inventory checkers the time and space to count carefully and check discrepancies, thus ensuring an accurate count. This type of check is a very expensive one because it often involves large quantities of outside and inside staff hours, many of which are overtime. A continuous process warehouse (i.e., one operating 24 hours a day, 7 days a week) also faces the added expense of a very costly complete warehouse shutdown. Despite their high cost, periodic physical inventory checks are highly valuable because they enable any discrepancies brought to light to be immediately investigated and they provide accurate evaluation figures for annual balance sheets and accounts.

In a ***continuous physical inventory check***, a selection or section of items is checked every week. Throughout a twelve-month period, every item in inventory will have been physically counted and checked without having to close the warehouse. Thus, a continuous physical inventory check allows a warehouse to continue operating 365 days a year; reduces the disruption caused by inventory checking because it spreads the disruption across the year; and, if the checking schedule is not disclosed to warehouse staff, can act as a form of spot-checking (see below). When inventory discrepancies are found, however, a significant amount of time is needed immediately for investigation. Unlike periodic physical inventory checking, continuous physical inventory checking offers only limited time for immediate investigations as the warehouse continues its standard daily operations.

Finally, *physical spot-checking* is used primarily as a security and anti-theft measure within warehouse control. Spot-checks are designed to verify the inventory held, without a prior warning to warehouse staff, which might otherwise allow for stolen inventory to be illegally replaced. Physical spot-checking, which is simple to arrange and conduct on a large scale, acts as a deterrent against those who might contemplate theft or fraud, knowing that a discrepancy highlighted in a sudden check may be the catalyst for a full-scale investigation of all inventory. Because physical spot-checking is limited in its full inventory counting applications and does not provide sufficient data for financial calculations, it is typically used in addition to an additional form of inventory checking, such as periodic or continuous physical inventory checking.

Most warehouses use digital computer systems to show a quantity of inventory that should be in stock. Warehouses use one of the three methods above to see if the actual amount of physical inventory in stock matches the amount shown in the computer system. If the numbers don't match up, inventory can be immediately rechecked and reconciled. Regardless of the specific type of method used to check inventory, the way in which personnel are used to conduct the check may vary according to: the size of the inventory operation, the size of the warehouse facility, the inventory staff and resources available, the experience of the inventory checkers, and the extent of the inventory variation. (An entire warehouse full of one type and model of computer chip is far, far easier to count than half a warehouse full of 500 different types and models of computer chips!) When conducting a physical inventory check, different ways in which personnel can be used include:

- **one person** checking the entire warehouse or set of warehouse facilities without assistance;

- **a team** of inventory checkers working through large warehousing areas; and

- **two inventory checkers working independently** of each other but counting the same inventory. This final approach is the most accurate because, when the inventory checkers compare each section counted, it provides an instant double-check of that inventory.

To ensure that a physical inventory check is an accurate and meaningful exercise, those in Warehouse Control must organize and control all inventory check activities. For a physical count to be effective, the inventory check demands a high degree of care and a very acute attention to detail. One of the toughest problems facing inventory checkers is a tight deadline. Inventory counts are often due by a set date, such as the end of the fiscal year, and any inventory not counted by that date will have to be counted later, which the necessitates additional complex calculations for inventory issued and received after the count deadline.

In order to have a timely and effective physical inventory check, warehouse managers often use standard steps for conducting an inventory check operation, such as the ten steps listed below:

1. **Appoint a controller.** For an effective physical inventory check, one individual should be appointed to have full authority over all those involved in the inventory check, producing clear lines of authority and responsibility for all involved in the operation. Sometimes outside professional organizations are hired to conduct physical inventory check and have their own controllers for the check.

2. **Allocate personnel by area.** When using teams to conduct large inventory check operations, inventory areas are allocated to each team to check and count. It is good industry practice to have teams or members of the teams work in pairs. In order to provide needed local knowledge to speed up the checking operation, one member of the pair should be someone who normally works in the area being checked. In order to provide an outside view and deter internal fraud, the other member of the team should be someone from an outside department, such as Accounting.

3. **Acquire the tools and space needed.** Adequate equipment must be made available to all inventory checkers before the counting can begin. Such equipment can range from pens, pencils, and clipboards to scanners and hand- held computers. Adequate office space will also be needed for checkers to do calculations and make comparisons.

4. **Hold a comprehensive meeting.** Several days before the actual inventory check, the controller should hold a comprehensive inventory check meeting to explain to all involved: the operational procedures of the check; what is to be checked and counted; how and where quantities are to be recorded; inventory check location assignments; the division of teams and pairs; and the timetable of events for the entire operation.

5. **Highlight what to count.** The inventory to be counted and recorded must be clearly highlighted. The inventory to be counted typically includes all normal inventory, inventory under inspection, scraps, packaging, and items on loan. Inventory to be counted but recorded separately on different sets of inventory check sheets include damaged inventory, deteriorations, and goods in-transit.

6. **Clean up!** To help make the actual physical inventory check more accurate and efficient, organizations often perform a pre-inventory check clear-up/clean-up of all inventory rooms, inventory yards, and warehouse buildings.

7. **Close the warehouse.** When conducting a complete periodic physical inventory check, the warehouse and its installations must be completely closed and all other activities must be stopped. An accurate comprehensive inventory check cannot take place when the inventory being counted is constantly being issued and received.

8. **Separate the counts.** All equipment and inventory that does not belong to the organization, such as rented equipment, must be counted, recorded, and documented separately from other inventory classifications.

9. **Don't forget in-transit...** All inventory in-transit (i.e., currently between the warehouse and some other installation) or inventory held in satellite warehouses and external inventory yards should be accounted for at the same time as the main warehouse inventory check. This practice ensures a complete and accurate picture of the organization's entire current inventory.

10. **Do the documentation.** All previously active warehouse documentation, such as issue notes, delivery notes, and quality control documents, should be documented and filed before the physical inventory check begins to ensure that all inventory records are up-to-date.

When conducting a physical inventory check operation, sufficient documentation is required throughout. This documentation may be paper- based, electronic, or a combination of both, but generally includes: inventory counting sheets, a master inventory sheet, an inventory certificate, outside warehousing installation inventory reports, and interred transfer notes.

Inventory counting sheets, produced specifically for physical inventory checks, are designed to be used by an individual inventory checker for a specific classification or type of item to be counted. These counting sheets may be in paper or electronic form on handheld tablets and connected via wifi or Bluetooth to the ERP system. Therefore, every classification or type of inventory held will have its own inventory counting sheet. These sheets must be numbered consecutively to avoid the possibility of the same items being counted twice. A standard inventory counting sheet also contains a great deal of useful reference data for the inventory checker and provides space for collection of the following data: the date of the inventory check, the description and code numbers of the inventory to be counted, the inventory unit of issue and physical location, the quantity of physical units counted, and the name and signature of the checker along with general comments on the inventory and its condition from the checker.

The controller then produces the ***master inventory sheet*** by collating all individual inventory counting sheets from each of the various warehouse locations. Each contribution from the inventory counting sheets is added to produce a total inventory quantity for each type of item held. While this may be done in paper form by smaller organizations, this is likely to all be done electronically for most mid- to large-sized organizations.

The ***inventory certificate*** is a formal document, which indicates the value of the total inventory held as of the date of the physical inventory check. The inventory certificate is checked and signed by a member of the organization's senior management team, most often a member of the financial auditing team. ***Outside warehousing installation inventory reports*** are smaller versions of the master inventory sheet produced by the individual warehouse, depot, and outside warehousing unit managers and controllers. The counts they contain are also included within the organization's total inventory calculations. Finally, ***in-transit transfer notes*** are used to account for inventory that is in-transit on the date of the physical inventory check.

During a physical inventory check, all inventory, tools, and other equipment held within a warehouse are checked, counted, and measured. The inventory check's item counts (quantities per item) are compared to the inventory levels counts calculated by the inventory control process. The inventory check controller, who has both sets of these actual and calculated inventory figures, can compare the quantities and verify whether or not the two sets of figures are the same. When they are the same, the controller may then report a final, verified inventory quantity. When they are not the same, a *discrepancy* has occurred.

Every seasoned warehouse manager and inventory controller has likely experienced the challenge of ***inventory discrepancies***, i.e., differences between the calculated and physical inventory quantities. In large, complex warehouse operations, discrepancies are inevitable but must still be investigated and corrected. The two primary types of discrepancies are: an *inventory surplus* and an *inventory deficiency*. An ***inventory surplus***, or ***positive inventory***, occurs when more inventory is physically counted than is indicated in the calculated inventory figures. An ***inventory deficiency***, or ***negative inventory***, occurs when less inventory is physically counted than is indicated in the calculated inventory figures.

There are three main classifications of inventory discrepancies, each of which denotes the amount of time and control energy expended in isolating the cause of the discrepancy and the steps needed to prevent future discrepancies of this type. These three inventory discrepancy classifications are:

- **Minor discrepancies**, which exist when the variation between the calculated and physical inventory is very small when compared to the overall inventory quantities involved. For example, in a sewing supplies distribution warehouse, which holds an inventory of 10,000 sewing needles, an inventory discrepancy of 2 sewing needles was found. With a minor discrepancy such as this one, the inventory controller would not waste time and resources on an inventory discrepancy investigation.

- **Major discrepancies**, which exist when a very large and valuable variation between the calculated and physical inventory is detected. Because of their accountability and responsibility for consistent and accurate inventory levels, warehouse managers insist on a complete investigation into the causes of major discrepancies.

- **Operational discrepancies**, which exist when the variation between the calculated and physical inventory is small but the items involved are vital to the operation of the organization. Although the variation may be small, a major investigation into the discrepancy may be launched to determine fault and ensure that the inventory of the vital items is secure and definitively known. For example, a car dealership, which holds 500 new cars in its external inventory yard, has found an inventory discrepancy of one car. A major investigation must be carried out to investigate this discrepancy of only one item because, not only is the item extremely valuable, but it is a core element of the car dealership's operation.

Once a major or operational inventory discrepancy has been identified, an organization will investigate its cause so that it may find the "lost" inventory and prevent similar discrepancies in the future. First, the controller and the inventory check team will check all inventory records and inventory control calculations for mathematical errors. They will also check the area of the inventory involved using a non-warehouse employee to establish a new physical inventory count. The controller and inventory team will also check to see if all units of issue are correct for each item of inventory taken, which includes checking inventory packaging and units of issue on all relevant documentation. They will also ensure that all rejected goods, typically those that have deteriorated or become damaged, have been formally reported and recorded within the inventory records system.

In addition, the controller and inventory check team may also investigate the discrepancy with the appropriate user department. For example, a missing inventory of light bulbs in a refrigerated fish warehouse might mean that the user, the warehouse maintenance department, had been removing the light bulbs without permission or proper documentation. Once such a user discrepancy has been found, an issue note can be created to balance the inventory record.

When inventory discrepancies are found and investigated, their causes may often be innocuous and quickly rectified. For example, incorrect inventory checks; mathematical errors on inventory cards; confusion of units of issue; misplacement of inventory on the wrong shelf or in the wrong place; lost or incorrectly entered documentation; and incorrect documentation from previous inventory checks may all lead to inventory discrepancy detection although no inventory has actually been lost. Discrepancies may also be detected when damage or deterioration has occurred or when inventory has been taken from the warehouse legally but without completing required documentation or notification. Finally, inventory discrepancies may also be the result of more purposive and malicious acts, such as fraud or theft.

Identifying and correcting any major inventory check discrepancy can be a drawn-out and costly process, often ending with the inventory simply being written off as "lost." To avoid such costly processes in the future, it is vital for an organization to identify the cause of the inventory discrepancy and take measures to prevent similar discrepancies during the next inventory check. A few inventory discrepancy prevention measures include:

- *Studying the existing system of control to detect and eradicate faults.*

- *Closely examining warehouse documentation to ensure that all inventory control data is provided clearly, quickly, and accurately.*

- *Holding consultations between the warehouse and other departments whose actions affect the accuracy of inventory checks (such as the transport, purchasing, distribution, and manufacturing) to ensure that all parties are aware of how their actions may positively and negatively impact the accuracy of inventory counts.*

- *Conducting a complete review of security systems if fraud or theft is suspected.*

Once an actual inventory discrepancy has been found and its cause isolated, both the inventory records systems and warehouse accounts must be adjusted to balance the organization's books. An ***inventory discrepancy adjustment report*** must also be completed. This official document is signed by a senior member of staff and contains the relevant data needed by the warehouse accounts, inventory records, and inventory control teams to write-off the amount of inventory involved. This data includes: the calculated inventory; full descriptions and code numbers for each item; a physical count of the inventory found; the total discrepancy involved; the value of the discrepancy; and the unit of issue and unit price. In order to avoid fraud within the organization, only the highest-ranking members of staff are typically permitted to write-off valuable inventory.

Because it is costly to hold inventory, organizations do not typically plan to waste their resources by holding inventory that they no longer need. During a physical inventory check, however, it is sometimes found that the organization is holding inventory that is obsolete or no longer of value. As inventory loses its value to the organization, it goes through the four-staged ***inventory obsolescence process***. During the first stage of this process, inventory becomes ***obsolescent***, i.e., it will soon be of no use or value to the organization. Inventory obsolescence often occurs as the result of changes in manufacturing or technology. As a result, an organization will often have to carry two lines of inventory as a new line is being phased in while the old one is being phased out. For example, an organization may decide to change from one form of packaging to another. The old packaging will still have some use until the changeover is complete.

During the second stage of the inventory obsolescence process, the inventory becomes ***obsolete***, i.e., it becomes completely worthless to the organization. A second organization may not have experienced the changes that set the inventory obsolescence process in motion for the first organization and may therefore find the inventory useful and be interested in purchasing it. For example, an organization that once used color ink jet printers has now switched all of its printers to color laser printers. The organization may now sell its obsolete inventory of ink jet printer cartridges to another organization that still uses ink jet printers.

During the third stage of the inventory obsolescence process, the inventory becomes **redundant**, which means that it is no longer of use to anyone, including both those in the organization holding the inventory and other organizations. For example, when the silicon chip was developed, traditional electronic circuits soon became redundant for many industries. During the fourth and final stage of the inventory obsolescence process, the inventory is considered **scrap** and, if possible, is sold off for the value of the components and raw materials within the items, rather than for any higher value the items might previously have held in it its own right. For example, an organization has switched its packaging from tin cans to plastic pouches. Once this change is complete, the organization decides to scrap its inventory of pre- formed tin cans by selling them to a metal raw materials provider for the value of the metal in the cans.

Thus, it is the goal of inventory management to reduce an item's inventory levels as soon as it becomes obsolescent. An organization can take steps to minimize its losses incurred during the inventory obsolescence process by: *encouraging other departments within the organization to accept and use second-hand equipment; marketing its scrap inventory to multiple organizations;* and *establishing raw materials sell-back agreements with suppliers,* in which original suppliers are encouraged to buy back inventory that is no longer needed.

Several factors can set the inventory obsolescence process in motion, most of which are outside the control of the organization now holding the soon-to-be obsolete inventory. The four most common are:

- **Changes in manufacturing methods.** An organization often finds that newer and more efficient methods of manufacturing are being introduced throughout its industry. As a result, the organization will often have to consider changes in its existing inventory of raw materials, component parts, and/or packaging.

- **Technological changes.** In today's world of rapidly advancing technology, major steps are made every day that introduce sweeping changes into various areas of industry and commerce. Aside from raw materials, inventory across most industries is not impervious to technological changes, which can quickly make component parts, work-in-process, finished goods, and supplies obsolete and even redundant.

- **Changes in customer demand.** Changes in customers' tastes and buying habits also lead to inventory obsolescence. Changes in customer demand can also be induced by changes in the customer's own manufacturing system and methods.

- **Alterations by suppliers.** In some cases, a supplier may decide to stop manufacturing an item (such as a component part) that the organization has incorporated into the design of the finished product. If this halt in the supplier's manufacturing is very sudden, any of the organization's work-in- process is also in danger of becoming obsolete unless a suitable alternative supply can be located.

Although an organization may have little control over the changes occurring which initiate the inventory obsolescence process, it does control when it makes the decision to declare the inventory in question obsolete. It controls the timing of the inventory changeover rather than the fact that the inventory change will occur, which is actually an inevitable fact brought on by one of the changes listed above.

If an organization finds that it has a very large, expensive inventory of the item, it will delay declaring that item obsolete for as long as possible. If the item can be used in other capacities or within other areas of the organization, the organization may be able to minimize or even avoid redundancies. Also, if item usage has drastically decreased but not stopped altogether, the organization may decide to hold inventories of that item and bear the cost of storage in order to provide desired customer service levels. (This often occurs in the holding of spare parts for consumer durables, automobiles, and other machinery that has already become obsolete and is no longer manufactured.) Finally, when it faces aggressive competitors that have already made inventory changes and are taking away an organization's sales, it may have to follow suit and make an immediate change, bearing the losses in obsolete, redundant, and scrap inventory it is left with.

CHAPTER 6 REVIEW QUESTIONS

1. When an organization holds inventory, what types of activities does this entail?

2. With an increased push toward just-in-time systems, why would an organization want to hold inventory?

3. What impact would an organization's available financial resources have on its levels of inventory held?

4. What is inventory control? What are some of its objectives?

5. What is buffer inventory? How is it calculated? Why would this be an important concept for a manufacturer?

6. What are EOQ and FOQ? How are they related and how can an organization use them?

7. How can ABC analysis be used for inventory control?

8. What is physical inventory checking? Why is it an important part of a warehouse's operations?

9. How are a periodic physical inventory check and a continuous physical inventory check similar? How are they different?

10. Which type of physical inventory checking is a deterrent for employee theft? Why?

CHAPTER 6 CASE EXERCISE

Inventory Control and the Case of Purely Posh Pets

Everyone's favorite pet clothing retailer, Purely Posh Pets, relies heavily on a few core product lines for most of its sales. One of these product lines is "The Sherlock," a basic Harris Tweed coat for small to extra-small dogs manufactured by Dapper Dogs. Purely Posh Pet sells approximately 100 "Sherlocks" every week. Because it is such a popular item, Purely Posh Pets likes to keep 4 weeks worth of buffer inventory of the "Sherlock."

The length of time it takes from the moment of reorder to receipt of the Sherlock from Dapper Dogs is one week. Because of the bulk order discount Dapper Dogs offers, Purely Posh Pets places only 5 large orders for "The Sherlock" every year.

Using the information and formulas on pages 126 through 128 of this chapter, answer the following questions:

1.What is the lead time for The Sherlock?

2.How much Sherlock buffer inventory does Purely Posh Pets keep?

3.What is the Sherlock's reorder level?

4.What is its reorder quantity?

5.What is the progress level for this item?

6.What is the maximum inventory Purely Posh Pets holds of The Sherlock?

International canine superstar Yogi Harrison modeling the Purely Posh Pets Spring 2016 "Ruff and Ready" line. (Photo credit: Tom Harrison.)

Bonus Exercise: Inventory Discrepancies!

Based on what you have learned about inventory discrepancies in this week's assigned reading, please read each of the scenarios below and determine:

- *if there is an inventory surplus or deficiency;*

- *the inventory discrepancy classification (major, minor, or operational);* and

- *if the situation is worthy of further investigation.*

Scenario 1:
The computerized inventory control systems for a major department store's regional distribution warehouse shows that there are 242 pairs of True Blue brand men's socks, with a retail value of $10 each. The actual physical inventory count revealed that there are actually 244 pairs in the warehouse.

Scenario 2:
A small soft drink bottling company uses different colored caps to bottle different products in its product range. The company's inventory control system shows that there are 20,000 blue caps (for two week's worth of bottling its Fruity Fizz drink) in inventory, with a replacement value of $0.01 each and a replacement lead time of 2 weeks. The actual physical inventory count revealed that there are actually 16,000 blue caps in inventory.

Scenario 3:
An airline flight from Los Angeles, California to Anchorage, Alaska shows that there are 134 people on its passenger manifest. A head count of oncoming passengers (and a subsequent recheck) reveals that there are actually 135 passengers on the plane.

Scenario 4:
The shipping warehouse of a computer chip manufacturer has 12,035 X-Pan-Sive chips, valued at $925 each, listed as in the warehouse and ready for distribution in its computerized inventory control system. The physical inventory count has revealed, however, that there are actually 10, 036 chips in the warehouse.

Chapter 7

Outbound Processes: Inventory Issue

Now that we have reached the halfway point of this text, you are an absolute expert on inventory! Well, perhaps you have an introductory understanding of: *what inventory is*; *what happens when it arrives into the warehouse*; and *how it is standardized and coded*.

If your goal is to live in a rich-eccentric-recluse-style warehouse with more and more goods coming in, piling stories high around you, and not being ale to find the exit thanks to the never-ending amassing of your precious goods, you can skip this chapter and move on to the next one. If this is not the case, however, we must now consider the exit of goods from our inventory and the *inventory issue process*.

The **inventory issue process**, also called *picking*, is that process in warehouse management of receiving and responding to demands for inventory held, typically within a warehouse or external inventory yard. In its simplest form, the inventory issue process involves hearing what people want and giving it to them in the right quantity, of the right quality, at the right time and place and minimizing the cost of the service to the warehouse customer. Typically, it means getting a product from its location, such as a slot within a warehouse, and bringing it to a packing and shipping area to prepare it for distribution to the person or company requesting the product. Raw materials, work-in-process goods, finished goods, and supplies are all types of inventory involved in the issue process. The demands for this inventory may come from a range of individuals or departments within or external to the organization. For example, the manufacturing department might request raw materials, while a retailer might request an organization's finished goods. In addition, an organization's maintenance department might request spares from inventory while its transportation and distribution department might request work-in- process goods to be shipped to a variety of regional assembly facilities.

As mentioned above, *picking* is a commonly used word to refer to the order issue process. When we talk about picking, we generally are referring to one of two types: *case picking* or *broken case picking*. **Case picking** involves taking items from the warehouse by the unit load, such as a in boxes or drums, typically using a larger piece of materials handling equipment, such as a forklift truck. When case picking involves taking an entire palletized unit load, it is called **pallet picking**. **Broken case picking**, also called **each picking**, involves taking individual items from a "broken case" or opened unit load. This might involve an individual picker taking items and placing them into a cart as an order is picked or it may be part of an automated system. More than half of the labor time in a distribution center is spent picking, specifically traveling to and from locations where the items are picked, so many distribution centers and warehouses have invested in automated picking processes and equipment to bring greater efficiency to the operation.

As we have stated before, the items that are held by a warehouse are called inventory, but when taking about them in the context of picking and inventory issue, these items are also called **issues**. In addition to standard issue held to meet customer demands, a warehouse might hold a variety of other types of issue, including:

- **replacement issue:** A piece of equipment or supply of goods that is held in case active pieces of equipment or supplies of goods become nonfunctional or obsolete.

- **scheduled maintenance issues:** Items held that are needed for regularly scheduled maintenance, such as on production equipment or company vehicles.

- **impress issues:** Items required by the user to be constantly on-hand, even without specific orders for them being placed, such as frequently ordered, maintenance, and service items. In cases where very large quantities of these items must be held, organizations sometimes utilize small, outlying unit warehouses.

- **loan issues:** Most often tools and equipment required by specific departments within an organization for specific jobs. The warehouse loans out the equipment when needed for limited periods of time.

- **allocated issues:** Inventory that has been allocated by the manufacturing schedule to a specific operation in a given function or section, such as manufacturing, packaging, engineering, etc.

- **general issues:** The general items of inventory needed by various departments for the day-to-day running of the organization. This could range from engineering spare parts to office light bulbs.

- **capital issues:** The major pieces of equipment purchased and issued by an organization. In most cases, large capital items are not held in inventory but are instead issued as soon as the items are delivered to the organization.

- **project-specific issues:** Items that are held for a limited period of time for dedicated use for specific projects, such as a new research and development project, a customer loyalty program, or a temporary marketing initiative.

Throughout the inventory issue process, data and additional information is requested, given, and processed. This data-driven and IT-based function is called ***order processing***.

THE ORDER CYCLE PROCESS

One important part of outbound logistics management and effective physical distribution management is an organization's ability to respond to the *order cycle*. The ***order cycle*** is the entire time involved and process undertaken beginning with the placement of an order by a customer and ending with the receipt of the shipment by the customer. The order cycle process outlines the order of goods and how the order is filled from the supplier's perspective.

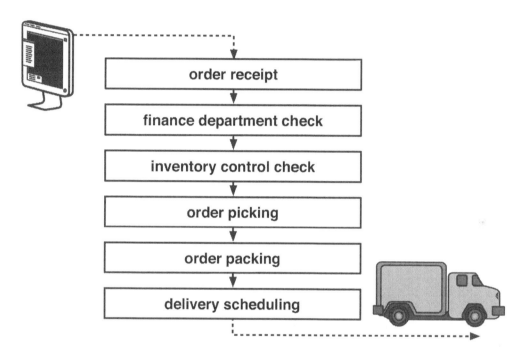

Figure 7.1 - The Order Cycle Process

For efficient and effective physical distribution management, an organization must respond to the six steps of the order cycle process efficiently and effectively. One of the goals of physical distribution management is to achieve competitive advantage for the organization. One way this can be accomplished is by reducing order cycle time, i.e., reducing the time it takes to complete the entire order cycle through its entire six steps. These six steps (and the ways in which they have an impact on overall order cycle time) are:

1. **Order Receipt.** Before the order receipt stage begins, the users of an organization's inventory first decide: what they need and in what condition; how much of it they need; and where and when they need it. As previously stated, these inventory users range from an organization's internal departments, such as manufacturing and maintenance, to

external users, such as wholesalers and retailers. When a user has determined its need for an organization's inventory, it makes a formal request for this inventory. The internal user's request may be a paper document, an electronic document, or part of a larger IT-based MRP (materials requirement planning) or JIT (Just-In-Time) system. In most cases, the user submits a request for goods to the organization's warehouse (or external inventory yard) in the form of a document called a ***requisition***. This may also be called a ***request for issue*** or an ***issue note***, depending on the preference and tradition of the organization. External customers may also place a *purchase order* through the sales department and this purchase order is another form of requisition. The degree to which an organization's order receipt procedures are automated and computerized have a substantial impact on overall order cycle time. For example, during the order receipt step for Company A, purchase orders are received from buyers by fax, manually entered into the company's computer system, and then printed and hand delivered to the company warehouse for order picking. Its competitor, Company B has streamlined its order receipt procedures by receiving buyers' purchase orders through a web-based ordering system, which are sent directly to the warehouse computer system for pre-approved buyers. Order receipt at Company A may take up to one hour, but takes only one second at Company B!

2. **Finance Department Check.** After the buyer's order is received, it is sent to the supplier's finance department to verify the customer's status. This check determines if the customer: is a preexisting one, is in good credit standing with the organization, and has preexisting sales and service terms, such as whether or not an order can be sent before its payment is received. This would apply to both orders from external customers and from customers internal to the company. As with the order receipt example given for Companies A and B, the degree to which the finance department check is automated and computerized influences the speed of this stage of the order cycle process. Even for smaller organizations, where large-scale computer automation may not be as cost effective as it would be for a larger company, accurate and thorough computer-based record keeping can make a world of difference to a company's order cycle time and its bottom line. If a supplier does not have well kept records about its previous transactions with buyers, the finance department may spend ridiculously large amounts of time checking up on past buyers and extra resources in unnecessary credit checks. It may even mistakenly approve buyers who have defaulted in the past!

3. **Inventory Control Check.** After the buyer's order is approved by the finance department, it is sent to the inventory control department or system, which then checks on the availability of the finished goods requested in the order. If it is, the requested quantity of the item is allocated to the requestor within the order processing system. If the item is not in stock, an order request is made to the organization's purchasing or manufacturing department, depending on the item's point of origin. When the request for items held within a warehouse come from the manufacturing department, however, the manufacturing department supplies those handling warehouse requisitions with a ***Manufacturing Materials Schedule***. This document provides details of manufacturing activities over a given period of time, enabling the warehouse to ensure that the correct inventory (and their corresponding services) required for manufacturing are readily available. Thus, through an MRP system, the Manufacturing Materials Schedule contains

information on: the amount of inventory needed; they types of inventory required; and the timetable of requirements.

In the previous example, the manufacturing department itself is the "authority" and is automatically granted its warehouse inventory requests. In most cases, however, someone within the warehouse or issuing department is the "authority" and their approval and signature must be sought before inventory is released for issue. This person is responsible for ensuring that the demand is real and that limits imposed by the organization are not being exceeded. In MRP, JIT, and other electronically-based systems, this authorization may be automatic, with specific quantities of items over a specific timeframe pre-approved/pre-authorized for issue to a specified requestor. At the risk of sounding like a very broken record, this stage of the order cycle, too, can be made an instantaneous one with order processing automation and computerization.

4. **Order Picking.** Now that the customer's financial status and the availability of the items in the order have been verified, the organization can now begin to physically fill the order. The items requested are *picked* (or selected) from the warehouse shelves. Later in this chapter, we will explore some of the techniques used for more efficient order picking, which focus not only on automation and computerization, but also on how a company actually plans the pick in terms of which items will be picked when and by whom.

5. **Order Packing.** After the items in the order are picked, they must be prepared for shipment. An order is *packed* when its items are placed into packaging, *unitized* (placed into unit loads, such as onto pallets or into containers), and physically prepared for shipping. We will also explore order packing in greater depth later in this chapter and the importance of effective packing to a company's bottom line.

6. **Delivery Scheduling.** Finally, after the inventory is picked and packed, a delivery time and place is scheduled with the customer through the organization's transportation system. The delivery is scheduled and subsequently conducted through the *distribution channel*, the route and means by which an organization distributes its finished goods. As with all steps of the order cycle, organizations can achieve greater delivery scheduling efficiency and effectiveness when the process is automated and computerized. Imagine, for example, a Walmart regional distribution center with 40 goods-in and loading bays and a steady stream of container trucks both bringing goods in from suppliers and taking them away to retail stores. If the scheduling of the bays alone wasn't precise down to the minute, chaos might reign, with container trucks backed up for hours waiting for available bays.

The first three steps of the order cycle process are increasingly automated and handled by computer systems, even in smaller companies, thanks largely to web-based apps and handheld devices. When, we get to the fourth stage of the order cycle process, *order picking*, we move out of the world of information and into the world of hands-on, physical action! We'll cover the exciting realm of order picking in the rest of this chapter. We'll then move on to the fifth and sixth stages of the order cycle process, order packing and delivery scheduling, in the next chapter.

WHAT IS VENDOR MANAGED INVENTORY?

Not all inventory goes through the order cycle process in exactly the same format as described above. In some situations, the supplier of an item keeps track of its inventory levels at an organization and they supplier handles most of the heavy lifting (and paperwork and record keeping) for its items in the customer's inventory.

Vendor managed inventory (VMI) is the practice of a buyer allowing a seller (or *vendor*) to monitor product demand and inventory levels in order to forecast demand patterns and set product shipment levels and schedules. The ultimate goal of VMI is to ensure that the buyer has enough inventory needed while keeping inventory holding costs at a minimum. The vendor makes sure to maintain adequate inventory levels and quality because the vendor is not paid until the items are picked from inventory.

Alaska Communications, a provider of broadband and managed IT services to businesses and residential customers across Alaska, has installed innovative vendor managed inventory systems at its central warehouse in Anchorage, Alaska. Most of the items in the warehouse are picked by their internal end users, such as the company's repair technicians who pick tools and suppliers to work on broadband cables and business network systems. To keep track of some of the higher value items in its VMI inventory, the organizations uses a vending machine that resembles those that sell mp3 players and other electronic devices at airports. The vending machines have scanning technology that allows vendors and Alaska Communications end users to use their identification cards or type in identification codes to access empty slots to fill them with inventory (vendors) and to take needed items from inventory (end users). This process lets Alaska Communications' inventory systems immediately know how much of which items are in stock and who has taken items and what department they should be charged to.

THE ORDER PICKING STAGE

Order picking is selecting and retrieving the correct type and quantity of inventory from a warehouse or external inventory yard based on a specific user's request or customer requirements. Order picking may range from retrieving individual items from storage to retrieving entire pallet- or container-loads of items. In the order cycle process, the order picking stage can have a great impact on an organization's revenue saved or lost. When goods are retrieved from storage quickly, an organization can fill and ship its customers' orders quickly, get paid sooner, and then move on to the orders of its next paying customers. When goods are retrieved from storage slowly, perhaps taking three days instead of the one day it takes for its quicker-picking competitor, an organization loses money because more money is tied up in warehouse space and inventory holding and customers are far less willing to pay premium prices because the inventory issuing time is soooo slow. Therefore, the ultimate goal of warehousing in the order picking process is that customers' needs are picked quickly and accurately.

The first step in rapid order picking is finding the item to be picked. Could you imagine if every organization's order picking system operated the way we do when we've parked our cars at the mega-mall multi-story parking garage or when we are in a frantic search for where we've placed our keys?! To avoid similar time traps, warehouses use **_inventory location systems_**. With these location systems, items (and their corresponding item codes) are assigned a location code, which represents a specific location within the warehouse. Even the most basic computers can house the most intricate and detailed inventory location systems, with the user simply typing in the name or item code of the desired item and immediately being supplied with the item's exact location!

Both bar coding and RFID systems (and their accompanying techno-toys, i.e., scanners, readers, transmitters, etc.) can also be used to further enhance the benefits of inventory location systems, with rapid bar code scanning of item codes and their corresponding location codes or even more rapid automatic location and item data collection from RFID tags.

Once an inventory location system is in place and you have pinpointed the exact location of the item desired, that item must now be "picked," or retrieved from storage. At this point, companies typically create a **_pick list_**, a document that lists the order number, the specific items to be picked, and the quantity of each item to be included in the shipment. Also typically included in the pick list is the location for each item, such as the aisle and bin number. For orders that are picked manually with no technological assistance, the information on inventory location can be the most critically important information on the pick list. When location information is not correct, pickers can waste valuable travel time searching for items. When companies use computer- and web-based systems, pick lists can be automatically generated as soon as customers place their orders.

When it comes to physically picking an order, there are a variety of manual or automated systems of order picking. The means of order picking an organization chooses to utilize depends on many factors, such as the size and weight of the items or unit loads, the value and possible hazardous nature of the items to be picked, an organization's financial resources and long-term goals, available warehouse space, and ergonomic considerations in item picking.

Order picking systems based on how products are taken from inventory include:

1. **The picker goes to the part.** The *picker* is the human worker retrieving the item. The *part* is the item being retrieved. Rather than having the picker spend his/her entire day walking up and down the long warehouse aisles retrieving items of varying sizes and weights, warehouses use technology to speed up the process. Pickers can get to their desired parts quickly and retrieve them effortlessly while operating pallet trucks or powered carts or even riding within Man-Aboard Storage/Retrieval Systems. Picker-to-part systems are generally the least expensive and most commonly used order picking systems.

2. **The part comes to the picker.** There are many quick and laborsaving systems by which stationary pickers can have desired items come to them. When there is adequate warehouse space and when the size and volume of items merit it, conveyors, carousels, and automatic storage retrieval systems (AS/RS) can all be used as effective and efficient means of bringing the part to the picker. The part-to-picker systems generally require a more expensive initial investment in machinery, but offer long-term savings in reduced labor costs. They are used more often in warehouses with a very large and rapid order throughput flow, such as

worldwide or regional distribution centers for computer components or central shipping warehouses for online mega-stores.

3. **The entire process is automated and operated under computer control**, with the picker simply pushing a button on a computer or supplying a voice command. When a very large quantity of items must be picked regularly within very short periods of time, fully automated picking systems can offer critical speed and efficiency. Examples of automated order picking systems include: *case and item dispensers*, in which items or cases of items are dispensed horizontally from a conveyor or vertically through a gravity-based system; *unit load AS/RS*, in which automated guided vehicles, conveyors, and/or monorail systems are used to automatically pick and dispense entire unit loads; and *robotic elements*, such as robotic arms and two- and three-axis gantry mounts are used to pick and dispense items and/ or unit loads. Because of their great expense and limitation of movement, these fully automated order picking systems are those least commonly found. They are, however, invaluable, in handling hazardous materials, very large throughput volumes, and those situations in which repetitive picking movements might cause ergonomically related injuries in pickers.

Figure 7.2 - Order Picking Systems: the picker goes to the part (*left*); the part goes to the picker (*center*), and automated process under computer control, sometimes with robotic elements (*right*)

As mentioned earlier, more than half the labor time in a warehouse is spent on picking an order, especially traveling to the item to pick it. The Warehousing Education and Research Council (WERC) found that an astounding 54% of labor time in a distribution center was engaged in order picking activities while less than half of that amount (24%) was spent in receiving items and putting them away into storage. To make order picking faster and more efficient, warehouses and distribution centers can utilize technology and automation in a variety of ways, with new forms of order picking technology becoming popular every year. A few of the ways in which technology is used in order picking include:

- *pick to light*. When a warehouse has smaller items that are stored in bins on rows of racks, pick to light can be a highly useful order picking technology. With pick to light, an indicator light above or adjacent to the bin holding the item that needs to be picked will light up. In many pick to light systems, a digital display will also indicate how many of that item must be picked. Some pick to light systems have eliminated the possibility of human error of picking from the wrong bin (despite the correct one being lit) by also installing a *weight check system* under each bin that measures the weight of the bin. With a weight check system, when an incorrect bin suddenly gets lighter, the picker will be immediately alerted, usually from a sound, light, or digital display system.

- *voice recognition technology.* In voice picking, pickers wear a handheld device or computer and a headset with a microphone. Pickers receive picking commands through their headsets, with the computer system verbally telling them which items to pick and exactly where they are located. When pickers find the item and begin to retrieve it, they read the item's identifying code into their headset's microphone so the compute system can verify that the right item was picked and then record the picking action into the inventory control system. This system of double-checking the pick through voice recognition has made this one of the most highly accurate forms of order picking technology available when a human picker is still involved in the process. Because voice picking is a hands-free system, it saves time because the picker doesn't have to stop and look down at a paper, clipboard, or hand-held computer. It also brings safety benefits because the picker has his/her eyes up and scanning the warehouse environment. Finally, it can reduce language-related error rates significantly because the system can be set to the picker's native language instead of the the default preferred language of the company.

- *RF-directed technology. Radio frequency directed* (or *RF-directed)* picking technology is part of a warehouse management system that has RFID (radio frequency identification) tags on all the items in a warehouse. The picker is directed to the items and scans them using an handheld RFID scanner as the items are picked. Although resulting in highly accurate picks because the pick is double-checked with the RF system, many warehouses have found that this form of picking technology takes longer than pick to light and voice recognition systems because of the time spent by pickers using the hand-held scanning devices.

- *AS/RS. Automated storage and retrieval systems*, also called *AS/RS* or *A-frame picking systems*, have goods in bins or totes that move along conveyors and shelving systems that are hundreds of feet wide and multiple stories high. This system brings the bins containing the items being picked to one location where the order picker can quickly pick an entire order with almost no travel time from item to item. Like KIVA robots, AS/RS requires a significant financial investment and would likely only be used by larger operations.

- *AGVs. Automated guided vehicles*, or *AGVs*, are machine operated vehicles, such as an industrial forklift truck, that does not require a human operator. An AGV can move goods along a fixed path, such as with a rail-guided system, or a variable path, such as with laser-guided systems. AGVs can be useful in operations that require the picking of larger, palletized unit loads.

- *Kiva robots.* Kiva, a wholly-owned subsidiary of amazon.com, manufactures robots that picks items from the warehouse or distribution center and brings them to the order picker, also known as *goods-to-person picking*. Kiva robots operate much faster and with greater accuracy than human pickers but are extremely expensive. Only organizations with large, high-volume picking operations would likely consider robotic picking.

When deciding which type of technology to use, or whether to use technology at all for order picking, a company must consider the expense of the technology and the *return on investment* it will get from each of the technology options being considered. A **return on investment**, or **ROI**, is how much the company will save or receive in additional financial compensation compared to the amount it spent on a particular investment, such as order picking technology. When determining the ROI for each order picking technology considered and comparing them, a company should look at the cost of the technology, the operating cost to run the technology, how productive the technology is to the operation, how long the technology will last and how far its reach is into the organization, how well the technology integrates with other systems within the company, how accurate the technology is, and how safe the technology is for both goods and people. Depending on the ROI of the systems, the eventual picking system selected could be any of the following, in order of increasing accuracy, complexity, and cost: **manual system**, in which the picker picks and moves items by hand; **mechanized system**, in which the picker uses materials handling equipment, such as dollies or forklift trucks, to assist in picking and moving the order; semi-automated system, in which the items to be picked are brought to the picker through an automated or robotic system; and **automated system**, in which a computer systems directs and controls the picking operation, which is handled entirely by robotic and automated picking technology with no humans involved.

Just as there are different systems used for order picking, there is also a variety of styles of order picking. Styles of order picking can be used individually or in combination with one another. A few of these styles include:

- **Order picking.** The spartanly named **order picking**, also called **discrete picking**, is the simplest and most common of the three order picking styles. In order picking, each order is picked by one person working from a single picking document, picking one item at a time until the entire order is filled. Order picking is not scheduled and orders may be picked at any time within the picker's work schedule, as long as he/she meets the delivery deadline. This simple style offers many advantages, including reduced errors and increased accountability. Its main drawback, however, is that it is at the mercy of human limitations (i.e., how fast one person can fill one order), making it the slowest style of order picking.

- **Wave picking.** One variation of simple order picking is **wave picking**, in which orders are picked by one picker, one item at a time, but orders are scheduled to be picked within specific timeframes, largely driven by shipping timeframes. For example, if FedEx is coming to pick up one of your orders at 10am for a same- day delivery to one of your biggest customers, wave picking would allow you to schedule that order to be picked within a shorter timeframe, not just within the picker's work shift.

- **Batch picking.** In **batch picking**, one person picks multiple orders (a **batch** of orders), following multiple picking documents, at the same time. When the same item appears of multiple orders, the total quantity of the item from all of the orders is picked together and separated later or immediately into small containers. Batch picking reduces the traveling labor time of the picker by picking multiple orders at once, but can increase the risk of incorrect picking and sorting. These risks are greatly reduced in computer-based automated picking systems, however.

• **Zone picking.** In *zone picking*, a warehouse is divided into sections (or zones). A different employee is assigned to and responsible for picking items within his/her section. Once picked, these items are brought to the central order consolidation and issue section where the entire order, with items picked from each of the warehouse's multiple zones, can be consolidated. While zone picking alone does not reduce the labor used in basic order picking, it does speed up the order picking process. It is also useful in warehouses using a variety of materials handling storage and transportation equipment. For example, within one warehouse, one zone may contain palletized unit loads with pickers on forklifts, another zone may contain small oft-used quantities of items delivered to stationary pickers via conveyor belts, and a third zone may contain extremely heavy items which picked and transported by crane operators.

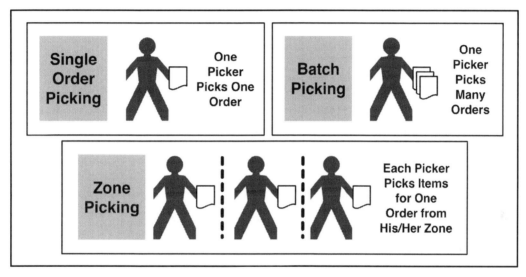

Figure 7.3 - Styles of Order Picking

• **Omnichannel picking.** For large companies with complex operations, picking has traditionally been considered in terms of batching orders to create larger picks and increase picking efficiency and cost-effectiveness. However, in today's world of internet and mobile phone shopping, manufacturers and retailers must consider omni-channel fulfillment. People and companies may order from a wide range of places and systems at any time of the day or night - and expect immediate results! For example, internet orders may have to be filled immediately, with no time to wait to consolidate a batch of orders to be picked at one time. For fast and accurate fulfillment, companies use software to determine the best picking location, such as which distribution center or warehouse around the country, for each customer's order. For example, an order might be picked from a distribution center located much further away from a customer simply because the software has determined that the distribution center selected has all of the items in stock or that the order could be picked much faster at that DC because of the location of the items to be picked. Companies like Google and Amazon are now using omichannel picking and related software systems in some markets to fulfill individual customer's orders on the same day the orders were placed!

CORE PRACTICES OF EFFECTIVE ORDER PICKING

Regardless of a warehouse's order picking system or style, there are core practices which enhance the efficiency and effectiveness of any organization's order picking. Four core practices for efficient and effective order picking are:

1. **Plan your pick.** When a picker has an order and is ready to begin picking, it is best if he/ she is simply not let loose in the warehouse to pick items from the order at random. While many of us have exceptional planning and spatial skills, we might not always choose the most efficient picking route every time. A pre-routed picking document, typically generated through computer optimization programs or a warehouse management system, can help a picker by providing the quickest, most efficient picking for each order. In addition, the way in which warehouse space is used can help increase picking planning efficiency. For example, those items that are picked most often can be located closest to the issue and consolidation section so the order picker does not often have to travel far.

2. **Clarify and reduce picking paperwork.** Without realizing it, pickers can spend many valuable minutes trying to decipher incomprehensible shipping documents or illegible handwriting when picking orders. Creating standard, easily read and comprehended picking paperwork can ensure that these wasted minutes are instead saved. Standard picking paperwork should include the following information about each item: a concise description, item code, location code, and quantity needed. It should not include extraneous information that is not only not needed by the picker, but that can also obscure the essential information. Confusing paperwork may also be eliminated entirely. Many organizations have moved to hand-held computer systems, bar code scanners, RFID scanners and transmitters, and voice recognition systems to ensure greater order picking efficiency.

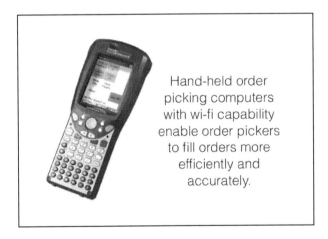

Hand-held order picking computers with wi-fi capability enable order pickers to fill orders more efficiently and accurately.

3. **Package in smaller, oft-used quantities.** When we have to count large quantities of items, we are almost certain to make at least a few mistakes from time to time. (As a fun, do-it-yourself experiment, fill your bathtub with individual jellybeans. Without eating any jellybeans or taking any of them from your tub, count them three times a day for three days. If you are a normal human being and not a bean-counting cyborg, all nine of your jellybean counts are not likely to be exactly the same.) To simplify order picking and reduce

miscounting errors, most warehouses ensure that items are packaged in smaller, oft counted quantities, such as pallet containing only 50 cans of tomato soup, even though the pallet is fully able to handle 500. (Imagine how much easier our jellybean experiment would have been if they had been packaged in bags of 25 or 1000 instead of one, huge, bathtub-sized container!)

4. **Make accountability count!** The fourth and final core practices for efficient and effective order picking is to make pickers accountable for the accuracy of the orders they pick. Although some warehouses make order checkers (individuals hired to "check" to ensure that the order has been picked accurately before it is shipped) accountable to order accuracy, greater efficiency can be achieved by going to the source. When a picker is responsible for his/her own order accuracy, a little bit more time may be spent filling orders, but far less time is spent checking and correcting orders!

THE ORDER CONSOLIDATION AND ISSUE STAGE

Once the order for inventory has been received and the items in the order have been picked from the warehouse, the items are consolidated and the order is issued to the customer. During the consolidation and issue stage, items listed on the user's order or *requisition*, which have been selected from the warehouse, are brought to a central place for consolidation and packing. This central place is usually a dedicated space located within the warehouse or external inventory yard and is often labeled with a self-explanatory name, such as *Issue and Consolidation Sector* or *Packing and Dispatch Area* or, simply, *Distribution* or *Shipping*.

In this issue and consolidation area, a pre-assigned warehouse supervisor or employee checks the order to ensure that it is correct (i.e., the requested items and quantities listed on the requisition match the items and quantities to be consolidated). Once the order has been checked, a ***consignment note***, also called a ***packing slip***, is created that lists exactly what will be packed within each receptacle, such as a carton, box, drum, pallet, or container. The items are then packed into their designated receptacles. Once the items have been consolidated and packed, transportation and, for international shipments, cross-border documentation is prepared. This is critical and very detail-oriented work in today's global market with ever-changing customs documentation and security issues. For example, unless the correct, up- to-date European customs paperwork has been completed, fresh, juicy Florida oranges will be forced to wait at European borders, growing less fresh and juicy every day the correct paperwork is not filed.

After the transportation and cross-border documentation has been prepared, a delivery or pick-up is scheduled for the order. At this point, the order then leaves the realm of materials management and, in most cases, enters the world of *physical distribution*.

CHAPTER 7 REVIEW QUESTIONS

1. What is the inventory issue process? At what point in the supply chain does it occur?

2. What is the difference between replacement issues and general issues?

3. What are some other names for a requisition? When and why is one used?

4. What happens in a warehouse after a requisition is received?

5. What does a warehouse strive for during the order picking stage? Why?

6. How does pick-to-light work? Based on the description of pick-to-light in this chapter, what kinds of inventory items do you think might be picked efficiently using a pick-to-light system?

7. What are the advantages and disadvantages of radio frequency directed technology in order picking?

8. What role does the "picker" play in the three primary categories of order picking?

9. In what type of warehouse might zone picking be most beneficial?

10. Why is it sometimes useful to package items for picking in smaller quantities?

CHAPTER 7 CASE STUDY

Secrets of the Order Picking Pros

Order pickers are the gatekeepers of our most cherished dreams. They influence how quickly we receive those things we desire most, perhaps your favorite flannel pajamas or the special order junk food from Japan that you have been craving. If order pickers are inaccurate or too slow, you might not get your pajamas and Pocky in time for this year's final episode of your favorite soap opera! Hopefully, you have one of the elite cadre of order picking pros picking your order. Those who work in the world of warehousing have a few tricks up their sleeve when it comes to efficient and effective order picking. Some of these tricks of the trade include:

- **Do NOT put different items (or SKUs) in the same bin!** Companies that don't know better sometimes think they are saving money on storage bins by putting multiple SKUs (stock keeping units) in the same bin. For example, the warehouse of a local printing company decided to keep all of its t-shirts in covered plastic tubs, which was a smart idea because it could keep the shirts clean and reduce the risk of damage. However, the tubs were a bit pricey, so the warehouse manager decided to buy only a few tubs and sort shirts into tubs by color, which meant all seven sizes of its glowing green t-shirt were in one tub. Great idea… Until it was time to do some order picking! The poor picker had to look at the label of every t-shirt in the tub just to try to find the one XXS in inventory.

At Once in a Blue Moose, order pickers have a much easier - and quicker - time picking t-shirts. Rather

than worry about pricey storage bins, the retailer uses cardboard boxes (*pictured left*) as storage bins and makes sure that there is a unique box for each unique SKU. For example, the small short-sleeve green t-shirt with two floatplanes on it is in a different cardboard box than the medium short-sleeve green t-shirt with two floatplanes. This speeds up the order picking process because pickers do not have to waste time searching for the correct item in the box. Instead, they simply grab a shirt from the box, confident in the knowledge that the correct item will be there.

- **Keep the "hits" coming!** Order pickers want to increase their hit density as much as possible, which means that they want items to be located near each other so they can pick as many items as possible within a set timeframe. Hit density can be increased by designing picks so that the picker is walking less and picking items that are near each other. At Alaska Communications, warehouse management noticed that most repair technicians who picked their own orders to fill their toolkits were picking the same items. Rather than waste the valuable labor time of highly skilled technicians by having them pick screws and tape out of warehouse bins, Alaska Communications decided to work with a vendor to create pre-supplied tool kits, based on the input of the technicians. With the availability of the new pre-supplied toolkits (*pictured right*), technicians now only had to pick one item instead of many, saving time and effort. When technicians want the toolkit restocked, they simply put the old toolkit in the return bin and grab a new one from inventory. With the vendor managed inventory system, the vendor makes sure to refill the toolkits on a regular basis and place them back into inventory.

- **Don't get touchy!** Items should be touched only once by the pickers' hands and automatic systems should be in place to double check order accuracy as orders are picked. Every extra time the picker touches an item, often when recounting or double checking, time is wasted and the picking process slows down. Larger warehouses and distribution centers now use scales integrated into their picking carts and forklifts. Thanks to the scale's readings, the picker can be immediately alerted if the weight detected does not match the weight expected for the item picked. Meanwhile, the picker can keep on picking!

- **Reduce walking!** Multiple time and motion studies have shown that warehouse workers are more accurate when they can be stationary or walk less during order picking. Walking takes time and energy, so a full day of order picking while walking around would exhaust even the fittest among us. As we mentioned earlier in this chapter, warehouses and distribution centers now work to try "bring the part to the picker." In their overwhelmingly large fulfillment centers, Amazon uses an inventive means of getting the parts to the picker… Robots! Amazon's Kiva Robots (*pictured right*) hold and move four-sided storage shelves, full of different SKUs in bins. These hard working little robots automatically bring the shelves to the order picker when needed.

- **Keep your pickers happy!** A relaxed, rested, and happy picker is an accurate and speedy picker. Alaska Communications created a dedicated break room for its hardworking warehouse staff. Rather than charge forward and create a break room with massage chairs and a meditation corner, warehouse management asked employees what they wanted in a break room. It turns out that a big-screen TV for down time and free snacks throughout the day (*pictured left*) keep people pretty happy and relaxed.

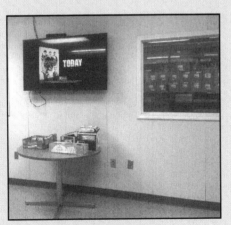

INSTRUCTIONS:

Based on what you have read in this book so far, what other secrets might order picking pros have? What advice would you offer for a more efficient and cost effective order picking process? Explain your answer.

Chapter 8
Outbound Processes: Distribution

After inventory has been picked, it is ready to be sent to the customer who has ordered the goods. This is part of the outbound processes of warehouse management known as **distribution**, but it is also referred to as **shipping** or **dispatch**. The work of a shipping function within a company (or the *distribution department* or the *shipping and receiving department*) includes: locating and checking the order to be shipped; scheduling a carrier to transport the goods; providing value-added services as needed; securing freight for outbound distribution; completing the corresponding paperwork for the outbound shipment, including a packing list for each box or container and a bill of lading to be given to the carrier; loading the vehicle for shipment; and alerting the customer that the shipment is being sent, often though an **advance shipment notice (ASN)**.

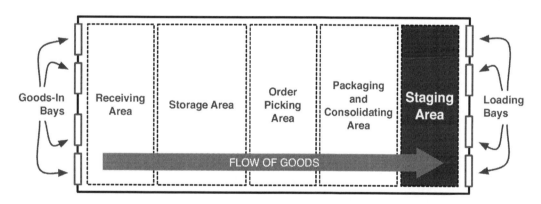

Figure 8.1 - Location of the Staging Area in a Warehouse Example

As part of the distribution process, items are first packed and prepared for an outbound shipment. When multiple items are picked for an order, they are typically brought to one central area of a warehouse to be consolidated and prepared for shipment. This area is known as the **staging area** or **marshaling area**. In cross-docking facilities, a staging area (and warehouse picking) might be bypassed entirely if goods are placed directly from one inbound truck or container onto a different outbound truck or container.

Figure 8.2 -The Staging Area (left) at the Tabali Winery in Limari Valley in northern Chile, where bottles of wine are placed into crates, which are stacked onto pallets and stretch wrapped for distribution to wine merchants and distributors around the world.

Figure 8.3 -Palletization in the Staging Area. Goods are often placed on pallets in a warehouse facility's staging area to prepare them for subsequent shipping, like the sacks of potatoes in this potato distribution center (*left*) and the IT equipment in this telecommunications company's warehouse (*right*).

Figure 8.4 - Retail Staging at the Local Level. At the Once in a Blue Moose warehouse in Anchorage, Alaska, operations are not large enough to justify the use of palletization. Instead, the retail chain warehouse uses color coded rubber totes in its staging area. Goods being distributed to a specific retail location are placed into totes for that location, as designated by color and a two-letter code. High priority items and important paperwork are placed in a special "Open Me First" tote.

When goods are picked and placed into a staging area, some warehouses or distribution centers may perform **value-added services (VAS)** for their customers. VAS are typically related to the specific products being shipped and can include: limited or light product assembly, such as installing plugs specific to the electrical current of the country to which they are being shipped; **product kitting** or **bundling**, such as combining a camera and camera case into one unit for a specific product promotion; **product postponement**, i.e., delaying finalized assembly or packaging until a customer has placed an order, such as waiting to place final consumer packaging on bags of chocolate until prior to shipment so the packaging can reflect the current holiday in the country to which they are being shipped; **product sequencing**, in which items are placed in a specific sequence prior to packaging to meet the needs of the customer, such as the order in which they are needed for a manufacturing operation; and inserting instructions or other paper materials into the packaging of each item, which allows for the instructions to be updated when needed and modified according to the language and cultural requirements of the country to which the items are being shipped.

Goods are prepared for shipment and sorted into sections according to customer or delivery route. Goods in the staging area may also be checked to make sure that items and their quantities are correct and match the customer's order. Typically, when there are multiple goods going to one customer at one location, the goods are unitized and secured, such as shrink-wrapped onto a pallet. Securing goods and stabilizing unit loads are critical on outbound trucks because they ensure that breakage and travel-related damage are less likely to occur. Shrink wrapping, stretch wrapping, and strapping all offer protection for goods in transit.

A company supplying the goods may handle outbound transportation or a transportation provider may be used. If a transportation provider or outside company is used, they sign for the goods and ownership of them officially changes hands. Whoever is responsible for the delivery and owns the goods must ensure that the loads are secure and items make it to the customer in perfect working condition.

PREPARING GOODS FOR SHIPMENT

When goods are being prepared for shipment, they must be packed and labelled to ensure that they make it to the right customer at the right time and location in the right condition. Depending on the customer receiving the shipment, it might also be important that the packaging makes a good initial first impression upon receipt This is less important for regular, recurring business-to-business orders but can be critical for orders being received by end users. Think about how you feel when you receive poorly packed goods or expensive items shipped in inexpensive looking packing materials. Compare this to the first time you received an Apple product, shipped in its streamlined, futuristic-looking, all-white packaging. Even though goods might be received in the same condition regardless of packaging, for some customers, the look of the packaging may have to be considered.

However, the most critical elements related to preparing goods for shipment is ensuring that the *packaging* keeps the items undamaged and that the packing *label* gets the goods to the correct location at the correct time. **Packaging** is the term used for the physical materials into which an order's items are placed. This also includes additional materials used to secure the items within

Figure 8.5 - Packaging. Not all packaging involves heavy cardboard boxes, pallets, and stretch wrap. At Dunkin' Donuts, fresh donuts are placed into retail packing, or the boxes you see in your grocery store (*right side of the picture on the left*). The boxes are then placed into an insulated rolling tray to keep them warm (*left side of the picture on the left*). When the insulated tray is full, it is zippered up and rolled onto the delivery truck (*center*), so it can be delivered to your local grocery store (*right*).

the package, such as straps or styrofoam package filler. The packaging used during the order packing process has an enormous impact on the efficiency and effectiveness of the supply chain. Poor packaging can lead to stolen or broken products, less efficient use of transportation and subsequent storage space, and materials handling equipment malfunction. Efficient and effective packaging, however, should:

- *Keep items safe and secure.* When packaging is insufficient or inadequate, items can be damaged in transit. When packaging can be opened too easily, items can be stolen by "opportunity thieves" at any point along the supply chain. Items may also have specific packaging instructions, including how they should be wrapped and placed in a container or stacked on a pallet or what specific types of packaging materials should be used to avoid environmental damage from water or extreme temperatures.

Figure 8.6 - Safe and Secure Packaging. At the Tabalí Winery in Chile, extra precautions are taken so that the bottles of wine are packaged safely and securely. Bottles are placed into individual slots in custom plastic crates, which are block stacked, placed on multiple-use pallets in a 4x4x4 configuration and extensively stretch wrapped. These glass bottles and their precious contents must travel all around the world to reach Tabali's customers, who are expecting delicious bottles of wine and not bits of damp, shattered glass.

- *Be easily labeled, transported, and stored.* Packaging must be easily labeled so that the customer's inventory receipt department can identify its contents. Packaging must also meet an organization's and its customers' requirements for transportation and storage. For example, packaging may have to be designed so that it can be placed and stacked easily onto pallets or into containers. It may also have to be placed onto storage racks of specific dimensions.

- *Be handled properly by materials handling equipment.* It is inevitable that packaged goods will be handled at both the producer's and customer's facilities. Packaging must be easily handled by both the producer's and the customer's materials handling equipment, which are not necessarily the same. For example, packaging may have to be handled by a forklift truck at one location and a conveyor at another.

Packaging provides necessary safety and security for valuable goods. Without it, goods can lose all of their value in transit. Just imagine the mess, spoilage, and smell of a truckload of raw eggs being transported loosely in a 3'x3' boxes! Within the world of physical distribution management, packaging presents a bit of a conundrum. For items to be the safest and most secure, extra layers of thick packaging are required. Both the materials used and the extra space consumed for this safe and secure packaging are quite costly, however. Therefore, many organizations are now looking at cost efficient yet effective packaging. For example, organizations are looking for "greener," reusable packaging and for packaging that allows for more space utilization.

When preparing goods for shipment, packaged items must be labelled. **Labeling** is the term used for creating, printing, and adhering piece of paper (or **label**) to a package to convey information about the package, such as its intended shipping address or contents. Barcode labels are commonly used to provide a unique identifier for each package, which can reveal detailed information about the package, its source, its destination, and its contents. Like barcode labels, Radio Frequency Identification (RFID) tags may also be used providing information about packages and both can also be scanned and used for tracking packages in transit. RFID tags provide the additional benefit of being able to be tracked wherever they are in the world through global positioning satellites (GPS).

CARRIERS AND TRANSPORTATION MODES

When preparing to ship goods, a company's shipping and receiving department must consider transportation. What provides, supports, and propels the flow of goods from the company to the customer? Transportation! **Transportation** is the act of using a vehicle to move goods or people from one place to another. Within the realm of warehouse management, transportation is the movement of goods, not people, to a desired location. Transportation of our finished goods forms the critical bridge between *where stuff is*, such as manufacturing or warehousing facilities where the goods are located, and *where stuff needs to be*, such as the immediate customers' locations or a distributor's regional distribution center along the supply chain.

One of the roles of a company's distribution (or shipping or dispatch) function is to coordinate and control the outbound transportation of an organization's finished goods. Transportation decisions play a significant strategic role in determining total supply chain costs and levels of service for an organization, often by striking a balance between the advantages and disadvantages offered by the following six criteria:

1. **Cost.** Obviously, transportation costs increase as delivery distances increase, making cost a central factor in determining the geographic limits within which a product can be sold cost-effectively.

2. **Speed.** For many products or situations, a speedy delivery time may be more important than delivery cost. For example, speedy delivery is essential for perishable goods (such as Maine lobster and Alaska King crab, both of which must be flown to their hungry customers) and goods immediately essential to a large manufacturing operation (such as a spare part needed to repair an ice cream producer's freezer, which will be flown in as quickly as possible before too much product melts).

3. **Safety & Security.** An organization's goods are often its most substantial financial assets. To protect the value of these assets, the organization must ensure that the transportation system handling its goods keeps them safe from damage and secure from theft at all times. Safety and security are especially important criteria for transportation decisions involving high-cost or hazardous goods.

4. **Convenience.** For a transportation plan or system to be the successful backbone of any logistics or supply chain, it must be convenient to all members of the chain. Transportation decisions made must consider how easy it is for customers, retailers, wholesalers, distribution centers, warehouses, and manufacturers to interface with those transporting goods.

5. **Reliability.** Even when costs are low, deliveries are fast and convenient, and goods are kept safe and secure, a transportation system or agent creates problems for an organization when it is not reliable. If transportation can't consistently and reliably get goods where they need to be when they need to be, an organization loses the time and place utility that reliable transportation provides.

6. **Flexibility.** For organizations that need to transport a wide range of goods of different sizes, weights, and handling needs, a flexible transportation system is essential. For example, the transportation system of warehouse-style retailers carrying goods from regional distribution centers to individual stores would need to be flexible enough to handle a wide range of goods within one shipment, from dish detergent to televisions to king-size mattresses.

Now that we have discussed the six criteria that are weighed against each other when transportation decision are being made, let's address two important transportation decisions, typically asked and answered in conjunction with one another: *Who will handle the transportation?* and *What mode or modes of transportation will be used?* When an organization has goods to be moved from one location or one terminal to another, it must first decide who will physically move these goods: the organization itself or a *carrier*, a second company that transports goods. An organization typically uses a carrier when it must move goods a great distance and/or using specialized transport modes, such as by rail or ocean cargo ships - because most companies don't own their own rail lines or cargo ships!

A single carrier may use any combination of one or more of the five modes of transportation (road, rail, water, air, and pipeline). Carriers also may own or lease the vehicles and vessels they use. For most carriers, the cost of delivering a container of goods is just about the same no matter how empty or full the container is. Therefore, it is less than ideal to have a situation of *less-than-truckload (LTL)* shipments. A *consolidator* works to combine small shipments to create full container-load or truckload shipments, thus achieving a significant cost savings for the organizations shipping smaller quantities of goods. A *freight forwarder* is a type of consolidator that specializes in combining smaller shipments for subsequent road or rail transportation.

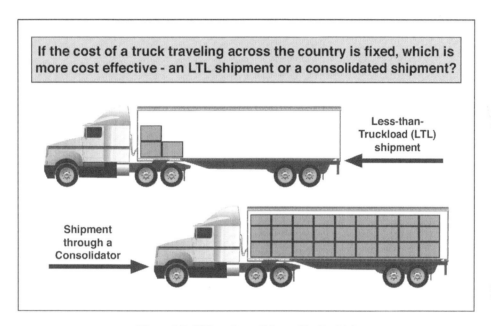

Figure 8.7 - LTL or Consolidator: You Decide!

Transportation involves more than an organization or a carrier simply picking up and moving goods from one location to another. Transportation includes the complex world of transportation management, i.e., planning, directing, and controlling how goods are moved and handled throughout the transportation process. Most raw materials and consumer goods today are not only moved across countries, but also across oceans. To navigate the murky and complex waters of transportation management, companies often turn to *third party logistics service providers*, also known as *3PLPs* or *3PLs*, to provide some or all of the transportation and transportation management services needed. 3PLPs typically bundle a range of these services under one cost structure. Some of the transportation management activities covered by a 3PLP might include: *planning shipments and selecting transport carriers; keeping track of shipments in transit; determining freight costs prior to shipping; checking and paying carriers' freight bills; filing claims with carriers for damaged goods; transportation budget planning and management; transportation administration and human resource management; monitoring and maintaining service quality; conducting carrier rate negotiations; keeping up with local, state, federal, and international transport regulations; planning and handling transport information systems;* and *conducting transport systems analysis.*

When a company is deciding who will transport its goods, it must also decide the mode by which its goods will be moved. In the world of logistics and physical distribution management, a mode of transportation is the physical means across or through which the goods are carried. The five **modes of transportation** are: *road, water, rail, air,* and *pipeline.*

Figure 8.8 - Road Transportation: a truck transporting wind turbine nose cones across the Arizona desert.

At the risk of stating the extremely obvious, a **road** is a surfaced route used by vehicles for moving goods or people. Within most countries around the world, road is, by far, the most commonly used mode of transportation, with approximately 70% of U.S. goods (by weight and by value) traveling by road. The primary advantage offered by road as a mode of transportation is that, within most countries, more locations are accessible by road than any other mode of transportation. In the United States, the National Highway System measures approximately 160,000 miles and vehicles can operate on this extensive road network 24 hours a day, 7 days a week. Road is cost-effective for smaller deliveries and shorter distances and is highly flexible, allowing for last minute changes and adjustments. However, traffic jams, congestion, and adverse weather can all affect road delivery times. Road-related labor costs can be high because the number of drivers or operators required per amount carried is much higher than for other modes of transportation. For example, one truck driver can transport one or two container loads of goods while a crew of five people can transport over 1000 forty-foot containers by way of cargo ship.

Figure 8.9 - Road Transportation Doesn't Always Equal Highways and Trucks:
propane tank deliveries by truck on the cobblestone streets of Valparaiso, Chile (*left*)
and by bicycle on some of the city's narrower and more congested streets (*right*).

Water is a mode of transportation used to transport large quantities of nonperishable and bulk goods both domestically and internationally on ships across waterways. In domestic trade, goods travel by water within and along the United States through the ***inland and intracoastal waterway system***, which serves 38 states and carries one-sixth of the U.S. intercity cargo by volume. In international trade, the majority of goods travel by ocean and enter and leave through ***container ports***, which are facilities that receive and dock cargo ships. They use specialized equipment, including a variety of cranes, to transfer containerized goods to and from the ships. As a mode of transportation, water can move massive quantities of goods and bulky items, is reliable and has very few traffic delays, and can also be less costly because it is far less expensive than air for international trade and there are no costs for using ocean waterways. Water is, however, often the slowest mode of transportation, making it unrealistic for shipping perishable or time-sensitive goods. Long transit times also increase the insurance costs of goods and fog or severe weather can easily cause sailing cancellations.

Figure 8.10 - Water Transportation: the Port of Boston

The transportation mode of ***rail*** is commonly used to transport large, heavy, and bulky items and large quantities for long distances across railroad tracks in railway cars. Rail is used to transport 4% of the total value of all U.S. goods and 15% of all goods by weight. Rail cars can accommodate very large, heavy items and rail is a less expensive mode of transportation for larger volumes over longer distances than road. Rail also offers greater reliability than many other transportation modes because it is less likely to experience traffic delays or adverse weather. Furthermore, most maritime cargo ports are connected to rail networks, making rail a vital

Figure 8.11 - Water Transportation: container ship (*top left*), canal locks (*top right*), and tanker (*bottom*) at the Panama Canal

Figure 8.12 - Rail Transportation (*top left* and *bottom*) and Pipeline Transportation (*top right*)

element of global supply chains. However, rail has geographic and time limitations because they are in a limited number of fixed locations and typically only operate at specific times. There can also be very long transit times due to the labor-intensive nature of boxcar consolidation and it is less than ideal for fragile items and small shipments. An interesting side note: More than 90% of all U.S. freight railroads are privately owned and operated. Most of the track is also owned by the rail companies.

Air is the mode of transportation more commonly used for perishable and time-sensitive goods. It is used to transport only 2% of goods by value within the U.S. and less than 0.04% of goods by weight. It's the fastest mode of transportation available to get goods anywhere where there's an airport, making it suitable for perishable goods and fragile goods that are easily damaged in transit. As a mode of transportation, air is very costly and it allows for less scheduling flexibility. Flights are generally at fixed times and adverse weather can delay flights and cause transportation delays. Furthermore, airplanes are strictly limited in the weights and item dimensions they can carry.

Pipeline is the mode of transportation used for carrying goods from point to point through a steel or plastic pipe. While oil and natural gas are the goods most commonly transported by pipeline, any form of liquid, such as water or sewage, can be carried by pipeline. Although expensive to construct, pipelines yield extremely low transportation cost. Pipeline systems are used to transport 3% of all U.S. goods by value and 5% of all U.S. goods by weight.

When goods are transported, they are not restricted to a single mode of transportation. ***Intermodal transportation*** occurs when different modes of transportation are used to carry goods in the same through shipment. A ***through shipment*** is the entire transportation flow of goods from their point of origin to point of consumption. Intermodal transportation is especially common in global trade. As container ships arrive into U.S. ports, their containers are automatically transferred to rail or motor carriers. Multiple modes of transport are used to transport more than 15% of all U.S. goods by value.

Figure 8.13 - Intermodal Transportation from Water to Road

As companies look to the supply chain as a means of cutting operating costs, competition is heating up between transportation carriers. Two primary forms of this competition are: *intramodal competition*, in which carriers of the same mode of transportation compete, such as one container ship line trying to come in at a lower cost than another container ship line following the same route; and *intermodal competition*, in which carriers of different modes of transportation compete, such as a trucking company trying to cut costs to meet those of a railway following the same route.

PAPERWORK FOR OUTBOUND SHIPMENTS

As previously mentioned, there is paperwork and documentation involved with outbound shipments. This includes the creation of packing lists for each package, carton, or container shipped out from an organization. This *packing list* would include the sender's address, the recipient's address and customer identification codes, and an itemized list of everything included in that parcel's shipment, with item descriptions and item quantities. The customer receiving the package would then check the items received against the packing list to make sure all of the items arrived at their intended destination.

When shipments move from the realm of *domestic* (within one country) to *international* (from one country to another), the world of paperwork and documentation gets far more complicated.n In the world of international trade, documentation is a necessity. Without accurate and timely paperwork, companies would not be permitted to trade outside their own countries. Exporters, importers, shipping companies, freight forwarders, banks, insurance companies, the regulating authorities of the countries both importing and exporting the goods, consular offices, chambers of commerce, and a massive battery of attorneys are all involved in ensuring that global distribution's complex network of documentation is completed.

The amount of documentation required may vary according to the nature of the goods and the regulations of the countries importing and exporting the goods. In addition, some forms of documentation are multi-functional and can be found in multiple categories of trade documentation. While there are thousands of different trade documentation forms that vary from country to country and from company to company, there are a few categories of trade documentation that a warehouse shipping outbound goods might need to consider. These include:

- *Export documents*. Documents required by the export authority of a country are called export documents. When completed and approved, these documents allow goods to leave a country. Export documentation varies according to the country of export and the goods involved. Examples of export documents include: export licenses and permits; export declaration and inspection certificates; Bill of Lading; and Certificate of Origin. A *bill of lading* (also referred to as *BOL* or *B/L*) is a document issued by a carrier, which acknowledges that specific, listed goods have been received as cargo for conveyance to a specific, listed place for delivery to an identified consignee. A *certificate of origin* is a document that certifies the country of origin of a shipment. For example, a NAFTA certificate of origin is used by Canada, Mexico, and the United States to determine if imported goods receive reduced or eliminated duty as specified by the North American Free

Date:	**BILL OF LADING**	Page 1 of _____

SHIP FROM	
Name:	
Address:	
City/State/Zip:	
SID#:	FOB: ☐

Bill of Lading Number:_____

BAR CODE SPACE

SHIP TO	
Name:	Location #:_____
Address:	
City/State/Zip:	
CID#:	FOB: ☐

CARRIER NAME: _____
Trailer number:
Seal number(s):
SCAC:
Pro number:

BAR CODE SPACE

THIRD PARTY FREIGHT CHARGES BILL TO:
Name:
Address:
City/State/Zip:
SPECIAL INSTRUCTIONS:

Freight Charge Terms:
Prepaid _____   Collect _____   3rd Party _____

☐ (check box)   Master Bill of Lading: with attached underlying Bills of Lading

CUSTOMER ORDER INFORMATION				
CUSTOMER ORDER NUMBER	# PKGS	WEIGHT	PALLET/SLIP (Y or N)	ADDITIONAL SHIPPER INFO
GRAND TOTAL				

CARRIER INFORMATION								
HANDLING UNIT		PACKAGE		WEIGHT	H.M. (X)	COMMODITY DESCRIPTION Commodities requiring special or additional care or attention in handling or stowing must be so marked and packaged as to ensure safe transportation with ordinary care.	LTL ONLY	
QTY	TYPE	QTY	TYPE				NMFC #	CLASS
							RECEIVING	
							STAMP SPACE	
						GRAND TOTAL		

Where the rate is dependent on value, shippers are required to state specifically in writing the agreed or declared value of the property as follows:

"The agreed or declared value of the property is specifically stated by the shipper to be not exceeding

_____ per _____.

COD Amount: $_____

Fee Terms: Collect: ☐   Prepaid: ☐
Customer check acceptable: ☐

NOTE Liability Limitation for loss or damage in this shipment may be applicable. See 49 U.S.C. - 14706(c)(1)(A) and (B).

RECEIVED, subject to individually determined rates or contracts that have been agreed upon in writing between the carrier and shipper, if applicable, otherwise to the rates, classifications and rules that have been established by the carrier and are available to the shipper, on request, and to all applicable state and federal regulations.

The carrier shall not make delivery of this shipment without payment of freight and all other lawful charges.

_____ **Shipper Signature**

SHIPPER SIGNATURE / DATE	Trailer Loaded:	Freight Counted:	**CARRIER SIGNATURE / PICKUP DATE**
This is to certify that the above named materials are properly classified, packaged, marked and labeled, and are in proper condition for transportation according to the applicable regulations of the DOT.	☐ By Shipper ☐ By Driver	☐ By Shipper ☐ By Driver/pallets said to contain ☐ By Driver/Pieces	Carrier acknowledges receipt of packages and required placards. Carrier certifies emergency response information was made available and/or carrier has the DOT emergency response guidebook or equivalent documentation in the vehicle.

Figure 8.14 - Bill of Lading Form

Trade Agreement.

- *Carrier documents.* Carrier documents are those documents issued and used by a carrier or transportation provider such as a barge or shipping line, a railroad, an airline, an international trucking company, a freight forwarder, or a 3PLP. Examples of carrier documents include: bill of lading and insurance and inspection certificates.

- *Goods-specific documents.* Finally, goods-specific documents are those documents required for import and/or export based on special requirements for the nature of the items being trades. Goods-specific documents are typically required for international trade of goods including: arms and ammunition, radioactive materials, animals, and food products.

In exploring the world of international trade documentation, we must also discuss **INCOTERMS** (**International Commercial Terms**), the standardized international trade terms that describe the obligations of both the purchasers and the sellers under the contract of sale. Specifically, INCOTERMS are a set of eleven terms created and published by the International Chamber of Commerce (ICC) that clearly outline and allocate the costs, risk, customs, and insurance responsibilities of each the purchaser and the seller in the international transaction. The most

INCOTERM	Description
EXW or Ex Works	The exporter must make the goods available for collection from his premises by the importer or the importer's agent. The goods are generally packed ready for shipment.
FCA or Free Carrier	The exporter will transport the goods to an Inland Clearance Depot (ICD), where they will be consolidated into a larger consignment ready for shipment by an intermodal carrier.
FAS or Free Alongside Ship (waterway transport only)	The exporter delivers the goods alongside the ship that will carry the goods overseas. This is where the responsibility of the exporter ends. The Purchaser bears all costs and risks from this point on.
FOB or Free on Board (waterway transport only)	The goods are delivered by the exporter to the port of export, where they then become the responsibility of the importer as soon as they are loaded over the ship' side rail. The Purchaser bears the loss if the goods should fall and become damaged just after being loaded onto the ship.
CFR or Cost and Freight (waterway transport only)	The seller must pay the costs and freight as far as the port of destination, but the risk passes to the Purchaser as the goods cross the ship's rail in the port of shipment.
CIF or Cost, Insurance and Freight (waterway transport only)	The seller is in the same position as in CFR but must also provide marine insurance during the carriage. The risk passes to the Purchaser as the goods cross the ship's rails, but the insurance policy covers the Purchaser's risk.
CPT or Carriage Paid to	The seller pays the freight and the risk passes to the Purchaser once the goods are delivered to the first carrier, regardless of the type of transportation used.
CIP or Carriage and Insurance Paid to	The terms are the same as in CPT, but the seller also has to insure the goods for all modes of transportation to the Purchaser's destination. The risk transfers to the Purchaser when the goods are given into the custody of the first carrier, after which point the risk is covered by the insurance policy.
DAT or Delivered at Terminal	The seller pays for delivery to the terminal, not including import clearance costs, and also assumes all risk until the goods are unloaded at the terminal.
DAP or Delivered at Place	The seller pays for delivery to the named place or destination, not including import clearance costs, and also assumes all risk until the goods are ready to be unloaded by the buyer.
DDP or Delivered Duty Paid	This represents a maximum commitment from the seller and a minimum one from the Purchaser. The seller delivers to the Purchaser after paying the import duty to the country of destination.

Figure 8.15 - INCOTERMS

recent update to these terms was in 2010. Each of all of the eleven INCOTERMS is referred to by a three-letter abbreviation and one of these eleven would be used in international trade transactions. More information about INCOTERMS and descriptions of each of the eleven three-letter abbreviations can be found atvwww.iccwbo.org or www.export.gov.

THE FINAL STAGES OF OUTBOUND SHIPMENTS

After all of the paperwork for the outbound shipment has been prepared, it is now time to load the shipment onto an outbound vehicle! It may seem simple - taking goods from a staging area and placing them onto a truck or into a rail car. However, the person or company accepting responsibility for the goods while in transit want to make sure that the goods arrive safely and in good working order. As we mentioned previously, the party responsible for the goods might be the company selling the goods, a carrier or third party transportation provide, or the customer itself. Regardless of who is handling the transportation and accepts responsibility for the goods, there are a series of steps that take place to ensure that goods are loaded onto the outbound vehicle in a manner that will increase their likelihood of safe arrival.

First, the load is checked before it is moved from the staging area to ensure that there is no preexisting damage to any of the items. Not only are the goods checked, but the packaging is checked, too. For example, pallets are inspected to make sure they are in good working order and stretch wrap or strapping is checked to make sure it will secure the goods and keep them from falling off the pallet. Next, the trailer, container, or other vehicle into which the goods will be loaded is inspected. If there is anything that might lead to product damage during shipment, such as waterlogged surfaces or holes in the roof, it is addressed and repaired before any goods are loaded.

Assuming that everything has checked out, it's now time to load the goods! As goods are loaded, weight plays a key factor. Heaviest items and unit loads are stacked on the bottom of the container or trailer, with lighter or equal-weight unit loads placed on top. When appropriate, until loads are restrained in the truck or container with additional strapping materials. Weight of all unit loads are also tallied to make sure that the trailer weight does not exceed U.S. Highway limits for goods traveling by road. After a trailer or container has been loaded, it is secured with airbags or other restraining materials to ensure that goods do not shift in transit. The container or trailer is then sealed and ready to ship! As it leaves the facility, the customer is alerted that the shipment is being sent, often though an *advance shipment notice (ASN)*.

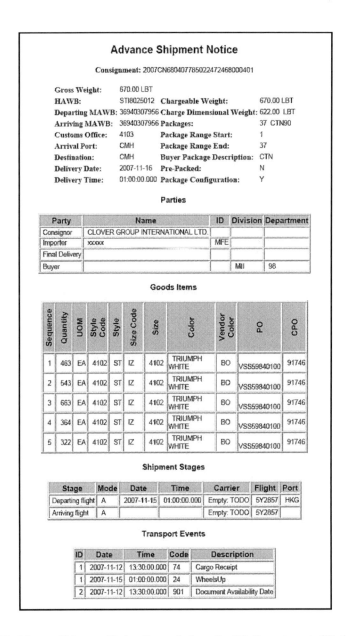

Advance Shipment Notice

Consignment: 2007CN680407785022472468000401

Gross Weight:	670.00 LBT		
HAWB:	STI8025012	Chargeable Weight:	670.00 LBT
Departing MAWB:	36940307956	Charge Dimensional Weight:	622.00 LBT
Arriving MAWB:	36940307956	Packages:	37 CTN90
Customs Office:	4103	Package Range Start:	1
Arrival Port:	CMH	Package Range End:	37
Destination:	CMH	Buyer Package Description:	CTN
Delivery Date:	2007-11-16	Pre-Packed:	N
Delivery Time:	01:00:00.000	Package Configuration:	Y

Parties

Party	Name	ID	Division	Department
Consignor	CLOVER GROUP INTERNATIONAL LTD.			
Importer	xxxxx	MFE		
Final Delivery				
Buyer			MII	98

Goods Items

Sequence	Quantity	UOM	Style Code	Style	Size Code	Size	Color	Vendor Color	PO	CPO
1	463	EA	4102	ST	IZ	4102	TRIUMPH WHITE	BO	VSS59840100	91746
2	543	EA	4102	ST	IZ	4102	TRIUMPH WHITE	BO	VSS59840100	91746
3	663	EA	4102	ST	IZ	4102	TRIUMPH WHITE	BO	VSS59840100	91746
4	364	EA	4102	ST	IZ	4102	TRIUMPH WHITE	BO	VSS59840100	91746
5	322	EA	4102	ST	IZ	4102	TRIUMPH WHITE	BO	VSS59840100	91746

Shipment Stages

Stage	Mode	Date	Time	Carrier	Flight	Port
Departing flight	A	2007-11-15	01:00:00.000	Empty: TODO	5Y2857	HKG
Arriving flight	A			Empty: TODO	5Y2857	

Transport Events

ID	Date	Time	Code	Description
1	2007-11-12	13:30:00.000	74	Cargo Receipt
1	2007-11-15	01:00:00.000	24	WheelsUp
2	2007-11-12	13:30:00.000	901	Document Availability Date

Figure 8.16 - Advance Shipment Notice: Example from the U.S. Department of Defense Columbus Electronic Freight Management Evaluation Final Report, www.ntl.bts.gov.

CHAPTER 8 REVIEW QUESTIONS

1. What happens in the staging area of a warehouse?

2. What is the difference between product kitting and product postponement? In what situations might a company use each?

3. What are some examples of materials that are used for packaging? What materials have you used for packaging when mailing items?

4. Why is packaging important for keeping items safe and secure in transit?

5. What kinds of information is contained in a barcode label or RFID tag? How can this information be read?

6. Why is it important for a company's mode of transportation to be flexible? How might a company benefit from using 3PLPs to achieve this desired flexibility?

7. What mode of transportation do most U.S. goods use to get to their customer? After looking around your house, what mode of transportation do you think most of the goods in it used to get to you? List five items and their probable mode of transportation.

8. Pipelines have extremely low transportation costs. Why aren't most goods transported by pipeline?

9. What is the difference between intramodal and intermodal competition in transportation?

10. What role does weight play when loading goods as they leave the warehouse? What might happen if warehouse workers don't pay attention to product and package weight?

CHAPTER 8 CASE STUDY

The Challenge of Bundling and a Possible 3PL Solution

In order to increase sales, introduce new products, or enhance customer service, manufacturers may decide to sell multiple products together as one product. This practice is known as **bundling** or **product kitting**. Companies often engage in bundling based on customer specifications, such as when you order a computer online and decide to include a specific upgraded hard drive or monitor with it or when you place an order for a new car to include an upgraded sound system or navigational system.

A company may also decide to bundle its own products together in large quantities, which is often done by cosmetics and fragrance companies to increase sales or expose consumers to new products. For example, U.S.-born cosmetics manufacturer Philosophy bundles its products together in both regular and promotional gift kits, often with fun and celebratory themes, such as "Birthday Girl," "I Think You are Wonderful," and "Here Comes the Bride."

Finally, a company may decide to bundle its products together with products from another company. Many companies work together to produce bundled kits, including video game console companies who parter with video game companies to produce promotional bundles. In 2015, an especially popular bundle was the Batman: Arkham Knight PlayStation® 4 Bundle, in which Sony sold its PlayStation game console together with a hugely popular video game produced by Warner Brothers Interactive Entertainment. In this case, two bundles were offered: a standard one, with the standard game and game console, and a limited edition one, which included a customer Batman faceplate on the game console and quickly sold out within weeks.

When a company's marketing department decides to offer a bundled package to increase sales, introduce new products, or enhance customer service, the company's warehouse must be ready to accomplish this task. For these bundles, products will have to be packaged differently, while the company will likely be continuing to package the products in their standard single formation, too. For a warehouse new to bundling, this may be a daunting challenge. Additional space or equipment may be needed to create these newly bundled product kits. Additional trained labor may also be needed to work just during periods of product bundle promotions, especially before the holidays when multiple

products are bundled in gift packages to entice consumers. There is also the IT challenge of creating a new SKU, the newly bundled product, and entering it into all of the company's information technology systems and inventory location software. When companies do not have the time, space, or labor to complete product bundling on their own in the warehouse, they may turn to a third party logistics service provider, also known as 3PLP or 3PL, to complete some or all of the tasks in the product bundling process.

GENCO Distribution System, Inc. is a third party logistics service provider headquartered in Pittsburgh, Pennsylvania that offers companies a wide range of inventory management and other supply chain solutions to customers at its 140 value-added warehouse locations or on the customer's site. The company became a subsidiary of FedEx in December 2014 and is now one of the largest third-party service providers in North America. One of the many categories of service that GENCO offers is Warehouse Kitting and Assembly Services, in which it helps companies with some or all of their product bundling tasks. GENCO can help a company create creative promotional packaging and displays for its product bundles, procure the equipment and materials needed to create the new bundles, assemble the bundles at the company's warehouse or at a GENCO facility, handle inventory management, install RFID chips, and provide temporary labor when needed for seasonal or promotional bundles.

INSTRUCTIONS:

Have you ever purchased any products that were bundled? If so, what were the products and were they manufactured by the same company? If not, visit your local clothing retailer or grocery store and find a product bundle and answer the same question: what are the products and are they manufactured by the same company?

Do you think these products were bundled by their manufacturer's warehouse or by a 3PLP, such as GENCO? Please explain your answer.

Chapter 9

Safety and Security in Warehouse and Inventory Management

On a whim, you've just purchased a new 54" flat screen television. You get it into your car and bring it home. You have no room for it in your living room until you rearrange your furniture, which may take a day or two. What do you do with your expensive new purchase, which you have now affectionately termed your new baby? Do you leave it in your front yard for a night or two, or perhaps put it on your front porch? Or, do you store it in another room of your house until your living room is ready? Unless you have more money than good sense, you almost certainly chose the last alternative.

Although your choice was an obvious one, exactly why would you prefer to leave a new, expensive item somewhere inside your home instead of outside? In two words: *safety* and *security*. You want your new television to be *secure from theft* (perhaps your less-than-law-abiding next door neighbor has always wanted a flat screen television) and *safe from harm and the elements* (perhaps a lightning storm is heading your way). While your purchase was expensive and may have cost you at least a month or two's salary, warehouse and inventory managers are often responsible for hundreds of thousands and even millions of dollars worth of inventory. Organizations entrust these managers with the very serious duty of keeping this inventory, the lifeblood of every production-based organization, secure and safe. Warehouse managers are responsible for keeping inventory secure from theft and fraud and safe from disasters and deterioration. They are also responsible for ensuring that all people inside the warehouse building or external inventory yard remain safe from harm. Similarly, warehouse employees are also responsible for keeping goods safe and secure. More importantly, they are responsible for keeping each other safe. Most warehouses now instill a culture of safety among all their workers, with safety a core part of job descriptions and training and with morning meetings regularly including a "Safety Minute" in which a volunteer shares a safety story or example for the day.

SAFETY: KEEPING PEOPLE AND INVENTORY SAFE

The warehouse manager is charged with keeping everything in the warehouse safe – both inventory and people. In this section, we explore how warehouse managers keep their people and inventory safe. If you ask almost any warehouse professional what their highest priority is every day on the job, they are likely to say *safety*. Many organizations, from oil companies to Disney World, have *safety* as their number one core value and have instilled a series of metrics to measure how well they are keeping people and inventory safe.

Within all warehouses, inventory faces two primary threats to its safety: *fire* and *deterioration*. A variety of disasters may strike a warehouse at any time. Many of these are location-specific and local warehouse managers know how to prepare for them. For example, warehouse managers in coastal Florida design their warehouse windows and layout to best combat the effects of hurricanes. Their counterparts in California and Alaska instead make sure that all hot water and dangerous chemical tanks are strapped down in case of earthquake. Depending upon where the warehouse is located, warehouse managers know that they must prepare for any of a variety of regional disasters, including droughts, blizzards, floods, raging forest fires, and tornados.

Figure 9.1 - Warehouse Fires: the most wide-reaching and pervasive of disastrous occurrences

All warehouse managers, regardless of location, must prepare themselves, their warehouses, and their staff for the most wide-reaching and pervasive disastrous occurrence of all: *fire*! In their 2013 report, *Structure Fires in U.S. Warehouses*, the National Fire Protection Association (NFPA) revealed that from 2007-2011, there was an annual average of 1,270 fires in warehouse properties and that every year, fires caused $188 million in direct property damage, 23 civilian injuries, and four civilian fatalities. Warehouse fires are extremely disruptive to an organization, not only because of financial loss and subsequent increased insurance premiums, but also because of the delivery delays fires cause, which may result in the loss of long-standing customers.

In order to decrease the risk of fire in warehouse installations, warehouse managers may take a variety of precautionary steps, including:

- **No Smoking!** One of the major causes of both commercial and domestic fires is cigarettes and matches that are carelessly discarded. Having a warehouse-wide *No Smoking Policy* and placing large, clear *No Smoking* signs in multiple areas throughout the warehouse is perhaps the easiest and most effective means of reducing the risk of cigarette-related fires.

- **Installing and Maintaining Firefighting Equipment.** Warehouse managers reduce the risk of fire in warehouse installation by placing various types of firefighting equipment throughout and inspecting and maintaining them on a regular basis. Some standard fire fighting equipment, which can be found in warehouse installations include:

    - **Fire Extinguishers.** A variety of gas-operated foam dischargers (i.e., fire extinguishers) have been developed to handle different types of fires, such as various chemical or hazardous material fires. Therefore, warehouse managers must take great care to understand the intended application of each fire extinguisher and place it within the warehouse installation according to this application.

    - **Hose Reels.** Hose reels are used for dealing with larger conflagrations and are typically linked to large reserve tanks or the main water supply.

    - **Sprinkler Systems.** When a major fire occurs, sprinkler systems are designed to saturate a given area with water or chemical foam. These sprinkler systems are controlled by a thermostat and smoke sensor so that small amounts of smoke alone (such as when your coworkers burn popcorn in the canteen microwave) will not set off the sprinklers.

    - **Fire Blankets.** Fire blankets are made of fireproof fabric and are used to smother very small fires or to wrap around a victim whose clothes have caught fire.

    - **Fire Buckets.** Fire buckets are another standard item of firefighting equipment. They are typically filled with sand and used to extinguish very small fires.

- **Installing and Monitoring Alarm Systems.** Alarm systems are a critical means of identifying fires and putting them out before they grow and spread. Good alarm systems link warehouse installations or even all parts of the organization, with a central alarm monitoring board in the security office. Within each warehouse installation, warehouse managers must ensure that there is a working alarm system for fire outbreaks. Warehouse staff must regularly check the alarm system to ensure that there are no obstructions covering the alarm unit.

- **Holding Regular Fire Drills.** Warehouse managers must ensure that regular, well-organized drills are held so that staff members are prepared to safeguard both inventory and people in case of fire. Clear fire instructions must be placed on the notice board and other central locations within the warehouse installations. These instructions must be precise and list the critical actions to be taken in case of fire, especially if any of the materials stored are highly flammable or dangerous.

- **Conducting Regular Inspections.** Warehouse managers must ensure that local fire department officials conduct regular inspections of warehouse installations. Such inspections, especially when conducted more often or in greater depth than legally required, help to ensure a safe and efficient fire safety system.

- **Marking All Exits.** Warehouse managers must ensure that all fire doors and emergency exits are clearly marked at all times and that passages and gangways are kept clear.

- **Segregating High Risk Materials.** Fire risks can also be decreased when high-risk materials, such as oil, gas, chemicals, explosives, etc., are stored in a separate, specially designed warehouse. While it may be somewhat more expensive to run a separate high-risk materials warehouse, there is actually a cost benefit to be offered because a smaller quantity of expensive, specialized high-risk materials firefighting equipment can be concentrated in this one area, rather than spreading greater quantities across all warehouse installations. Such high-risk material warehouses are also usually placed a set distance from the other warehouse installations. As a result, fires occurring in the main warehouse do not reach the high-risk inventory, thus staving off larger, more serious fires. Conversely, large fires occurring in the high-risk warehouse can be allowed to burn themselves out without posing a risk to the main warehouse or other installations.

Figure 9.2 - Segregating High Risk Materials. This port-side warehouse in southeast Alaska keeps its propane tanks and other flammable materials outside in a fenced and locked area away from the warehouse.

Those who work in warehousing and inventory management must also know about the ***National Fire Protection Association (NFPA) Chemical Hazard Label***, which uses a rating system for the health, flammability, and reactivity hazards of chemicals. Although this system was originally developed for emergency personnel and first responders, it is now used an information and warning system for anyone who must handle or work near potentially hazardous materials. The NFPA Chemical Hazard Label is a diamond-shaped placard that is placed on a container, such as a tank or drum, filled with a hazardous chemical. This diamond-shaped label has four diamonds of different colors inside it. Each colored inner diamond has a number or letter written in it which reveals information about the hazard level of the chemical founded inside the container. These inner diamonds and the information they contain are:

- **Blue Diamond - Health Information:**

    - *4 = Danger. May be fatal on short exposure. Specialized protective equipment required.*

    - *3 = Warning. Corrosive or toxic. Avoid skin contact or inhalation.*

    - *2 = Warning. May be harmful if inhaled or absorbed.*

    - *1 = Caution. May be irritating.*

    - *0 = No unusual hazard.*

- **Red Diamond - Flammability Information**

    - *4 = Danger. Flammable gas or extremely flammable liquid.*

    - *3 = Warning. Flammable liquid flash point below 100 degrees F.*

    - *2 = Caution. Combustible liquid flash point of 100 to 200 degrees F.*

    - *1 = Combustible if heated.*

    - *0 = Not combustible.*

- **Yellow Diamond - Reactivity Information**

    - *4 = Danger. Explosive material at room temperature.*

    - *3 = Danger. May be explosive if shocked, heated under confinement, or mixed with water.*

    - *2 = Warning. Unstable or may react violently if mixed with water.*

    - *1 = Caution. May react if heated or mixed with water but not violently.*

    - *0 = Stable. Not reactive when mixed with water.*

- **White Diamond - Special Notice Information**

    - *W = Water Reactive*

    - *OX = Oxidizing Agent*

In addition to the NFPA Chemical Hazard Label, there are also additional hazardous materials placards that warehouse professionals must know about. These include the ***U.S. Department of Transportation (DOT) Placard***, which provides hazardous cargo information to transportation workers and first responders, and the ***U.S. Department of Labor Occupational Safety and***

Health Administration (OSHA) HazCom 2012 placard, which provides information about the hazards chemicals in containers may pose to workers under normal working conditions.

Figure 9.3 - Find the DOT Placard! Can you find the DOT placards about the hazardous nature of the cargo in these tanker trucks (*pictured above and below*) outside the Cruzan Rum Distillery in the U.S. Virgin Islands? Do you notice any other safety placards?

Like fire, **deterioration** also poses a threat to inventory safety. All items in an inventory will deteriorate eventually, but ineffective storage and improper handling can cause inventory to deteriorate over a much shorter span of time. Such premature inventory deterioration can have disastrous results. First, poor storage of vital inventory can lead to substantial lost output and subsequent increased operating costs. In addition, the administrative costs of ordering are increasing rapidly. Every time inventory deteriorates, it must be ordered again, causing ordering costs to double - or even triple, if administrative costs have increased dramatically. Many factors can contribute to inventory deterioration, including:

- **faulty storage areas**, which allow for damp conditions due to broken windows, leaking roofs, and badly fitting doors;

- **lack of attention to storage instructions**, which are usually provided by the suppliers in the packaging or delivery documents;

- **incorrect storage conditions**, especially concerning temperature and humidity;

- **faulty or careless materials handling**, which leads to damage, breakage, or unintentionally opening airtight seals;

- **proximity-related materials contamination**, which is caused by storing different types of materials in close proximity and thus contaminating at least one of the materials (for example, most food items become contaminated when stored alongside oil drums); and

- **improper or nonexistent inventory rotation**, which allows newer inventory to be used while older inventory remains held and continues to naturally deteriorate.

Figure 9.4 - Deterioration (*left*) and Incorrect Storage Conditions (*right*)

When precautionary steps are taken, however, premature inventory deterioration can be avoided. The warehouse manager plays a pivotal role in preventing costly deterioration by following a series of steps, including:

- *Checking storage installation conditions.* The warehouse manager and his/her team can make regular inspections of all storage areas to ensure that they are clean and damp-free. Also, all doors, windows, and ventilators can be checked for leakage.

- *Regulating warehouse temperature and humidity.* When the temperature and humidity of a warehouse are carefully controlled, premature deterioration is avoided. To conserve effort and resources, warehouse managers often store inventory requiring similar temperature and humidity conditions together.

- *Adhering strictly to suppliers' instructions.* By ensuing that suppliers' instructions are followed, the warehouse manager extends the life of the inventory.

- *Handling materials properly.* Proper materials handling is an essential element of warehouse management. It reduces damage and breakage, thus preventing deterioration. To ensure that materials are handled properly, for example, warehouse managers may simply ensure that suppliers' instructions are followed (*Fragile — Handle with Care*), may send staff to specialized materials handling training, or may personally supervise the issue and loading of dangerous chemicals.

- *Hands-On Supervising.* By ensuring that all materials and storage handling is supervised by trained and experienced staff, warehouse managers can reduce the risk of bad storage and faulty handling.

Warehouse managers would all agree that even more important than keeping inventory safe is keeping *people* safe. According to the Department of Labor Bureau of Labor Statistics, the warehousing and storage industry accounted for 17 fatal occupational injuries in 2013. In this same year, there were many non-fatal work-related injuries and illnesses, translating to an incident rate of a startling 5.2 for every 100 full-time warehouse and storage workers! Furthermore, the transportation and warehousing industry had the highest industry-based incidence rate for cases that involved employees either having to take 4 or more days of leave and/or transferring occupations as a result of a work-related injury or illness. Thus, the warehouse manager's ability to keep warehouse staff safe from harm has moral, legal, and economic implications. It is also important to note the especially challenging safety task of the manager of a warehouse club store, like Costco or Sam's Club. In 2013, the warehouse club and retail super-center industry accounted for 8 fatal occupational injuries, but not included in those statistics are all the injuries for warehouse club *customers*. Warehouses can be dangerous places, with forklift trucks zipping around and heavy objects stored on high shelves with one small misplacement of goods causing potentially fatal accidents. In the 1990s, there was a series of preventable, location-related fatalities among warehouse club customers, which led to stricter OSHA regulations and an eventual reduction in fatalities.

Warehouse occupational injuries can be caused by a variety of accidents, including: *incorrect manual handling*, which can cause strain, muscle damage, and long periods of injury and recuperation; *faulty equipment*, which suddenly breaks down at a critical and dangerous moment;

poor storage conditions, such as weak or uneven floors and unstable racks, shelves, bins, and fittings; *overloaded or misused storage and handling equipment*, especially those used against the manufacturer's outlined specifications; and *lack of supervision* within the warehouse, which results in untidiness, carelessness, and other poor warehouse practices. In order to avoid the injury-causing accidents, the warehouse manager must create, issue, and ensure adherence to a warehouse *safety policy*, a company-wide policy document, which clearly outlines responsibilities and policies related to safety issues. An example of a warehouse safety policy is shown below.

STATEMENT OF XYZ, INC. WAREHOUSE SAFETY POLICY

(a) The Policies contained within the Corporate and Departmental Statements of Safety Policy and those matters referred to herein will be implemented to provide the means for all warehouse employees to work in a safe environment. The organization and arrangements for the time being in force for the implementation of the policy will be described in this statement.

(b) The warehouse manager has overall responsibility for ensuring that there are safe conditions of work within the warehouse; that sufficient information, instruction, training, and supervision is available to enable hazards to be avoided; and that each staff member may contribute to his/her own safety and health at work. They will take all reasonable steps to meet those responsibilities as set out in the employee's terms of reference and will issue codes of safe practice, which must be adhered to at all times.

(c) On a routine basis, the responsibility is assigned to the Warehouse Supervisor as set out in his/her terms of reference. The Warehouse Supervisor will make periodic visits to the various warehouse buildings and sectors within his/her control and will ensure that particular attention is paid to the provision and maintenance of the following:

     i. machinery, plant, equipment, and systems of work that are safe and without risk to health

     ii. safe and healthy arrangement for the handling and use of materials

     iii. adequate employee facilities

     iv. a clean and tidy workplace

(d) It is the duty of the warehouse manager to highlight hazards to safety and to compile lists of known hazards together with details of preventative and (when appropriate) emergency action to be taken. All employees must report immediately any accidents or unsafe/hazardous working conditions to their supervisor.

Figure 9.5 - Example of a Warehouse Safety Policy

After a company-wide warehouse security policy is issued, the warehouse manager must then also draft and issue codes of safe practice, or *safety codes*, which provide detailed guidance on safe practices and procedures for all those working in or entering the warehouse. The warehouse manager should first begin with the OSHA standards and then draft additional safety codes specific to the individual warehouse, industry, and inventory. *OSHA* is the *Occupational Safety and Health Administration*, which is part of the U.S. Department of Labor. Its role is to set and enforce standards, provide education and training, establish partnerships, and encourage continual improvement in workplace safety, all to ensure the safety and health of the U.S.

workforce. For any product that could be potentially harmful to people or the environment, OSHA requires a *Material Safety Data Sheet (MSDS)*, a document that provides details about the properties of the product, including its hazardous ingredients, fire and explosive information, reactivity data, health information, safe handling instructions, and first aid measures.

When OSHA classifies a material as hazardous, the material must have a MSDS that is often attached to the packing list and bill of lading. OSHA will also require that *HazMat* markings must also be on the container holding the material, such as on the tanker or trailer. *HazMat* is an abbreviated term for hazardous material, which can be any material in solid, liquid, or gaseous form, and also poses potential harm to people, property, other living organisms, or the environment. Materials classified as HazMat may be poisonous, flammable, explosive, or reactive and the HazMat marking required by OSHA will provide information on the nature of the danger the material poses.

Similar to the ways in which OSHA regulates and provides information about hazardous materials to keep people safe in the workplace, the U.S. Department of Transportation (DOT) has developed special guidelines and classification and labeling systems for hazardous materials to keep people, inventory, other living things, and the environment safe and free from hazardous when hazardous goods are in transit. The Pipeline and Hazardous Materials Safety Administration of the U.S. DOT has worked together with Transport Canada, the Secretariat of Transport and Communications of Mexico, and CIQUIME (a similar government agency in Argentina) to develop the *Emergency Response Guidebook (ERG)*, which is a guidebook for first responders to understand, interpret, and respond to hazardous materials and their corresponding information during transportation incidents. The ERG contains information about how to read the various hazardous materials placards in North America and how to respond to the dangers they pose. Free digital copies of this highly useful 300+ page guidebook are available on the Pipeline and Hazardous Materials Safety Administration website at http://www.phmsa.dot.gov/hazmat/library/erg.

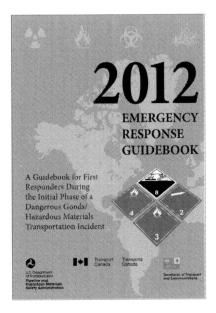 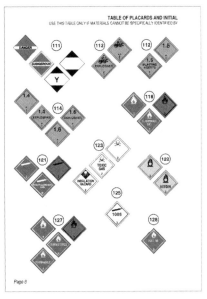

Figure 9.6 - Cover (*left*) and Sample Page (*right*) from the *Emergency Response Guidebook*

SECURITY OF INVENTORY AND PEOPLE

For a production-based company, inventory represents a major portion of its capital (i.e., its money). Any inventory a company loses due to theft or fraud will have to be replaced, which will increase the company's costs and reduce its profits. ***Inventory shrinkage*** is inventory loss resulting from internal and external theft, fraud, and administrative errors. In 2011, U.S. retailers' losses from inventory shrinkage totaled $44.25 billion - yes, BILLION! Employee theft alone accounted for 40.9% of this loss and shoplifting accounted for an additional 33.1%.

Figure 9.7 - Security Service Professionals Provide an Invaluable First Line of Defense Against Inventory Loss

When inventory shrinkage from theft and other factors occurs, not only does a company lose the monetary face value of the stolen or lost products, but also its operating efficiency dramatically decreases. Inventory records become meaningless for inventory control if inventory is lost and not recorded. In addition, production planning relies on inventory being available against a predetermined plan. If inventory is not secure, these plans will need to be constantly reformulated, resulting in lost output and decreased operational efficiency. Thus, inventory security is not only important but also extremely vital to the success of any organization.

Organizations typically rely on two groups of people for keeping their inventory secure: *security service professionals* and *warehouse management and staff*. For security service professionals, an organization may rely on an outside security service company or on members of its own Security department. Either way, these security service professionals are charged with protecting company inventory from theft, fraud, and other losses. They are trained to cope with a variety of difficult situations and can provide coverage up to 24 hours per day. Although they can be expensive to maintain, these security service professionals provide an invaluable first line of defense from the outside world against inventory loss. The degree to which an organization uses security service professionals and corresponding security equipment (alarm systems, video surveillance cameras, etc.) for inventory security will depend upon the value of the inventory being protected, the location of the warehouse, and the organization's goals and finances.

In every warehouse, the manager and staff are ultimately responsible for the warehouse's inventory. Thus, most organizations also rely on these warehouse managers and staff for a large portion of their inventory security needs. Not only do they have specialized knowledge of the warehouse and its inventory, but it is also in their best interest to keep goods secure and the organization profitable, especially when companies offer profit sharing or special loss- prevention incentives. Although security service professionals are trained in a variety of security techniques, warehouse managers and staff play an even more critical role in inventory security because they work closely with the inventory every day and may be the first to recognize when inventory is missing or in jeopardy. Furthermore, warehouse managers and their staffs offer the first line of security against employee theft. A variety of studies have shown that anywhere from 30 to 45% of inventory shrinkage is caused by employee theft and that 30% of U.S. business failures is linked to such internal theft.

Warehouse managers are directly responsible for inventory and warehouse security in all of the areas in which goods are received, stored, picked, and issued. Thus, they are responsible for: *the warehouse security policy*; *warehouse keys and alarm codes*; *the security of warehouse installations*; and *inventory marking*.

In most organizations, the warehouse manager plays a decisive role in setting and enforcing a warehouse security policy. This policy typically includes provisions for: appointing a senior manager with overall responsibility for security; allocating a reasonable budget to cover security costs; consistently enforcing stated company policies for theft; and allowing for regular discussions about warehouse security at the organization's managerial level.

The warehouse manager is also responsible for all of the keys, locks, and alarm codes used within the warehouse area. As with the security policy, the warehouse manager would be responsible for setting and enforcing rules regarding these keys, locks, and alarm codes. For example, a set of rules regarding warehouse keys might be:

RULES FOR WAREHOUSE KEYS AT THE XYZ, INC. WAREHOUSE

a.   All keys must be numbered so that the correct key can be matched to the correct lock quickly and efficiently.

b.   All keys must be registered in the central security log by the Security department.

c.   Members of warehouse staff are responsible for the keys corresponding to their area of the warehouse and will be held accountable for any losses in their area.

d.   Keys taken from the central key bank must be signed out only to those taking immediate possession of them. They must similarly be signed back in when they are returned.

e.   The number of duplicated keys made must be kept to no more than 2 for each master key to ensure adequate inventory control. This rule may be modified in case of emergency or urgent operational needs but only with the written approval of a senior departmental manager.

Figure 9.8 - Example of a Set of Rules for Warehouse Keys

The warehouse manager is also responsible for ensuring that all warehouse-related installations are secure at all times, whether or not they are operational. These installations include:

- **Warehouse buildings.** Warehouse managers, their staff, and corresponding security staff must ensure that all doors, windows, skylights, entrance ways, shutters, and other possible means of entry are secure to prevent unauthorized entry into the warehouse building. This focus on curbing unauthorized entry should apply not only to unwelcome people, but also to unwelcome pests, such as rats, mice, birds, and foxes, all of which can quickly cause a great deal of damage to inventory.

- **Warehouse offices.** Warehouse managers, their staff, and corresponding security staff must also ensure that all cabinets, filing systems, desks, and computers are locked and that no unattended and unsecured valuables are visible, which is often an open invitation for unauthorized entry and theft.

- **External inventory yards.** Warehouse and inventory yard managers, their staff, and corresponding security staff must also secure the entirety of the external inventory yard by regularly inspecting fencing and checking for complete coverage. Any portion of fencing damaged by foul play, natural events, or other occurrences must be repaired immediately. In addition, all external inventory yard gates and locks must be regularly inspected for security.

- **Marshaling areas.** While typically part of a warehouse building or external inventory yard, marshaling areas are worthy of a separate mention because they face the greatest security risk. *Marshaling areas* are those sections of a warehouse building or external inventory yard reserved for consolidation, packing, marking, merchandise sorting, inspection, and storage prior to shipment. A marshaling area is often a very difficult area to secure because many people from a variety of departments from both within and outside of the organization have access to the area while inventory within this area must be readily mobile. Some warehouse managers combat this problem of free access by multiple parties to mobile inventory by using secure mobile devices, such as locking pallet cages — metal cages with a locking entrance affixed to pallets.

- **Entrances.** Like marshaling areas, entrances to warehouse-related installations are also part of warehouse buildings or external inventory yards which merit special mention because of the security concerns they pose. As mentioned in the warehouse buildings bullet above, warehouse managers, their staff, and corresponding security staff must ensure that unauthorized personnel do not pass through the entrance to warehouse- related installations. Entry is restricted to prevent theft within the installation and to prevent personal injury occurring to those unfamiliar with the installation. (Imagine someone wandering in to a warehouse without authorization and without a hardhat walking near a forklift lifting heavy palletized material. The material was improperly stocked by the previous evening. The forklift has a difficult time securing the material and the pallets come crashing to the ground, perhaps near or even on the unauthorized entrant!) To combat such unauthorized entry, many warehouse buildings have entrance counters to deter easy entry. Similarly, both warehouse buildings and external inventory yards often use pass card systems, in which cards are either electronically or manually read, to restrict entry to cardholders only.

Figure 9.9 - Electronically Secured Entrance. Entrance to this port-side container and warehouse facility in Reykjavik, Iceland is accessed via electronic pass card.

Finally, in addition to security policies, keys and codes, and installation security, warehouse managers are also responsible for ensuring that materials held by the warehouse installation are clearly marked to identify their ownership and origin. When high cost inventory is involved, such *inventory marking* is a critical practice for two primary reasons. First, inventory marking discourages theft. Marked inventory cannot be easily sold or used outside of the organization, making it a less desirable target for theft. Second, inventory marking increases the likelihood of return of stolen inventory. If marked inventory is stolen and subsequently recovered by the police, its rightful owners can be readily identified. Types of inventory marking include:

- *Color marking.* The color used for marking is often related to the organization's trademark and will therefore be easily associated with the company if its inventory is stolen and later found. For example, the Yellow Cab Company uses yellow to mark its spare parts.

- *Trade marks.* Many organizations use the method of embossing or engraving their name and trademark on inventory. This method greatly discourages theft. If you were a less than honest person and you needed a set of plush towels for your guest bathroom, you might be tempted to steal hotel towels, but your temptation may wane if you see the hotel's logo emblazoned on them. After all, if you used hotel towels in your guest bathroom, your guests would then know about your somewhat dubious character.

- *Dye Marking.* Dye marking has been used for very valuable inventory items. Dye is placed on or within the item's packaging, which leaves dye marks on the hands of those who handle or open this valuable inventory. This system of marking allows organization officials and the police to quickly check and identify theft suspects.

In this discussion of warehouse and inventory security, it is also important to mention the issue of terrorism that has had an enormous impact on warehouse and supply chain facilities. External threats to security, such as through acts of international and domestic terrorism, mean that companies must become increasingly vigilant. Companies that deal with hazardous materials must be extra cautious because of the impact of a potentially far-reaching and lethal spread of chemicals from incidents at their facility. Managers of warehouses - and any other facility with goods and people in the supply chain - pay special attention to the U.S. Department of

Homeland Security's alert system called the ***National Terrorism Advisory System***, or ***NTAS***. In 2011, this system replaced the old color-coded system that had been in place since 2002. In the new NTAS alerts, there are two levels of threats:

- **Imminent Threat Alert.** *Warns of a credible, specific, and impending terrorist threat against the United States.*

- **Elevated Threat Alert.** *Warns of a credible terrorist threat against the United States.*

NTAS alerts also contain a ***sunset provision***, which, as defined by the DHS as: *An individual threat alert is issued for a specific time period and then automatically expires. It may be extended if new information becomes available or the threat evolves.* The Department of Homeland Security has also identified sixteen different critical infrastructure sectors and published free reports at www.dhs.gov on security guidelines for each of these sectors, including: the chemical sector, the commercial facilities sector, the critical manufacturing sector, the food and agriculture sector, the healthcare and public health sector, and the transportation systems sector.

CHAPTER 9 REVIEW QUESTIONS

1. In addition to deterioration, what is the other primary threat to the safety of goods held in a warehouse? What are a few precautionary steps a warehouse can take to minimize this threat?

2. Why is it important to segregate high risk materials in a warehouse?

3. If you see an NFPA Chemical Hazard Label on a container and it has a "4" in the red, yellow, and blue diamonds, what does this mean?

4. What is inventory deterioration? What are its causes? What impact does it have on an organization's bottom line?

5. What can a warehouse manager do to minimize warehouse safety-related incidents?

6. What is inventory shrinkage? What impact does it have on the U.S. retail industry?

7. In addition to security service professionals, who else helps to keep goods secure in a warehouse? How do they do this?

8. What is a marshaling area? Why is it difficult to keep secure?

9. What is inventory marking? How is it used?

10. What are the levels of threat in the National Terrorism Advisory System?

CHAPTER 9 CASE EXERCISE

Getting to Know OSHA

The U.S. Department of Labor Occupational Safety and Health Administration (OSHA) produces a wealth of human safety resources extremely useful for warehouse managers and staff. According to the administration's website, Congress created OSHA in 1970 "to assure safe and healthful working conditions for working men and women by setting and enforcing standards and by providing training, outreach, education and assistance." The primary tasks of OSHA are to set health and safety standards, conduct inspections to ensure that private businesses in the U.S. are compliant with these standards, provide assistance to employers that need help reaching compliance, and provide information and educational tools on workplace health and safety to both employers and employees. Two types of these educational tools provided by OSHA are their eTools and their printable publications.

OSHA's eTools are a series of online, interactive training tools relating to occupational safety and health, from potentially fatal situations and chemicals to workplace ergonomics. Many of the OSHA eTools would be useful for warehouse managers and employees, including: Powered Industrial Trucks; Eye and Face Protection; Respiratory Protection; Noise and Hearing Conservation; Baggage Handling;Beverage Delivery; and Grocery Warehousing. The eTools can be found online (https://www.osha.gov/dts/osta/oshasoft/index.html) and are available to use, download, and reproduce free of charge.

OSHA also has a library of health and safety resources that can be accessed online, reproduced, and shared. The administration encourages users to share and distribute this information, even without attribution, because it is their goal to extend the reach of health and safety information in the workplace as far as possible. A few of the many free OSHA resources that are related to warehouse operations are:

- *Materials Handling and Storage* (https://www.osha.gov/Publications/osha2236.pdf)
- *Safety and Health Topics: Powered Industrial Trucks* (https://www.osha.gov/SLTC/poweredindustrialtrucks/index.html)
- *Sample Daily Checklist for Powered Industrial Trucks* (https://www.osha.gov/dte/library/pit/daily_pit_checklist.html)
- *Controlling Electrical Hazards* (https://www.osha.gov/Publications/osha3075.pdf)
- *Personal Protective Equipment* (https://www.osha.gov/Publications/osha3151.pdf)

The most comprehensive publication for any warehouse worker to start with is OSHA's *Worker Safety Series: Warehousing* (https://www.osha.gov/Publications/warehousing.html). Included below are some excerpts taken from this publication:

Think Safety

More than 145,000 people work in over 7,000 warehouses. The fatal injury rate for the warehousing industry is higher than the national average for all industries.

Potential hazards for workers in warehousing:

- *Unsafe use of forklifts;*
- *Improper stacking of products;*
- *Failure to use proper personal protective equipment;*
- *Failure to follow proper lockout/tagout procedures;*
- *Inadequate fire safety provisions; or*
- *Repetitive motion injuries.*

Hazards & Solutions

Warehouse operations can present a wide variety of potential hazards for the worker. For warehousing establishments, the 10 OSHA standards most frequently included in the agency's citations were:

1. *Forklifts*
2. *Hazard communication*
3. *Electrical, wiring methods*
4. *Electrical, system design*
5. *Guarding floor & wall openings and holes*
6. *Exits*
7. *Mechanical power transmission*
8. *Respiratory protection*
9. *Lockout/tagout*
10. *Portable fire extinguishers*

The remainder of the *Worker Safety Series: Warehousing* publication describes each of the dangers listed above and offers possible workplace solutions. It also includes extensive information on where to find additional education and training resources related to warehouse occupational safety and heath.

INSTRUCTIONS:

Explore at least one of the five resources listed above and consider whether or not it would be useful in your workplace.

Read the rest of *Worker Safety Series: Warehousing* (https://www.osha.gov/Publications/ warehousing.html) online and answer the following questions:

+ **What should an employer provide near dock edges? Why might this be important?**

+ **How old must someone be before they are allowed to operate a forklift?**

+ **What should be maintained for each chemical in the facility where workers are present?**

+ **Why should floors be kept clean? (Hint: This is related to workplace safety.)**

+ **What is a Voluntary Protection Plan?**

+ **In the New Jersey success story, what were the hazards identified? How did the company address these hazards and what was the result?**

Chapter 10

Information Technology Systems

Information technology and information systems have become an integral and critical part of logistics, woven deeply and entirely into and throughout every supply chain. Although it would take many tomes to cover the broad spectrum of information technology and information systems used in global and local supply chain, this chapter provides a basic introduction to information technology systems and the role they play in warehouse and inventory management.

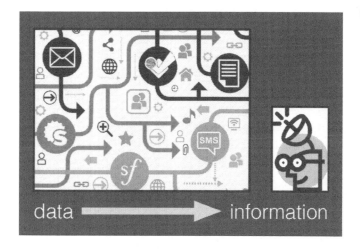

Figure 10.1 - The Relationship Between Data and Information... It's All About the Recipient!

Before exploring information systems and technology in the world of logistics, we'll first take a moment to discuss what we mean by *information* and the role it plays in decision-making. Let's begin where it all starts, with *data*. The terms data and information are often used interchangeably, but they are quite different. **Data** are facts gathered by research or observation and then represented by groupings of nonrandom symbols, such as letters, words, numbers, values, and other symbols. For example, an inventory checker in a warehouse counting the number of wobbly widgets counts that there are 432 Willamina's Wickedly Wild Wobbly Widgets in stock. The data regarding the quantity of widgets observed is 432.

The inventory checker then needs to enter this data (432 Willamina's Wickedly Wild Wobbly Widgets) into a hand- held computer or onto a piece of paper on a clipboard so that others may subsequently receive the message that there are currently 432 of these particular widgets in stock. By recording and transmitting this data that others receive, the inventory checker is transforming data into information. *Information*, therefore, is data that has been received and understood by the recipient of a message. In our example, the recipient may be the logistics manager or even the computerized inventory control system. Information is a critical component of decision-making. Without information, there is no basis upon which to make productive decisions. Imagine selecting a new car to buy without basic information such as gas mileage, safety ratings, and purchase price! In the world of warehouse management, information is used to make a wide range of decisions on an ongoing basis, including storage, materials handling, and transportation decisions. Clear, accurate, and timely information is critical to this process. Ultimately, decisions can only be as good as the information used to make them.

Information is used for decision-making throughout all supply chain processes, including all of those related to warehouse management and inventory control. Physical goods flow along a supply chain, but information must pervade every aspect of the chain and flow back and forth between members of this chain. The warehouse department and its warehouse management system (WMS) has information flowing to and from many others members of the supply chain, including:

- **the customer,** who provides information about product needs and requires information about product availability, quality, price, and delivery times, and to whom the warehouse department or WMS provides information about product availability and delivery schedules;

- **the Marketing Department,** which provides information about product needs and promotions and receives information from the warehouse department or WMS about product availability;

- **the Production Department,** which provides information about production lead-times and production capabilities and requires information about supply deliveries and receives information from the warehouse department or WMS about inventory availability in the warehouse;

- **the Purchasing Department,** which provides information on quantities of goods ordered and their delivery timeframes and receives information from the warehouse department or WMS about when the goods have been received, inspected, and put into stock;

- **the supplier,** who provides information about the availability of goods and means os transportation being used to deliver goods to the warehouse and requires information from the warehouse department or WMS about delivery times and receiving capabilities, such as specifics on the receiving docks and available receiving times.

As we've already mentioned, information is used for decision-making. In the world of warehouse management, information is used to make a wide range of decisions about: *inventory management and control*; *transportation*; and *physical distribution facilities placement and management*. When determining the optimal levels of inventory to hold, companies need information on inventory holding and issuing costs, customer demand patterns, and ordering costs. When selecting transportation routes, modes, and vendors, companies need information concerning transportation costs for various options, shipment frequency and size, and customer delivery receipt locations. Finally, when determining the optimal location, layout, scheduling, and management of a warehouse or distribution center, companies need information regarding customer demand and locations, local regulations and taxes, and inventory type and quantity. Throughout the range of a company's inbound, internal, and outbound processes, information is truly the lifeblood of efficient and effective warehouse management.

Because of its importance in so many of these decisions in warehouse management, the quality and accessibility of information are critical. Therefore, information must be:

- *Clear, complete, and accurate.* If information is incorrect or incomplete, decisions made will suffer a similar fate. Imagine placing a delivery order for eighteen pizzas for an office party and being misheard over the telephone, resulting in eighty pizzas landing on your doorstep!

- *Accessible in the right place.* Great information is as good as no information if it can't be found. A scene from the film *Zoolander*, a comedy about the world of male modeling, provides a great illustration of this point. While trying to stop an evil fashion designer from taking over the world, two heroic (but less than computer-savvy) male models are told that the files they need to find are "in the computer." As a result, the protagonists demolish the computer as they try to get the files they believe are literally "inside" the machine.

- *Accessible at the right time.* Needed information is of little use after a decision has been made. For example, a traffic light would be of little use if it were only visible from the middle of an intersection.

- *The kind of information needed.* If the information available is not relevant to the decision to be made or cannot be interpreted, it can be even more harmful that having no information at all. Imagine again that you are buying a car and the only information you have about it are its color and model name (i.e., no information about miles per gallon, safety features, and cost). Many of us might be tempted to select a car based solely on its color and model name, but, with this insufficient information, we might end up with a lemon that we can't even afford!

To ensure that logistics information is clear, accurate, and of the right type accessible at the right time and in the right place, warehouse management professionals have turned to *information systems* and *information technology*. Today, both information systems and information technology smooth logistics flow by efficiently and accurately recording, analyzing, and transmitting warehouse management and inventory control information. **Information systems** are the systems and software programs that manage the flow of data in an organization in a systematic, structured way to assist in planning, implementing, and controlling. **Information technology** is the hardware used to implement information systems to help achieve warehouse management and supply chain efficiencies.

INFORMATION TECHNOLOGY IN THE WAREHOUSE

In a warehouse or distribution center, information technology (IT) is used to assist in managing the information essential to the inbound, internal, and outbound processes of warehouse management. IT hardware is used to: *capture data; store data; sort information; complete calculations; analyze data and information; display information; track inventory and people; organize tasks; create reports;* and *manage and plan inventory control activities.* Over the past few decades, technology has developed at an astounding pace. Just when you think technological devices can't possibly get any smaller or faster, the next biggest advancement is announced and technology keeps jumping forward!

Thanks to technological advancements, especially, in mobile phones and other hand-held technology, warehouses of any size now use information technology for warehouse management and inventory control activities. Some of the types of inventory technology used in the warehouse include:

- **Computers.** Both stationary and mobile computers are used throughout the warehouse to store, process, analyze, and report information. Computers provide the backbone of the information systems in the warehouse.

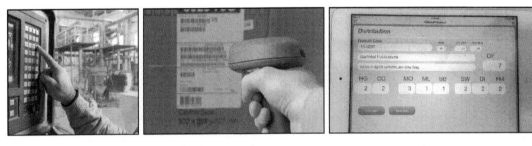

Figure 10.2 - Stationary Computer (*left*), Barcode Scanner (*center*), and iPad Handheld Device (*right*)

- **Mobile phones and handheld devices.** Mobile phones and similar handheld devices can be used in conjunction with computers or in place of computers when combined with cloud-based apps and computing. Because of the scanning capability of their cameras, mobile phones are now increasingly being used for taking in information for inventory management. To see an example of this, go to any 24-hour grocery store after midnight, casually stroll up to anyone who is checking inventory, and ask them what they re using to scan the bar codes on the inventory they are counting. Chances are, the device being used will either be an enhanced mobile phone or another handheld device that closely resembles a mobile phone.

- **Barcode scanners.** To take in information about incoming, stored, and outgoing inventory quickly and accurately, handheld scanners are used. Scanners are typically used to take in information from RFID tags and barcodes and then communicate this information to information systems and warehouse management software. A barcode scanner reads the label and communicates the information to a central inventory control system. Bar code technology is used within many logistics information systems, such as electronic point of sale and warehouse management systems. When we step into the self-scanning express aisle of a large grocery store, we ourselves become frontline users of bar code technology.

- **RFID readers.** An RFID reader with an antenna reads this information and transmits it to a central inventory control system. Like bar coding, RFID technology is used within logistics information systems, such as transportation management systems. Unlike bar codes, RFID tags can be programmed with additional information and can be read when not in the line of sight, at distances of 90 feet or more, and when the tagged item or load is in motion.

Figure 10.3 - RFID Tag (*left*). A stationary RFID reader can read tags on each of this train's containers as it speeds through the station (*right*).

- **GPS technology.** Global positioning technology (GPS) is the type of information technology used to locate goods and track them wirelessly using remote sensors and satellite systems. GPS is used to track goods on the move, which means that it is especially useful in tracking goods inbound to and outbound from the warehouse. This can help warehouses plan for inventory receipt and in conveying information about the anticipated delivery ties of outbound goods. Warehouses can also use GPS tracking of inventory for security, which provides an alert when items from inventory are removed from the warehouse, either accidentally or for more nefarious purposes.

- **Label printers.** When we think of information technology, we often think of high tech equipment. However, low tech equipment is also an important part of information technology in the warehouse. For example, printers are frequently used in warehouses to create labels that are adhered to incoming goods. These labels often contain barcodes or other inventory management codes that make it easy to track and record information about the goods as they become inventory within the warehouse's system.

- **Voice technology equipment.** Voice-activated or voice-directed technology can be used in systems that guide users to complete specific actions via voice commands. For example, voice technology is gaining popularity in warehouse order picking systems, in which an order picker wearing a hands-free headset listens to each item to be picked along with its location. The order picker then uses voice commands to confirm that the correct items and quantities have been selected.

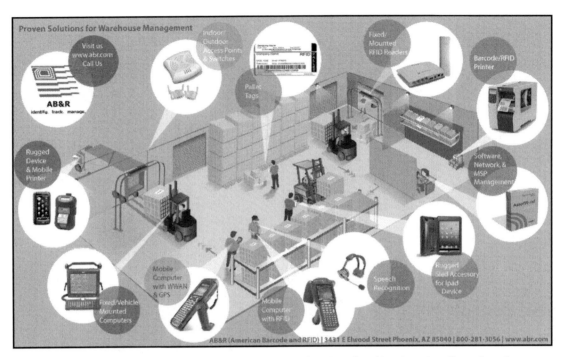

Figure 10.4 - Snapshot of an Inventory Management Solutions Provider. American Barcode and
RFID (AB&R) is a national third party logistics service provider (3PLP) located in Phoenix,
Arizona that helps companies manage their warehouses and inventory by using information
technology and information systems. The picture above is from the AB&R website (www.abr.com)
and highlights some of the inventory management services and solutions it provides.

INFORMATION SYSTEMS IN THE WAREHOUSE

An important part of warehouse management and inventory control is making sure that
companies have the exact goods they need to provide to either external customers or internal
operations when and where they need them in the quantity they need. This must also be balanced
with the cost of holding goods to make sure that too many goods aren't being stored
unnecessarily, resulting in unnecessarily high inventory holding costs. However, companies do not
want to cut their inventory holding levels too low or they might risk a *stockout*, a situation in
which there is no longer any stock of an item in inventory, which can result in lost potential sales,
operational shut-downs, and angry customers.

To help perform this balancing act in the warehouse, companies use *information systems*,
most often in the form of computer programs and apps, to manage the flow of data surrounding
inventory and determine when, where, and how much inventory should be held. In world of
warehousing, information systems are the software programs that manage the information
associated with the inbound, internal, and outbound processes of warehouse management. The
goal of warehouse information systems are ultimately to create efficiencies and minimize cost,
typically by creating a faster *dock-to-stock* process, or from an inbound receiving bay to a
warehouse shelf. *Warehouse management software* programs are used to manage
information relates to activities such as receiving, putaway, storage, inventory management,
picking, packing, and shipping.

A *warehouse management system (WMS)* is a software program or app that manages warehouse business processes and directs warehouse activities. These activities and processes include: order receipt and shelving; order picking and shipping; inventory cycle counting; integration with RFID or voice recognition technology; and layout planning. A WMS typically tracks the movement of goods into, within, and out from a warehouse or distribution center. The WMS interfaces with the *enterprise resource planning (ERP)* transaction system to provide real time visibility of inventory and orders. This integration provides a seamless transfer of order data to the WMS system, and a transmission of shipment and inventory data from the WMS to the ERP system.

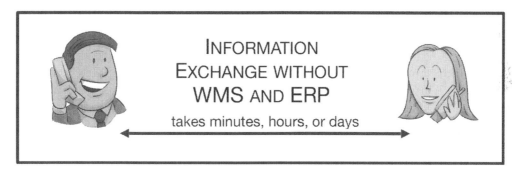

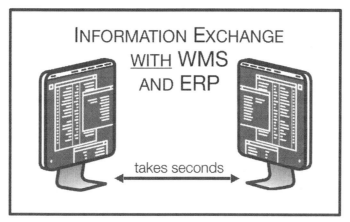

Figure 10.5 - The Time Benefit of Using WMS and ERP in the Warehouse

An *enterprise resource planning (ERP)* system is a type of software system used across an entire company for planning and managing its resources. It replaces a company's many, often incompatible information systems with a single, integrated database system with seamless, real-time information sharing, storage, and retrieval. Thus because the WMS system is integrated with the ERP systems it plays a large role in order receipt, shipments, and inventory management. ERP systems are typically inter-organizational, although aspects of a system may interface with customers and suppliers. The most commonly used ERP systems are those developed by SAP, Oracle, PeopleSoft, and BAAN. The WMS system is directly linked into the ERP system.

Warehouse management systems and their integration with enterprise resource planning are critical to the efficient warehouse management, especially for medium to large size warehouses. The core objective of a WMS is to reduce the number of movement warehouse operators and equipment must make while handling inventory to minimize the equipment, facilities, and labor costs to run the warehouse. Another objective is to provide speedier service, such as order picking and order fulfillment, for internal and external customers. A few additional objectives of a WMS related to specific warehouse management inbound, internal, and outbound processes include:

- **Inventory receipt:** match advance receipt paperwork, such as shipment notification documents, with the actual shipment as it is received, often using bar code scanning technology with automatic systems in place to pay the vendors when the correct order have been received

- **Put Away:** optimize locations, slotting, and materials handling vehicle routes for the most efficient put away process possible to maximize warehouse space, minimize equipment use and labor hours, and avoid traffic congestion inside the warehouse

- **Picking:** minimize equipment and human movement when picking orders, perhaps with multiple orders being picked simultaneously, again to minimize equipment use, make the most of each labor hour, and avoid traffic congestion inside the warehouse

- **Shipping:** check to ensure complete accuracy of every outbound shipment and even to increase the unloading efficiency when outbound goods are received by efficient placement inside outbound trucks and containers

Additional types of software used in warehouse management include:

- *slotting optimization software,* which helps a company identify the best locations within a warehouse to place slots to store SKUs based on using the space available in the most efficient and effective way possible

- *load optimization software,* also called load building software, which helps create ideal unit loads and suggestion the best transportation systems and plot the best routes to save both time and money

- *yard management system,* which helps organize containers and trailers in external inventory yards and outdoor waiting areas by showing where they are located, what the arrival and departure schedule for each trailer or container is, what inventory is located in each trailer or container, and when each trailer will begin to incur additional or unnecessary costs, such as excess rental fees

- *warehouse control system,* which is a type of software that keeps operations running smoothly in a warehouse or distribution center by directing operations and suggesting what should be done at what time in warehouse operations to achieve maximum efficiency and effectiveness

CHAPTER 10 REVIEW QUESTIONS

1. What is the difference between data and information?

2. How does the warehouse department and its warehouse management system (WMS) interact with the others members of the supply chain?

3. Because the quality and accessibility of information are critical in warehouse management, what must information be?

4. In two sentences or less, describe how a barcode and barcode scanner work. In what situation might you want to use barcode technology?

5. In two sentences or less, describe how RFID tags and RFID scanners work. In what situation might you want to use RFID technology?

6. In two sentences or less, describe how GPS technology works and how it is related to warehouse management. In what situation might you want to use GPS technology?

7. Does voice technology equipment involve listening to a voice or having your voice listened to? Please explain your answer. In what situation might a warehouse want to use voice technology?

8. What is a stockout and how can a warehouse prevent it?

9. What is a WMS and what is its core objective? Does is have any other purpose? Please explain your answer.

10. If your warehouse manages many containers in its external inventory yard and they seem to be piling up more and more every day, what type of software might be useful? If you have a warehouse that always seems to run short on space, what type of software might be useful?

CHAPTER 10 CASE STUDY

A Tale of Two Companies (and Their Information Systems)

When it opened its doors in 1996, very few people had heard of Under Armour, a Baltimore, Maryland based sports apparel manufacturer. But after becoming the outfitter of two Oliver Stone sports films, the official outfitter of the XFL, and developing a wildly popular marketing campaign ("Protect this house") in the short four years from 1999 to 2003, the company became an overnight sensation and grew exponentially. It quickly become a global brand and continues to have wildly successful growth.

With this initial growth, Under Armour's warehouses and distribution centers were becoming bogged down. There never seemed to be enough warehouse space and the warehouse management system could not keep up with the pace needed to get the products out to the rapidly growing consumer base. In 2006, the company decided to replace its warehouse management system to accommodate this growth. After exploring many of the top WMS providers, Under Armour decided to work with third party provider Manhattan Associates to help them develop the WMS they needed to attain the agility and speed they needed to keep up with their almost unbelievably rapid growth.

Because there never seemed to be enough warehouse space, no matter how big their warehouses were, Under Armour also decided to add Manhattan Associates' slotting optimization software to their WMS. This let the company utilize every available inch of its warehouse space and automatically placed the most highly picked items in the golden zone of each warehouse. The system was also highly flexible, which meant that slotting optimization could vary from warehouse to warehouse and placement of items varied on a seasonal basis, resulting in more efficient and streamlined picking processes throughout the year. As a result, Under Armour also experienced more accurate picking, packing, and shipping and saved money because warehouse overtime expenses were drastically reduced and even eliminated. The apparel manufacturer continues to use Manhattan Associates' customized WMS and slotting optimization software in its warehouses and distribution centers around the world.

While a global clothing manufacturer like Under Armour can interview the top WMS providers and receive custom-made solutions, the issue of information systems is more challenging for local businesses that does not have the size or volume of sales of global brands and national retail chains. One example of the struggle local companies face when searching for WMS solutions can be found in the tale of Once in a Blue Moose, a locally popular retail chain of nine gift and souvenir stores in Alaska. A few years ago, the retail chain knew it needed an information system to manage its incoming, internal, and outbound inventory across its nine retail location and its warehouse in midtown Anchorage. One of the company's owners was also an IT guru and made it her job to search high and low for the perfect (or at least a pretty good) system that would work on the company's Apple computers and meet the ERP and WMS needs they had outlined.

Once in a Blue Moose quickly found that its options were limited when you're not a retail giant who can afford to get custom-built solutions. The systems available were either far too expensive or were not flexible enough for the retail environment for a business of their size. For example, one brand of software was great for many business functions but was not designed to track and manage inventory at multiple retail locations. Another brand of software could handle multiple retail locations but was rigid in its inventory coding and forced users to have a coding system that did not make sense for Once in a Blue Moose and its inventory. Fed up with limited possibilities that didn't meet their needs, the company's IT-loving co-owner decided to create an information system herself using File Maker Pro.

It has been a labor of love for many months and Once in a Blue Moose now has an inventory management system that meets its needs perfectly. The customized system, called "Mercury" (the Roman messenger of the gods) is a blend of ERP and WMS, with all of its functions designed to meet the inventory management needs of a retail environment with one central warehouse and countless retail outlets. It serves to manage and locate off of the inventory held by the company at all of its locations.

It also has a special function to create inventory codes for new items based on the inventory and location coding system used company-wide. Mercury is tied in to wireless barcode scanners and has an app for handheld devices, such as iPads, used across the company.

While the system is working well for Once in a Blue Moose, there are more developments on the horizon. The company is continuing to develop it to meet their needs for more efficient and streamlined operations, such as introducing a GPS component for inventory tracking and streamlining the distribution process. It is also exploring converting to a cloud-based system for greater flexibility and real-time information sharing.

INSTRUCTIONS:

If Under Armour had not replaced its WMS in 2006, what might have happened? Do you think the company would have continued to grow to become as popular as it is today? Please explain your answer.

If you were the owner of Once in a Blue Moose but did not have a co-owner who was an IT genius, what would you have done to meet your company's needs for an information system to manage inventory?

BONUS ASSIGNMENT:

Visit two businesses near you: one large, national chain and one small- to medium-sized local business. Ask them about the types of information systems they use to manage their inventory.

Do you notice any similarities or differences between the businesses you observed and the businesses in this case study?

Chapter 11

Customer Service and the Warehouse

A system of efficient and effective warehouses and distribution centers is vital to a successful supply chain. Every link in the supply chain involves a warehouse or some type of warehouse management activity. The objectives of warehouse management throughout the supply chain are the same as all other logistics and supply chain activities: provide a service valued by customers at a minimum cost and at a service level that meets or exceeds customers' expectations. This involves getting the right product to the right place, in the right quality, in the right quantity, at the right time when the customers wants it... and doing this consistently every time it's done!

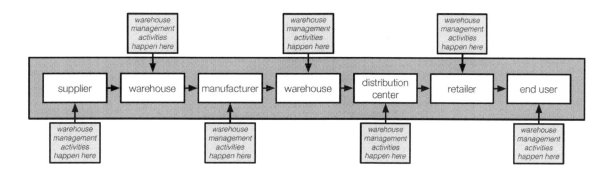

Figure 11.1 - Warehouse Management Activities Can Be Found Everywhere Along the Supply Chain

Customers and their needs drive the supply chain and determine so much in warehouse management, from whether an organization uses a traditional warehouse or a cross-docking regional distribution center to what type of packaging is used when shipping plastic toy trains. These customers have an enormous say in warehouse management and inventory control, but who *are* these customers?

WHO ARE THE CUSTOMERS OF WAREHOUSING?

Let's begin by defining the meaning of the word *customer*. A ***customer*** is a party who receives a product or service from another party. Although we usually think of customers as people, customers may also be organizations. For example, Walmart is one of Coca-Cola's many customers. When looking at customer service, organizations must consider the service they provide to both individual people and other organizations.

Warehouse customers can be either *external* or *internal* to the organization providing the product or service. When we think of customers, we typically think of ***external customers***, or those who receive a product or service who are private individual end users or organizations other than the company providing the product or service. For example, when you buy a bag of tortilla chips from a grocery store or when the Taco House Restaurant chain buys the same chips from the tortilla chip manufacturer, both you and the Taco House Restaurant are external customers.

In the world of warehousing, ***internal customers*** are those individuals or departments within an organization who receive goods or services from a warehouse or warehouse function within their own organization. For example, at the tortilla chip production facility, the production department creates, fries, and salts the chips, which are then sent to the production department's internal customer: the packaging department. After the packaging department places the chip into bags and seals them, it sends the bags of chips to its internal customer: the finished goods warehouse. This process of sending goods from internal customer to internal customer continues until the product reaches the external customer and, eventually, the end user.

When developing warehouse customer service policies and standards, companies must have a clear understanding of exactly who their customers are. Many companies create great global customer service policies for their external customers, but fail to address their own internal customers. Companies with exceptional customer service not only have external customer service policies, but their functional departments also have policies and procedures for their individual internal customers.

Regardless of whether its customers are internal or external, an organization that provides goods or services must focus on the concept of customer service to achieve financial success and part of this focus on customer service must be within the warehouse management function. But before we go any further, what exactly does the term *customer service* mean? ***Customer service*** is simply the service (or everything an organization does and the actions it takes) while providing a product or service to a customer (the person or organization or internal department) in order to meet or exceed its customer's expectations and result in *customer satisfaction*. Although there may be only one employee or a small team of employees within warehouse management who are officially responsible for customer service, everyone in the warehouse function contributes to customer service! For example, although there may be only one person in the shipping and receiving department who send outs picked orders to a customer, everyone in the warehouse who comes into contact with the products picked have an impact on customer service. Despite the fact that there may be the most diligent employees providing customer service in shipping and receiving, if the employees doing the inventory putaway are not focused on customer service, items might be put into the wrong slots and it might take much too long to pick and fill customers' orders because items can't be found in the warehouse.

As we've already established, warehouses have both internal and external customers. *External customers* are any people or organizations receiving the product from the warehouse who are not part of the organization itself, such as people and companies who use, sell, distribute, or deliver products from the warehouse, including third party logistics service providers. When we think of *customers*, we generally think of these external customers. A harder group to picture are a warehouse's internal customers. For employees in a warehouse, *internal customers* include, people in the *purchasing, manufacturing, maintenance, finance,* and *marketing departments*. Listed below are examples of the types of customer service warehousing operatives provide to each of these departments:

- **Customer Service from the Warehouse to the Purchasing Department.**

  - *Provide information on when the goods they have ordered have been received, inspected, put away into inventory, and are ready for issue.* This tells the purchasing department that they can start the process for payment to the supplier.

  - *Gather information on key performance indicators (KPIs) on the service that suppliers are providing.* This helps the purchasing department identify which suppliers perform well and do what they have promised and which are poor performers and should no longer be used or have specific areas that need improvement.

- **Customer Service from the Warehouse to Incoming Inventory Deliverers**

  - *Assist the productivity of those delivering goods to the warehouse from the company's suppliers by ensuring a fast unloading and turnaround time.* A large amount of goods are delivered to the warehouse from suppliers by truck. The warehouse can ensure a fast turnaround time at the unloading dock by ensuring adequate people and machinery are available immediately when the truck arrives for a fast unloading and checking of the goods. Today, truck drivers' hours of service are legally tightly controlled. Unnecessary time spent at unloading or loading bays must be avoided through efficient scheduling of incoming inventory. Fast unloading turnaround also helps the supplier because the purchasing department of the organization receiving the goods will receive the receipt information and can process payment quickly to supplier.

Figure 11.2 - Internal Customer Service at the Tabali Winery Warehouse. The warehouse department at the Chilean winery lets their purchasing department know as soon as new bottles have been received, inspected, and ready for issue for the wine production process (*left* and *center*). The purchasing department can then pay the bottle supplier and set up the next bottle order. The warehouse department also provides customer service to the wine production (or manufacturing) department by delivering the received bottles in the right quantity, quality, time, and place to the production floor so that they are ready to go for the wine bottling process (*center* and *right*). They also prevent inventory deterioration by keeping the glass wine bottles secure until ready for use.

- **Customer Service from the Warehouse to the Manufacturing Department**

  - *Ensure that production inputs are delivered in the right quantity, quality, time, and place to the production floor.* By making sure that all incoming goods are of the required quality and that the quantities are correct, this ensures that the manufacturing department will have sufficient inventory to meet production needs.

  - *Prevent inventory deterioration.* By storing inventory in the warehouse in the proper conditions, this can prevent goods from deteriorating, ensuring that they are of a good enough quality to be used in the production process.

  - *Keep inventory safe from theft.* This ensures that the quantity of goods listed in the inventory control system is accurate and there will be no surprises when goods are needed for production due to inventory shortages from stolen goods.

- **Customer Service from the Warehouse to the Maintenance Department**

  - Keeping needed spare parts and inventory for maintenance and special projects. Keeping accurate control over spare parts and a proper account of equipment issues on loan to maintenance staff allows the warehouse to make sure that they always have needed spare parts, maintenance equipment, and inventory for special projects on hand for the maintenance department. These spare parts, machinery, and special projects supplies for maintenance are often isolated from the organization's main inventory and are stored in a special section of the warehouse.

Figure 11.3 - More Internal Customer Service at the Tabali Winery Warehouse. Tabali's warehouse department makes sure to keeps its outbound bottles of wine in a safe and secure environment, crated, wrapped, and palletized to protect them from spilling and breaking (*left*). The warehouse department also ensures that the promises of the marketing department are met by helping get the wine out the door so that they arrive to the customer when promised and in the condition promised. This internal customer service helps to drive repeat business with external customers.

- **Customer Service from the Warehouse to the Finance Department**

  - *Ensure that the receipt and inspection for quality and quantity of all incoming inventory is accurate.* This prevents the finance department from paying for quantities not received and for quality that does not meet specifications.

- *Hold inventory in a safe and secure environment.* Every inventory item that is stolen or deteriorated costs money that must be replaced out of profit, causing headaches for the finance department!

- *Provide access and resources necessary to carry out the end-of-year physical inventory check.* This annual physical inventory check must be reconciled with the company's annual financial statements.

- *Investigate inventory check discrepancies.* Ensuring that any discrepancies, either under- or over-stock situations, are investigated urgently and accurately helps to make sure that the company's financial records are accurate and balanced.

- **Customer Service from the Warehouse to the Marketing Department**

  - *Ensure that marketing's promises are met.* A company's marketing and sales staff makes promises to customers, from delivery times to the condition of products delivered. The warehouse can help to ensure that many of the promises to the customer are kept, resulting in a happy customer and repeat business.

  - *Process incoming orders quickly and accurately.* Companies aim for zero defects in their orders. The customer must get the right quantity, of right quality, at the right time, and at the right place. The warehouse can make sure that this happens by filling orders quickly and accurately. If there are any unforeseen delays, the warehouse provides good service to the marketing department by advising them immediately and providing suggested solutions so they can communicate this information to the customer.

  - *Respond professionally and empathetically to customer-driven changes.* For any number of reasons, customers can request any number of changes at the last minute when interacting with the marketing and sales department. The warehouse can provide a good level of customer service to the marketing department by addressing all last minute, customer-driven changes communicated by the marketing department.

THE CUSTOMER SERVICE PROCESS AND RELATIONSHIPS

Warehouse management also plays a critical role in all three phases of the *customer service process*. The **customer service process** has three primary phases that cover the entirety of the relationship between the customer and the organization supplying the desired goods or services. The phases are: *pre-transaction*, *transaction*, and *post-transaction*. Warehouse management and operations play a significant role in providing effective customer service during all three of these phases.

Figure 11.4 - The Three Phases of the Customer Service Process

The *pre-transaction phase* of a customer service relationship between a customer and a supplier takes place before the sale has occurred, often before the customer has gone anywhere near the supplier. During this initial phase, companies establish their customer service policies and procedures, working closely with their warehouses and the shipping or physical distribution departments or their third party logistics providers to ensure that these policies and procedures are realistic and can be consistently delivered to customers. For example, you might initially attract customers with a customer service policy that states "We promise to deliver your order to you less than one hour after you have placed it," but this is likely to be impossible for your physical distribution department to carry out, especially if it takes that amount of time alone to pick and package an order, leaving you some very unhappy, unsatisfied customers.

Figure 11.5 - Inventory Visibility. With inventory visibility, companies know exactly where their products are during the distribution process. This allows them to inform customers of delays and early deliveries.

During the pre-transaction phase, companies also ensure that they are ready for upcoming potential sales by forecasting customer demand and maintaining enough stock or ready access to enough stock to fill future orders. Companies also ensure that all of their information technology and communication systems are in place and in working order for upcoming sales so that products can easily be found and tracked as orders are filled and products are delivered to customers. In today's age of immediate gratification and rapid advances in information technology, a critical element of customer service is *inventory visibility,* the ability of organization and its customers to know exactly where a specific product is in the supply chain at any time as it is being delivered to the customer. Think about the last time you placed an order for something online and the company provided inventory visibility as the item was prepared and shipped to you. Didn't it give you a happy feeling in the pit of your stomach to know exactly when your order left the warehouse and when it arrived it Houston, Texas on its way to you in Anchorage, Alaska?

The ***transaction phase*** of the customer service relationship is the actual sales transaction: the customer placing an order for a product or service and the company delivering that product or service to the customer. When a customer places an order for goods with an organization, warehousing plays a vital role in fulfilling the order. The order is picked from the warehouse, packaged for delivery, and transported to the customer. Although an organization's marketing department typically makes the sale, it is the warehousing and physical distribution departments that do all the grunt-work during this phase.

Finally, the ***post-transaction phase*** of a customer service relationship between a customer and a supplier takes place after the sale has occurred and the product or service has been delivered. This phase is largely the domain of a *customer service and support department*, who handles customer complaints, returns, recalls, customer satisfaction surveys, and post-sales service, such as warranties and repairs. However, warehousing also plays a significant role during this phase, especially in dealing with the reverse logistics aspects and physical handling of goods in product returns and recalls. ***Reverse logistics*** is a specialized area of logistics that is concerned with the backwards or reverse flow of goods up the supply chain, i.e., moving goods from the customer back to the supplier as a result of product returns and safety or quality recalls.

On a daily basis, warehouse professionals interact with many types of people. Throughout the customer service process while also performing warehouse management and operations functions, warehouse and supply chain professionals form a variety of relationships with others both *internal* and *external* to the company they represent. They also engage in a variety of both *vertical* and *horizontal* relationships. In the warehousing organization, ***vertical relationships*** are those that flow up and down a vertical chain of command, such as the relationship between you and your boss or you and your staff or between the warehouse manager and warehouse employees. ***Horizontal relationships*** are those between peers across an organization, such as the relationship between a warehousing manager and a manufacturing manager.

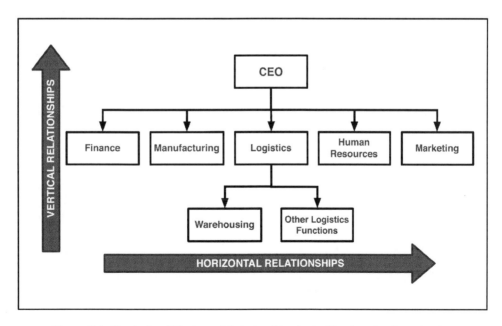

Figure 11.6 - Vertical and Horizontal Relationships in the Warehousing Organization

When we think of supply chains, we often think of a physical flow of goods, initiated by a user's need, purchased from the supplier by the user, and then moving seamlessly from materials' suppliers to factories, warehouses, distribution centers, and, eventually, to the retailer and end user. Often overlooked are the people involved in theses processes and the importance of their interpersonal relationships. People and their relationships are the essential solder of the customer service process of warehouse management and the links within the supply chain. As shown in Figure 11.7, there are many horizontal relationships across a variety of departments within an organization.

Figure 11.7 - The Warehouse Department's Horizontal Relationships

All of the relationships shown in both images above are relationships between members of the warehousing department and others within the same company. These are all examples of *internal relationships*. Warehousing professionals also have many relationships with people from other companies, such as the suppliers' delivery people and customers receiving people. They may also have relationships with the staff of a 3PLP if there organization outsources all its transportation and often direct contact with customers if there is a problem with their delivery schedules.. These relationships with others from other companies are called *external relationships*. The chart below highlights the locations of people and their external relationships in a simple supply chain.

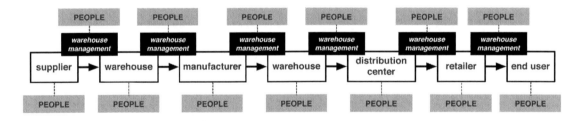

Figure 11.8 - People and External Relationships in the Simple Supply Chain

Warehousing professionals have to manage all of these internal and external interpersonal relationships to ensure that a warehouse can successfully complete its role as an important link in the total supply chain. *Interpersonal relationships* are social associations, connections, or affiliations between two or more people. They vary in different levels of intimacy and sharing, implying the discovery or establishment of common ground. Typically, they are centered around something shared or in common. For interpersonal relationships within the warehousing world, those involved may work for the same company, have similar work methods and personalities, and be working toward identical goals. They often share much in common and often form easy, immediate, and successful interpersonal relationships. There are also interpersonal relationships within the warehousing world where the members of the relationship have far less in common, however, often with the need for the warehousing transaction being their only common bond. Most participants in supply chain and warehousing relationships will have a variety of differences, including the companies or departments for whom they work, their work methods and goals, or even their perception of the relationship and the work to be done.

Successful relationships, in both warehousing and the world at large, often depend on our ability to understand others and build relationships. Before we explore the skills needed to build relationships in warehouse management, lets's examine the *people* who work in the warehouse.

THE PEOPLE OF WAREHOUSING

There are a growing number of positions available in the workforce for people interested in working in professions related to warehouse management and inventory control. Baby boomers are retiring from the workforce and the work required in warehousing has become increasing complex, resulting in greater numbers of positions that are harder to fill. In the world of warehousing, long gone are the days of purely physical labor in which Henry Ford wanted his workers to leave their brains at the door. Supply chain jobs, including those in warehousing, have become increasingly complex, and require employees to understand the importance of warehouse management to a corporate bottom line, the technological tools and programs needed to operate a warehouse and control inventory, and the complex interpersonal relationships in a supply chain, some of which span across cultures and continents. With corporate continuous improvement initiatives like *lean* (as covered earlier in this text), warehouse employees must also now be problem solvers, ready to identify and articulate a workplace problem and provide possible solutions for it. With advances in information technology and systems almost happening on a daily basis, the information technology and information systems to manage a warehouse and control inventory change on a regular basis and today's warehouse employees must also now be ready to adapt to the changes and learn new systems. Gone are the days of going to work and expecting to do the same job every day for the next twenty, ten, or even two years!

In the world of warehousing, there's not the heavy lifting that there used to be. Forklift trucks can do that! Instead, warehouse employees must be highly computer literate and ready to learn new systems and tools. Warehouse job, along with other jobs found in the supply chain, are extremely important because they influence how quickly and in what condition people get their stuff (almost *all* their stuff), giving them an enormous influence on a company's financial bottom line. Almost everything we see around us to help us in our daily lives has passed through the hands of warehouse workers. When goods arrive into a port, a distribution center, or a warehouse at the back of a store, it is primarily warehouse workers who handle and are responsible for these goods along the way until they reach the end user. These employees are the guardians of all the precious cargo that we need every day to thrive and survive in our lives. For example, imagine a poorly trained warehouse staff for a pharmaceutical company that produces one-of-a-kind lifesaving drugs. If these drugs don't make it to pharmacies and hospitals on time because of the poor training (or laziness or ineptitude) of the people picking, packing, and shipping the orders, lives could be lost.

These important positions found in warehouses are related to the inbound, internal, and outbound processes of warehouse management. A few of these jobs and their descriptions are:

- *Warehouse Manager*, who plans, controls, directs, and administers all of the inbound, internal, and outbound processes of a warehouse or warehousing facility. This position will generally report to a company vice president or director and will be responsible for all of the employees in the warehouse.

- *Warehouse Coordinator*, who oversees all of the day-to-day operations in the warehouse. This position might be found in larger warehouses and would likely report to the warehouse manager. By running day-to-day operations and paying attention to the details of immediate operations, the warehouse coordinator frees up the time of the warehouse manager to focus more on the big picture, continuous improvement initiative, and top-tier corporate strategic planning.

- *Inventory Receiving Operator*, who physically moves goods from an inbound truck or container into the warehouse. This position generally also checks to make sure the right quantity of the correct goods are received. Depending on the goods being received and the materials handling equipment used, this type of position may have physical criteria, such as requiring potential employees to be able to lift a specific number of pounds.

- *Inventory Receiving Clerk*, who handles the paperwork when inbound orders arrive to the warehouse facility. For example, a person in this position might enter information into a computer system about the order that has come in and might also schedule the inbound trucks so that no truck drivers have to waste valuable labor hours sitting outside waiting for a dock or loading bay to free up.

- *Quality Control Associate*, who checks the quality of incoming inventory. Although an initial eyeball check of items is done by inventory receiving operators, those in quality control professions make sure that the items received are up to the quality specifications as promised by the supplier.

- *Putaway Operator/Stock Handler*, who uses their hands, hand trucks, or other materials handling equipment to put goods away into the warehouse after they have been received and checked. People in these positions might put goods away onto warehouse shelves or, in the case of a cross-docking facility, into staging areas to be immediately shipped out on outbound trucks. Like inventory receiving operators, this type of position may have physical criteria regarding the ability to lift a specific number of pounds.

- *Inventory/Stock Checker*, who helps an organization control its inventory by counting the amount of inventory in stock to make sure that the physical count matches up with the quantities shown as available in the warehouse information systems. This type of position may be full time or temporary, depending on how often the company conducts physical inventory check. It may also be a position with a third party provider, such as an external company that provides inventory checking services.

- *Inventory Picker*, who helps to fill customers orders by taking items in the order from the warehouse shelves and placing them in a staging area to be prepared for an outbound

Figure 11.9 - Forklift Operator. Because their jobs are dangerous, forklift operators must be trained and highly focused. Untrained or careless drivers could be lethal to themselves and those around them and can easily damage inventory.

shipment. People in this position might use their hands, hand trucks, or other materials handling equipment and might also have physical criteria regarding the ability to lift a specific number of pounds.

- *Forklift Operator,* who moves inbound, internal, and outbound palletized and non-palletized goods using a forklift truck. All forklift operators must undergo safety training as required by OSHA.

- *Packer*, who packs products into protective materials and packaging for subsequent shipping by truck, container, or third party delivery system, such as FedEx, UPS, or the U.S. Postal Service.

- *Shipping Clerk*, who processes outbound shipments from the warehouse. The person in this position would typically enter information about the outbound shipment into the computer and make sure that all necessary documentation has been completed for international shipments.

- *Shipping Operator*, who, like the inventory receiving operator in reverse, physically moves goods from the warehouse to an outbound truck or container. Depending on the goods being shipped and the materials handling equipment used, this type of position may have physical criteria, such as requiring potential employees to be able to lift a specific number of pounds.

We previously explored how positions related to warehouse operations or inventory control are critically important because they all make sure that the goods we need to survive and thrive get to us when and where we need them in the quantity and of the quality we need. While there are a wide range of positions in a warehouse requiring different skill sets, people applying for jobs related to warehouse management and inventory control should expect to have a set of common competencies.

- **Reading and math skills.** Most warehouse workers will have to be able to read shipping documentation, some of which can be a little complex with larger orders or when suppliers and customers have different systems of documentation. They will also have to be able to understand inventory item numbers and location systems, which are often made up of a series of letters and numbers. Finally, some basic counting and arithmetic skills could be required for counting incoming, internal, and outbound inventory.

- **Technical aptitude or interest.** As we discussed earlier in this chapter and previous chapters, information technology and information systems play a significant part of most warehouse operations. Basic computer skills are required for most warehouse positions and an ability to learn warehouse management and inventory control software systems is essential. Today, working in a warehouse requires so much more than lifting boxes! If you're a technophobe, any job in supply chain management might not be the right fit for you.

- **Flexibility and adaptability.** The business world is changing rapidly. With the rapid pace of technological advances, warehouse workers have to be prepared to be flexible and adapt to new information technology and information systems. Also, because of technological advances, products and how they are handled may also change. Any position in a warehouse must be filled by someone who is ready to learn new things on a regular basis.

- **An eye for detail and accuracy.** Much of any job in the warehouse involves looking at the details of item numbers and descriptions or warehouse location numbers to make sure the right quantities of the right items are being received, stored, or picked. There's lots of checking and double checking involved, especially when the differences between items held in inventory are not readily apparent, such as 5/8" silver wood screws versus 3/4" silver wood screws. There is also a considerable amount of paperwork checking to make sure that orders received and shipped match corresponding paperwork. For example, even if a customer has ordered and paid for 10 bicycles and 10 bicycles are shipped, if the packing slip that is sent with the order contains a typo and reads "11 bicycles," there will be confusion on the customer's end and unnecessary labor hours will be used to clear up the mistake.

- **A focus on quality and improvement.** As previously mentioned, in order to save money and become more efficient and effective, companies are adopting a LEAN philosophy by asking employees in the warehouse and other locations along the supply chain to identify inefficiencies and suggest ways in which to improve. Companies can gain a competitive advantage through supply chain improvements, making them reliant on those at the front line at the warehouse to suggest ways in which to improve processes and procedures. Warehouse employees must also have an eye for quality to make sure that goods received, stored, picked, and packed are always in the condition that the customer expects. For example, if an order picker at a regional distribution center for a grocery store chain picks and ships a pallet-load of brown and rotting bananas, the customer seeing the rotten bananas come in to their neighborhood grocery store will question the quality of the produce and all other goods sold by that company.

- **A focus on safety and security.** As covered in an earlier chapter, warehouses can be dangerous places. They contain heavy equipment moving large and sometime dangerous goods. Warehouse employees must always be mindful of the safety of themselves and others. Goods also equal the financial future of the company. If goods are not kept secure and are stolen or damaged due to the negligence of warehouse workers, the company loses potential profits, resulting in lower employee salaries and lost market share.

- **Ability to work independently.** Although warehouse workers are an important team and must work well together, many of the tasks completed by warehouse professionals involve hours spent working independently. People often work singly to put away and pick orders, count inventory in physical inventory checks, package and ship goods, and complete paperwork. It is important for warehouse workers to be self-motivated and complete this work quickly, accurately, and on their own.

- **People skills.** Although you must be able to work independently, in a warehouse you must also be able to work well with others. Warehouses are full of people who are handling goods as they move through a company and on to a customer. These people in the warehouse must be able to communicate well with people both internal to and external to their organization. If you have poor people skills and upset those working around you, they may be distracted and less productive or even more likely to want to take extra sick days from work. Therefore, it is important for those working in a warehouse to have good communication skills and a fair amount of emotional intelligence. This is especially important for those in management or supervisory positions because their primary job is to get the work of the warehouse done through other people, i.e., the people who work in the warehouse.

CHAPTER 11 REVIEW QUESTIONS

1. Where do warehouse management activities happen in the supply chain? Please explain your answer.

2. What is the difference between internal and external customers? In your work, school, or home life, whose external customer are you? Whose internal customer are you?

3. Is a company's purchasing department an internal or an external customer of the same company's warehouse? How does the warehouse provide customer service to the purchasing department?

4. What is inventory visibility and how is it related to the three phases of customer service?

5. What are vertical and horizontal relationships? Provide a few examples of these relationships from the point of view of a warehouse employee.

6. Why are warehouse workers important to you? What distant yet important role do they play in your life?

7. What is the difference between a warehouse manager and a warehouse coordinator? Which position would you rather have? Why?

8. What special requirement is required of forklift operators?

9. Why might someone working in a warehouse need an eye for detail and accuracy?

10. Of the list of common competencies for people working in warehouse management and inventory control, which two are your strongest? Which two are your weakest? Please explain your answer

CHAPTER 11 CASE EXERCISE

Customer Service, ABC Analysis, and Charlie's Chewy Chowder

One of the most darkly kept secrets of the business world is that, despite our best customer service intentions, all customers are not created equal. Some customers purchase more from us than others and thereby contribute more to the success of our business. Because these customers are vital to the life and longevity of our company, we must always ensure that they receive top class customer service. Let's explore this a bit more by examining the case of Charlie's Chewy Chowder, a soup manufacturer located in New Winterfell. Charlie's Chewy Chowder delivers all its manufactured goods to its customers using its own fleet of trucks. Sometimes, especially during the coldest and bleakest months of deepest winter when chowder orders are high, there is not enough available capacity on Charlie's own trucks to distribute the chowder to all of the company's customers. The company's only option is to rent transportation from a local logistics service provider with a a spotty customer service record called Lazy Larry's Languid Logistics. Charlie's Chewy Chowder must decide which customers' orders will be shipped using Lazy Larry's Languid Logistics, which means that they may receive their deliveries late. This situation of running out of space on their own trucks does not happen often enough to justify the purchase of more trucks, which would site idle for more than 360 days a year. Patty Pennypincher, the distribution manager of Charlie's Chewy Chowder, has asked you to use the technique of ABC analysis that we covered on pages 136 through 138 of Chapter 6 to determine who Charlie's Chewy Chowder's top priority customers are to ensure that their deliveries are never placed in the hands of Lazy Larry's Languid Logistics.

INSTRUCTIONS:

From the customer information in the table below, please determine who the A, B, and C customers are for Charlie's Chewy Chowder. This will give the company a list of all the A customers, who should never have their goods delivered using Lazy Larry's Languid Logistics, and the C customers, who may have to suffer an occasional delivery from Lazy Larry when there are transportation space shortages.

CUSTOMER	ANNUAL SALES ($)
University of New Winterfell	$2,000
Narniaville Navy College	$1,600
Poodle Palace	$110,000
Fabulous Floating Ferries	$6,000
Goode's Not Great Goods	$1,800
We Heart Crabbin'	$2,200
Quick Stop Shop	$14,000
Grabby Groceries	$50,000
Happy Hippy Hotels	$2,400
McShab's Fun Time Bars	$10,000
TOTAL SALES (IN MILLIONS)	$200,000

Chapter 12
The Rapidly Changing Future of Warehouse Management

As our global business environment becomes increasingly competitive and interconnected and as information technology tools and techniques become increasingly more sophisticated, warehouse management and inventory control face a rapidly changing present and future. Successful companies and their warehousing departments today must harness these technological advances to achieve competitive advantage. Organizations must be vigilant and continually scan the highly dynamic external business environment for changes in both technology and customers' expectations. Companies must look to their warehouse management and inventory control tools, systems, practices, and procedures to gain competitive advantage through adapting to a changing environment and implementing efficient and cost effective changes. Five of the areas in which warehouse management and inventory control are impacted by the changing business environment are: *standardization and visibility, the impact of e-commerce, delivery personalization, mobile and wearable technology*, and *robotics, driverless vehicles, & 3D printing*.

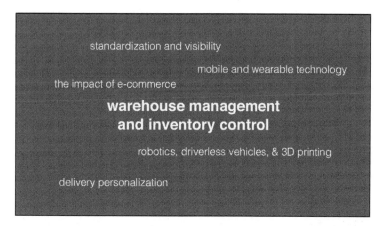

Figure 12.1 - The Changing Business Environment for Warehouse Management and Inventory Control

STANDARDIZATION AND VISIBILITY

As we mentioned in previous chapters, global positioning systems (GPS) technology now allows inventory to be tracked during its entire route inbound to a warehouse, within a warehouse, and outbound from a warehouse on its way to the customer. Different locations and organizations within the supply chain can use information technology to share accurate, real-time information about inventory location, making inventory visible to a company, even when the inventory is no longer under its control. This *inventory visibility* helps reduce cost by allowing an organization to move more to Just-in-Time (JIT) operations and hold less "just-in-case" inventory. It also enhances customer service because it helps an organization control the process of getting the right quantity and quality of finished goods to the exact time and place a customer desires. Inventory visibility has become possible only through advances in information technology, including: computerized inventory information systems; bar code printing and scanning; RFID (radio frequency identification) technology; GPS (Global Positioning System) technology; and wireless connectivity.

 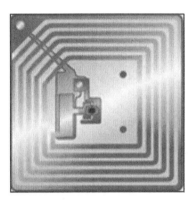

Figure 12.2 - Inventory Visibility. Both bar code technology, which uses optically scanned codes printed on label and adhered to inventory (*left*), and RFID technology, which uses radio frequency scanners and RFID tags adhered to or hidden within inventory (*right*), have played a significant role in the increasing visibility of inventory in the supply chain.

Advances in information technology now make it possible for all members of a supply chain to instantly and easily share information, such as information about inventory location and visibility. Information that once could travel only as fast as a courier could carry it or as fast as someone could convey it by telephone can now travel instantly in the blink of an eye. This now opens up a wide range of possibilities in information-sharing between a customer and its suppliers and even its suppliers' suppliers to create even greater supply chain efficiency and effectiveness. Advances in technology and information-sharing also allow for more seamless supply chain operations through increased standardization. Companies can now standardize logistics processes and supplies so the supply chain into, within, and out from warehouses is a leaner and more efficient one, meshing seamlessly into the supply chains of suppliers and customers. Immediate information sharing has led to *standardization* in supply chain management, which is the process of creating and implementing sets of standard or agreed-to processes and rules regarding sizes, quality, and interoperability of systems. For example, in a previous chapter, we discussed how the sizes of shipping containers have become standardized, primarily 20 and 40 feet long for worldwide shipping, but that standardization has differed in different parts of the world, with 10 foot containers more standard in Europe and 53 foot containers more standard in North America.

Inventory visibility and supply chain standardization has led to the development of a concept called the *Physical Internet*. The **Physical Internet,** also known as **PI** or **π**, is a concept of a standardized and highly visibly supply chain currently in development in the United States and Europe. It is called the physical *internet* because, like the digital internet which transmits packets of information, it is focused on the concept of moving packets or containers of goods across the world. Goods would be moved across the world in standardized containers using standardized systems and processes worldwide. In the United States, research into the design and feasibility of a physical internet is being conducted by the Center for Excellence in Logistics and Distribution (CELDi) and funded by the U.S. National Science Foundation. In its initial studies, CELDi has found that implementation of a Physical Internet in the United States would result in $100 billion in supply chain cost savings and reduced carbon dioxide emissions of more than 200 Tg. They also found that driver turnover would be greatly impacted, with a 75% reduction of driver turnover. A similar PI research project being conducted in Europe is the Modulushca Project, which is funded and run by a consortium of universities, research centers, consultancy companies, and commercial companies. The goal of the Modulushca Project is to develop a road map for a fully interconnected logistics system across Europe by 2030.

IMPACT OF E-COMMERCE

In the past decade, we have become increasingly dependent on *e-commerce* as private consumers. *Electronic commerce*, known primarily as *e-commerce*, is a system for a company to sell its goods or services to other business or end users using computer systems and/or the internet. For example, when you buy and download this week's Top Ten songs on iTunes, you are using Apple's e-commerce system. Similarly, when you place any order for goods online, whether it's an order for a pair of Italian, handmade shoes from a small, family-run business in Milan or an order for a pepperoni stuffed-crust pizza from the Pizza Hut around the corner, you are using e-commerce. As our use of e-commerce has increased, so have our expectations. We can easily do shopping and supplier research in our pajamas from the privacy of our homes at any time of the day or night. This research allows us to not only find the lowest price, but we may choose one supplier over another because it is the supplier that get us our goods the quickest. As a result, for companies to stay competitive, picking and delivery times must continue to become shorter in the future as our expectations increase for shorter and shorter delivery times. As you will see in the "Personalization" and "Robotics and Automation" sections below, companies are now beginning to invest in systems and research to bring significantly shorter delivery times in the future.

E-commerce has also changed the nature of the *distribution channels* for companies and their outbound goods. A *distribution channel* is the route and means by which an organization distributes its finished goods. Like a supply chain, a distribution channel is the structure of the physical flow of goods and includes all members involved in this physical flow, such as the organization itself, distribution centers, third party logistics service providers, wholesalers, and retailers. However, unlike the supply chain which covers both the inbound and outbound flow of goods, the distribution channel is concerned solely with the physical *outbound* flow of goods.

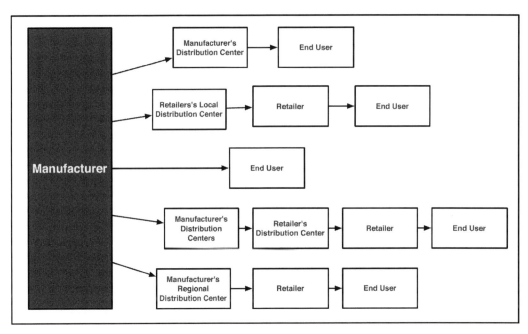

Figure 12.3 - Omni-Channel Distribution

Most warehouses and distribution centers have traditionally been designed with one distribution channel in mind, such as distribution goods just to retail store locations or to other companies buying the goods. E-commerce has changed the nature of distribution channels and warehouse design because companies must now plan for multiple distribution channels because any company or any one can but the company's goods at any time from any location thanks to e-commerce. This approach is called **omni-channel distribution**. Warehouses, especially distribution centers, must now design or re-examine their picking, packing, and distribution methods to accommodate for more complex omni-channel distribution in the future.

One example of how China is dealing with omni-channel distribution from international goods purchased through e-commerce is the creation of government-run bonded warehouses. Like online shoppers everywhere, individual shoppers in China were turning to online stores overseas to find cheaper goods or goods that were not available in their area of China. Goods were sent through regal and express mail services, but the Chinese government was not able monitor and collect the required import tax duty on all of the incoming goods. To help legitimize and control this process of incoming goods from other countries, as a test run, China set up *free trade zones* in six cities across the country. A *free trade zone*, also called a *foreign trade zone* or *FTZ*, is an area within a country in which tariffs, quotas, and bureaucratic requirements have been eliminated or minimized in order to attract foreign companies by providing incentives for doing business there. The Chinese government established *bonded warehouses* and worked and operated in partnership with private companies to receive and distribute the desired foreign goods. When moving goods internationally, most organizations consider the option of a **bonded warehouse**. When goods arrive from another country, the company receiving the goods must immediately pay excise taxes and customs duties. If a company secures a bond for potential taxes and duties of future incoming goods, it may them temporarily store foreign inbound goods in a bonded warehouse. The company may then legally defer the payment of taxes or duties until the goods are removed from the bonded warehouse. In addition, not only can goods be stored in a bonded warehouse, but they may also be assembled or partially assembled there. Establishing bonded warehouses and increasing the free trade zones across China is allowing the government to regulate and collect duties on incoming foreign goods while allowing the consumer to continue to purchase these goods from overseas for a reduced cost. The international explosion of e-commerce may have other countries around the world considering China's approach to establishing bonded warehouses in multiple free trade zones nationwide.

DELIVERY PERSONALIZATION

Thanks to e-commerce, as individual consumers, we are now able to easily compare and select how quickly we want items delivered and at what price. Online companies like Zappos and LLBean offer free delivery and returns. Brick and mortar companies like Apple and Lowes let you place your order online and have it waiting for you when you get to the store, which comes in handy by letting you skip the line when Apple comes out with its newest iPhone. Both individual consumers and companies are becoming increasingly demanding in their expectations of suppliers, expecting them to personalize delivery methods to meet their needs, just like their favorite retailers now do. Some companies, like Amazon, have begun to offer same-day delivery and are beginning to explore *same-hour delivery*!

Figure 12.4 - Delivery Drones. While drones in 2015 are being tested to deliver critical medical supplies to rural areas, in a few short years, drones may be your dinner delivery agent.

Varying delivery expectations to omni-channel customers, from free two-day delivery to same-hour delivery, will put great pressure on the warehouses and distribution centers of the not-too-distant future. Warehouse facilities will need to focus on high-speed picking and packing operations. Much of this will likely be accomplished using automated order picking systems, as will be described in the "Robotics, Automation, & Additive Manufacturing" section below. Similarly, same-hour delivery will also require the development of new delivery technology, such as the delivery drone technology that Amazon is now testing. *Delivery drones*, also called *parcelcopters*, are unmanned aerial vehicles that are used to transport goods. While the technology is almost ready for unmanned delivery, the regulations and government systems to allow them are not as of the publication date of this textbook. Complications exist because of the complexity of regulating airspace. However, on July 17, 2015, the first commercial drone delivery that was approved by the U.S. Federal Aviation Administration took place in rural Virginia, delivering medical supplies from an airfield to a nearby medical clinic.

Even without drones, one-hour delivery is being tested by Amazon in London through their ***central delivery slot*** system. For a fee of approximately $10, Amazon Prime members within certain zip codes can have a one-hour delivery of any of over 10,000 available products. Also, for no fee, customers can pick a two-hour window within the same day to have their goods delivered. As same-day to same-hour delivery becomes a reality, warehouses and distribution centers will have to keep items in stock that can be picked, packed, and shipped immediately. To meet the immediate delivery needs of customers, warehouses and distribution centers will have to be located within population centers to save on delivery time. However, in areas with high population density, available warehouse space is harder to find and more expensive than out-of-town warehouses. Therefore, warehouses and distribution centers of the future will have to maximize every inch of their valuable urban storage space with ***high-density storage systems***, which maximize warehouse floor space by minimizing aisles. Instead, shelves move so human and automated pickers can access goods as needed, with the shelves moving using anything from tracks to shelf-shifting robots.

A final development in delivery personalization is the increasing trend of *customized packaging*. With orders of varying sizes coming in from a variety of omni-channel customers, warehouses' shipping departments traditionally stocked a range of boxes and delivery packages in a few different shapes and sizes. These packages would usually not fit each shipment perfectly, with much wasted space and increased delivery costs. Larger warehouses and distribution centers have now begun to turn to ***customized packaging***, in which a company uses packaging machines from companies like Packetize that automatically and rapidly build each shipment's corrugated cardboard packaging to the exact specifications of the size of that shipment. This helps a company reduce shipping costs and minimize the specialized packaging products, like boxes of different sizes, that a company has to keep in inventory.

MOBILE AND WEARABLE TECHNOLOGY

In previous chapters, we have mentioned the proliferation of mobile computers, tablets, and cell phones in today's warehouse management and inventory control operations. Warehouse workers are now using mobile computing devices to assist with a wide range of inbound, internal, and outbound warehouse management activities. For example, cell phones are now used to scan items during putaway or picking processes to let the inventory location system know where the item is and how many of them item can be found there. While mobile technology is already a reality, its use will only continue to grow and become more accessible to smaller and smaller companies and warehouse operations through more affordable cloud computing apps.

In addition to mobile computing technology, warehouses are beginning to increase their use of *wearable technology*. ***Wearable technology*** are forms of clothing or accessories that can

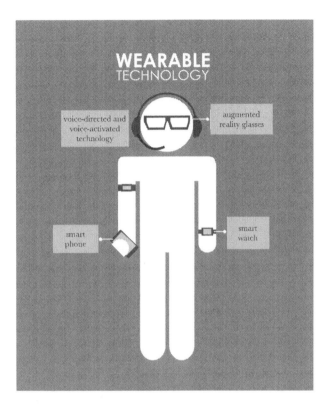

Figure 12.5 - Wearable Technology in Today's Warehouse

comfortably be worn on the body and complete sensing, communications, or computing functions. We previously covered ***voice-activated*** or ***voice-directed technology***, which is a form of wearable technology, often a headphone-microphone headset paired with a mobile computing device, that can be used to guide users to complete specific actions via voice commands. It is often used in order picking systems, with an order picker wearing a hands-free headset and listening to which items need to be picked and where they are located. However, the warehouses of the future are likely to see further advances in *voice control technology*, such as that used by a grocery store distribution center in Sweden. ***Voice control technology*** is a similar form of wearable technology utilizing a headset and either a mobile computing device or wireless transmitter to use voice commands to control equipment to perform specific actions. In the case of the Swedish grocery distribution center, order pickers use their voice to control automatically guided vehicles that follow them around and perform actions to assist them as they pick orders.

Another form of wearable technology that is likely to be found in warehouses of the future are ***augmented reality (AR) glasses***. AR glasses, like Google Glass, act as a wearable computer monitor. In warehouse operations, they are being tested to show maps of warehouses and guide pickers to each location they need to find as they pick orders. They would also allow warehouse workers hands-free access to any other type of information they would normally see on a computer or tablet screen.

In September 2015, Tokyo's Haneda Airport introduced eleven robotic helpers into its workforce to help with moving luggage. In an exciting leap forward in wearable technology, Cyberdyne, the Japanese robotics company that developed these robot helpers, is also planning to equip airport workers with ***wearable robotic power suits***. These robot suits contain Hybrid Assistive Limbs (HAL), which increase workers' speed and strength and allow them to lift heavier loads. This is especially useful in Japan, a country with an aging workforce and more than a quarter of its population over the age of 65.

ROBOTICS, DRIVERLESS VEHICLES, & 3D PRINTING

It's hard to picture a warehouse of the future without robots. According to the International Federation for Robotics, there are currently 1.5 million industrial robots in use worldwide. We are currently at the cusp of major developments in robotics in materials handling. Kiva is a company that has been creating materials handling robots since 2003. ***Kiva robots*** operate by lifting shelves weighing up to 700 pounds and bringing them to putaway workers and order pickers in the warehouse. These robots are only sixteen inches tall, but they weigh 320 pounds and can perform much of the heavy lifting in a warehouse. Amazon used Kiva robots in their distribution centers and had so much faith in their future that they bought out the company for $775 million in 2012. Kiva is now a wholly owned subsidiary of Amazon and has more than 15,000 robots operating in ten Amazon distribution centers across the world. Other companies that use Kiva robots in their warehouse management operations include Office Depot, Crate & Barrel, Diapers.com, Dillards, Gap, Toys-R-Us, and Saks Fifth Avenue.

As we stated earlier in this chapter, warehouses of the future will need to putaway goods and pick and pack orders rapidly to meet customers' needs for same-day and even same-hour delivery. Settling for Kiva robots to do all the heavy lifting alone will not be enough to speed up the order picking process. In order to spur the development of ***robotic order picking technology***, Amazon held its first robotic picker competition, called the Amazon Picking Challenge, in June 2015. The company invited mechanical engineering and computer science students from around the world to design and develop robots that can pick items from warehouse shelves and place them in bins. Teams of students from 31 universities competed in this first annual challenge, with the winner, the Technical University of Berlin, successfully moving ten of the twelve objects tested. While this robotic order picking is still not nearly as successful as human order picking, it was an important first step in encouraging the ongoing development of robotic order picking.

Another change we may see that impacts warehouses of the future are *driverless vehicles*. You may already have seen one of Google's self-driving cars moving slowly up and down the streets of your city, taking photos for Google Street View, a function of Google Maps. Like Google's self-driving cars, a ***driverless vehicle*** is an autonomous, automated, or self-driving motor vehicle that is able to sense its environment and drive without human input. Although popular in television series since the 1980s, these vehicles are currently in the research, development, and testing phases. At the time of the publication of this text, Nevada, Florida, California, Michigan, and Washington, D.C. allow driverless cars. A 32-acre fake, unpopulated city was opened in Ann Arbor by the University of Michigan in July 2015, solely for the purpose of testing driverless cars. The next move forward is driverless trucks, which are anticipated to reduce transportation costs because of increased safety and reduce driver labor costs. It is unknown yet whether or not driverless technology will eliminate truck drivers or supplement an actual driver's driving activity for improved safety.

Finally, you cannot mention the future of warehousing with mentioning the most Star-Trek-style technology of all - *additive manufacturing*. Like replicators on Star Trek, that produced anything from a laser gun to a t-bone steak on demand, additive manufacturing technology can create something out of almost nothing. **Additive manufacturing**, also known as **3D printing**, uses a powder or other raw material to create a three dimensional version of almost any object that can be represented in digital form. In warehouses of the future, additive manufacturing may be used to create replacement parts for industrial vehicles and other less-often used items. This would free up warehouse shelf space because warehouses would no longer be required to hold single quantities of less often picked items in inventory because they could be created immediately when needed. It may also allow for enhanced personalization and minor manufacturing in the warehouse just before distribution.

Figure 12.6 - Additive Manufacturing. With the drop in price of 3D printers, they are likely to be used more for business and personal applications.

ARMING YOURSELF FOR A WORLD OF CHANGE

Over the past decade, the role of the warehouse and methods of inventory management have changed with advances in information technology equipment and systems. To confront, tackle, and gain the greatest competitive advantage from this rapidly changing present and future, good warehouse and inventory managers arm themselves with the most potent weapon available: *knowledge*!

To keep abreast of advances in warehouse and inventory management, managers and their companies stay informed using the resources of core warehousing, inventory control, and supply chain management professional organizations. These organizations typically hold annual conferences and issue both trade and academic publications covering the latest theoretical and practical advances in their fields. Their websites also provide a wealth of up-to-date information and useful links related to their fields. Many also offer a variety of free e-learning opportunities.

Core professional organizations utilized by warehouse and inventory managers include:

- **WERC (www.werc.org):** The Warehousing Education and Research Council (WERC) is a professional organization devoted to warehouse management and its relationship to the supply chain. WERC publishes a wide variety of research papers and trade materials for its members and also includes member searches for both suppliers and employers.

- **MHIA (www.mhia.org):** The Material Handling Industry of America (MHIA) is a professional association for those who provide materials handling and logistics services. The MHIA website contains a variety of free online educational resources for those who want to learn more about current practices in materials handling.

- **CSCMP (www.cscmp.org):** The Council of Supply Chain Management Professionals (CSCMP) is the largest professional organization in the United States whose members represent those working and studying within the field of supply chain management. CSCMP's annual conferences and academic periodical, the *Journal of Business Logistics*, supply warehousing, inventory management, and other supply chain professionals with information on the most recent research, practices, and technologies available across the supply chain.

- **APICS (www.apics.org):** The Association for Operations Management is a professional association for those interested in operations management, which includes the fields of production, inventory management and control, supply chain management, materials management, purchasing, and logistics. In addition to information on recent research and trade publications, the APICS website also provides useful information on professional certifications within a variety of fields of operations management.

CHAPTER 12 REVIEW QUESTIONS

1. What role does RFID technology play in inventory visibility?

2. What is standardization and why might it be useful for warehouses and for global supply chain management?

3. What is the physical internet? What benefits will it bring? Do you think you are likely to see it become a reality in your lifetime?

4. What impact has e-commerce had on distribution channels?

5. What innovations are making "same-hour delivery" a possible delivery timeframe in the future?

6. Where are more warehouses of the future likely to be located and why will they need high density storage systems?

7. How is voice-directed technology different from voice-control technology? How could both be used in the same warehouse?

8. Which form of wearable technology mentioned in this chapter would you most like to try? Why?

9. Why might robotic order picking technology be important to Amazon's future operations?

10. How could additive manufacturing be used in the warehouse?

CHAPTER 12 CASE EXERCISE

Final Project: Time to Visit a Warehouse!

Now that you have read all about warehouses, it's time to visit one! If you do not have access to an industrial warehouse, you many visit Costco, Lowes, Home Depot, or any other warehouse-style store or a personal storage facility. During your visit, take photographs (if permitted) and complete the following:

1. Write a description of the location you have chosen and why you believe it is a warehouse.

2. What type of building is your warehouse? Is it single-story or multi-story? Does it have an external inventory yard?

3. Is your warehouse building a publicly owned building or is it privately owned (or leased) by the company whose products are stored there? If it is privately owned, was it a purpose-built or converted building?

4. In ten sentences or less, please describe the basic warehouse operations or functions that are undertaken at this warehouse.

5. Draw a rough diagram of the layout of your warehouse. Please be sure to include information about the receiving, shipping, storage, order picking, packaging, and office areas relevant to your warehouse.

6. What types of inventory does your warehouse contain? Are the items in inventory raw materials, work-in-process, finished goods, or MRO supplies?

7. Describe at least one example of standardization of inventory that you see.

8. Take three photos of how the warehouse or store uses inventory codes and write a description of the inventory codes you see (how many letters or numbers are there, are bar codes included, where the inventory codes are located, etc.). Next, write a description of what the inventory codes mean and how they are interpreted. You may have to ask someone at the warehouse or store for help with this.

9. Describe two pieces of materials handling equipment at your warehouse and where each piece of equipment is located. Describe the types of materials that are handled with each piece of equipment and evaluate whether or not each of the two pieces of equipment was the best equipment that could be used for that job. If not, suggest what type of materials handling equipment might be more efficient or effective.

10. Provide a description of the physical inventory checking you observe, if present. What type of physical inventory checking does your warehouse do?

11. What safety signs and placards do you see? How does your warehouse address the issues of safety and security?

12. What signs of internal customer service do you observe?

13. What information technology and information systems does your warehouse use?

14. Are any of the types of technology mentioned in this chapter present in your warehouse?

Index

About the Authors

Philip M. Price, Ph.D., is a Professor of Logistics in the College of Business and Public Policy at the University of Alaska Anchorage. Dr. Price has over thirty years of experience in university instruction and professional training in management and supply chain management settings. Before joining the University of Alaska Anchorage, Dr. Price was Professor of Logistics and MBA Director at the Kazakhstan Institute of Management, Economics, and Strategic Planning as part of a European Union initiative to develop an MBA program in post-Soviet Central Asia. Throughout his career, he has also provided training and consultancy services to a wide range of private and public sector customers, including Shell Oil, the Bureau of Engraving and Printing, the U.S. State Department, and the U.K. Ministry of Defense.

Dr. Price has co-authored a series of handbooks through Liverpool Academic Press, including *Stores and Distribution Management* and *Integrated Materials Management*. His research in supply chain management has appeared in the *Journal of Business Logistics*, *Journal of Marketing Channels*, and the *Central Asia Journal of Management*. His current areas of research include supply chain management in post-Soviet economies and the role of personality type within the logistics chain.

Natalie J. Harrison, M.Ed., is the owner of Access Education, a publication, training, and research firm focusing on issues within business management and logistics. She is also a former Adjunct Professor at University of Alaska Anchorage and Kenai Peninsula College and has been involved with corporate communications and training for almost twenty years, delivering programs to a wide range of government and commercial clients, including the Bureau of Engraving and Printing, the U.S. Department of State, the National Institutes of Health, the U.S. Peace Corps, U.S. Forest Service, U.S. Bureau of Land Management, Arctic Slope Regional Corporation Energy Services, Federal Management Systems, Alaska Communications, Carlile Transportation, and the State of Alaska Division of Public Health. For the past fifteen years, she has worked extensively with the Myers-Briggs Type Indicator and is certified to administer and interpret the MBTI, the MBTI Step II, and the MMTIC.

Dr. Price and Ms. Harrison have additionally co-authored *Looking at Logistics* and co-edited *Fundamentals of Purchasing and Supply Management*. They are currently developing an instructional model of supply chain education for secondary school classrooms and are conducting research on the role of personality type within the supply chain.

Printed in Great Britain
by Amazon